In reading this wonderful tome on spiritual gifts, not only will you find it inspiring, but you will also be presented with insights into what differences can be made in your life's journey. Not only is it an honor to be invited into the life of Jay Morris and his trials, it is also a series of powerful lessons on how one might learn to discern the voice of God and serve the world in magnificent ways that continually prove to be of value to the world and a blessing to you. The power of this writing will leave you in a place that is closer to God than you are today.

Dr. Leon Bailey, DMin, MDiv, MPA
Senior HR Vice President for Community Foundation
for Greater New Haven, New Haven, Connecticut

Dr Morris' love for Jesus and the scriptures has evolved over the years through an amazingly wide spectrum of life experiences. Not unlike the Apostle Paul, Dr. Morris has learned to be content, to be full and to be hungry, to abound, and to suffer need. With the Holy Spirit as His trusted guide, he has learned that he can indeed do all things through Christ who strengthens him.

You'll laugh with him, cry with him, and most of all learn from Dr. Morris as he takes you on his own spiritual journey of discovery.

Reverend Todd Foster, Director of
Global Missions at Cornerstone Christian Center,
Former Senior Pastor at Church on the Rock, New Haven,
Connecticut

Dr. Jay Morris' skill in telling his story through the perspective of scripture caused me to consider how the Holy Spirit has guided, protected, and delivered me through very challenging times. I would strongly recommend reading this book.

Dr. Gerard Rabalais MD, MHA
Associate Vice President for HSC Faculty Development,
Chairman Emeritus, Department of Pediatrics, and Professor of
Infectious Diseases, University of Louisville Health Sciences Center,
Louisville, Kentucky

This book will transform your life into the original masterpiece you were created to be. It teaches you how to unleash the power of the Holy Spirit so you can develop unshakable faith, and spiritual discernment when you commit to doing the work that your spirit requires. Dr. Morris takes you deep into self-reflection as you imagine the possibilities for your life when you completely surrender to the Holy Spirit.

Karen Hinds, CEO of Workplace Success Group,
Loxahatchee, Florida

Masterpiece takes readers on a captivating journey with a young man and the Holy Spirit. The book prompted me to evaluate my life and reflect on how the Spirit of God protected and led me over the years. I highly recommend it.

Patrice Covington Green, MA/MPH Broker/Realtor, Covington Realty LLC, Charlotte, North Carolina

Those who have gone through great challenges, as I have, will find great value and hope in *Masterpiece*.

Gail Adams, Vice President, Communications and External Affairs at EnerGeo Alliance, Houston, Texas

If you are interested in next level living, then you must take this reading journey into the Holy Spirit. Dr. Morris expertly demystifies that which is unseen and helps connect the reader to tangible and deeply enriching experiences. This book helps us understand how the Holy Spirit shows up and works within our lives. Dr. Morris provides the reader with keen clarity on how to reap the fruit of the Spirit in an exceptional and timely way. This book is a spiritual gift to the soul.

Jen Olson, Co-Founder/Principal KGO | Knowledge Growth Opportunity, Washington, DC

My abuela used to say, "Orar y Obrar," which means 'keep praying and don't forget to do the work.' *Masterpiece* artfully combines those virtues and avoids inspirational happy-talk; it is deeply sincere, deeply substantive, and deeply serious. Bracingly beautiful . . . Morris gives one part memoir, one part psalm book, and one part workbook.

Read and remember how special you are, how loved you are, and how well made you are. You are a magnificent masterpiece capable of great things when you trust God, read the Word, and decide to work out your purpose. You'll find yourself aware and connected as you've never been before.

Dr. Marcia Dawkins, PhD, Author, Speaker, Media Commentator, Educator, Long Beach, California

Masterpiece is an engaging personal recollection by a writer who makes our individual journey of life more relatable through memories, experiences, and correlations between universal law and spiritual realms that drive our human-centered maturation; the content will captivate readers immediately.

Nkanta N. Hines Sr., President and CEO Capital Strategy Group, Richmond, Virginia

Jay Morris' *Masterpiece* takes the reader on a journey through which we come to see *our own lives* as God's *masterpiece*! Faith doesn't have to be complicated or over-spiritualized, but it must be nourished. Through a transparent narrative of his own personal life, Jay demonstrates how the Holy Spirit is present and active, and, as we take simple daily steps, we come to see the hand of God working in and through our lives. Jay helps us see that our highs and our lows, our good times and our bad times, can all reflect God's love for us and His plan for our future.

Deacon Richard Louis, Board Chairman,
Cornerstone Christian Center, Milford, Connecticut

How to recognize the Holy Spirit's presence in our life and deepen the intimacy of our relationship with Him are mysteries unto themselves. Morris' account of reading scripture into His life story is both graceful and timeless. At once, a meditation and guide to prayer, this book will serve others in their own journeys, whether their spiritual practice is newfound or well-established.

Anthony Nicoletti, MFA, MA
Program Analyst for Physician Assistant Education,
Yale School of Medicine, New Haven, Connecticut

I just finished reading, *Masterpiece*. It was so meaningful to me. I loved the way it interspersed personal stories with focus on God's Spirit leading or his protecting Jay along with scripture. The examples of biblical character stories as examples of people led by the Spirit were really enlightening.

I would definitely recommend this book to friends…It was clearly an encouragement to walk in the Spirit, with many examples…even when others may not consider it to be led by the Spirit.

Wanda Sindorf, Wife of Pastor Fred Sindorf, Former Senior Pastor at
North Shore Assembly of God, Williams Bay, Wisconsin

Masterpiece

**Our Journey to
Spiritual Transformation**

Jay Morris, JD, PhD

Masterpiece

Our Journey to
Spiritual Transformation

Jay Morris, JD, PhD

credo
house publishers

Published in the United States of America by Credo House Publishers,
a division of Credo Communications LLC, Grand Rapids, Michigan
credohousepublishers.com

ISBN: 978-1-62586-252-5

Cover and interior design by Believe Book Design
Editing by Donna Huisjen

Printed in the United States of America
First edition

For we are God's masterpiece. He has created us anew in Christ Jesus, so we can do the good things he planned for us long ago.

Ephesians 2:10

"Thank you for making me so wonderfully complex! Your workmanship is marvelous—how well I know it."

Psalm 139:14

Contents

Preface

You are one of the most valuable and precious treasures in all the universe. Yes, you! Do you understand that God created you in His own image?

> *"So God created human beings in his own image. In the image of God he created them; male and female he created them."*

> *Genesis 1:27*

> *God describes you as a masterpiece: "For we are God's masterpiece. He has created us anew in Christ Jesus so we can do the good things he planned for us long ago."*

> *Ephesians 2:10*

The online Merriam-Webster Dictionary states that a *masterpiece* is "work done with extraordinary skill; especially; a supreme intellectual or artistic achievement." When the world envisions a masterpiece, people typically think of paintings like the *Mona Lisa*, created by Leonardo Da Vinci in 1506, or *The Creation of Adam*, painted by Michelangelo in 1508. Both are timeless pieces of exquisite art.

However, *You* are *God's unique masterpiece*, more valuable, irreplaceable, and more beautiful than anything else the world has ever seen or known. Your value exceeds human ability to calculate.

We, God's ultimate creations, can understand our purpose in life only, if we learn to see ourselves through the eyes of our Creator. Our lives are not merely timelines for the unfolding and development of our physical, emotional, social, and mental facets, although these components are crucial to our experience. Life is also, and primarily, a spiritual journey. Our physical bodies will die, but our souls will live on through eternity, with or without God. We are so precious that God sacrificed His Son to die for you and for me, so that we can finally thrive in our eternal relationship with Him here on earth, as it will be in heaven.

We all must ask crucial questions about life here on earth. Am I experiencing life the way God, my Master Creator, designed my life to be lived? Am I evolving and growing according to the Master's design for me? Or, am I living a lesser, devolving life of my own choosing?

This book was written for people like you; men and women, young and old, who have a deep soul yearning for something more meaningful in their lives. But before we can live in the fullness of our purpose, something deep inside of us must change. *Masterpiece* was written to help people embrace their spiritual DNA and walk in their authentic spiritual selves, with the same intimacy Adam and Eve enjoyed with God in the garden before the fall.

> *"You saw me before I was born. Every day of my life was recorded in your book. Every moment was laid out before a single day had passed."*
>
> *Psalm 139:16*

God has a unique, eternal purpose for your life. You are a one-of-a-kind creation. This book will help you learn how to listen for and discern the still, small voice of the Holy Spirit. It was written to guide you into the arms of the Holy Spirit, in part by teaching you practical steps I have gleaned over the course of my life (I also cull principles from the lives of various Bible characters, as well as relying heavily on what scripture itself has to say). I dearly wish someone would have taught me these helpful tools when I was young.

Was my life perfect? Absolutely not. Have I enjoyed my life? I can truthfully say that, yes, I have. When I look back I laugh and smile, for much of my journey has been fun and downright joyful. However, my life has not always been easy, or all fun and games.

I was born into poverty to two of the most loving, caring, and yet dysfunctional parents you could ever imagine. I wasn't aware of the Holy Spirit as a child, but God had His hand on my life. He allowed me to serve twenty-five years as a deacon and chairman of the board in diverse, Spirit-filled congregations in Skokie, Illinois; Northville, Michigan; Princeton, New Jersey; and Milford, Connecticut. I was also able to integrate my faith and spiritual values for over 35 years working in major corporations as life/health underwriter, supervisor, field underwriting manager, director, and vice president in companies such as Allstate Insurance Company, Ernst & Young, Computer Sciences Corporation (CSC), Merck & Company, Trinity Health, and Yale New Haven Health.

The following was written on September 30, 2021, by Kevin Myatt, Senior Vice President (SVP) of Human Resources in the companywide announcement regarding my retirement from Yale New Haven Health:

> "A passionate advocate for lifelong learning and personal development, Jay has a master's degree in organizational development, a doctoral degree in instructional management, and a juris doctorate degree. While these credentials are impressive and a well-deserved source of pride, we mostly know Jay as a gentle, thoughtful, and humble person. He is a man of great faith, one who is generous and caring, a role model and mentor to many, and someone known to take personal interest in the disenfranchised in our community. He makes a difference on many levels."

My hope is that *Masterpiece* will help you to:
- Recognize the Person and role of the Holy Spirit
- Understand the vital role of the Word of God
- Understand and appreciate who you are and fully use your gifts and talents
- Learn how to live as your best self
- Fall in love with reading the Bible
- Apply the Word of God in your daily life
- Walk intimately with the Holy Spirit

I pray that *Masterpiece* will awaken your spirit to live into the purpose God planned for you before you were born. Let this call sit in your spirit as you press toward a deeper intimacy with the Holy Spirit, and watch as He draws you into the arms of the Father through Jesus Christ.

Introduction

Saturday afternoon on August 26, 1972, in Durham, North Carolina, was a scorching, muggy 87 degrees in the shade. It was a great day to be inside, relaxing in front of an air-conditioned breeze, listening to silky jazz with friends I hadn't seen over the summer. I was perched in a tan wicker chair, staring out of the picture window of 410 Pilot Street, Apartment A7, mindlessly playing with my nickel-plated .25-caliber pistol while drinking wine and smoking weed. It was the gun cousin Bucky had given to me before I left Allentown, Pennsylvania, as I was preparing to head back to North Carolina Central University (NCCU) for my sophomore year.

As I look back over my childhood, I can clearly see that the Holy Spirit had been right by my side (although I didn't know it then), just as He was in apartment A7 on that unforgettable Saturday afternoon in 1972. This was two months after one of my closest friends, Dennis Blanks, had been killed the week before he was to start his dream job as a Pennsylvania State Police Officer. He had been elated after finally passing the entrance exam.

I sat alone in the dark sanctuary of St. James AME Zion Church on the night before his funeral, questioning God through my tears and agony. Why had He taken my dear friend, the big brother I never had? My heart was crushed.

Dennis had the most giving heart. Joy flowed from his soul, and I later realized he had glimpsed heaven the weekend before his death, when, on two separate occasions, he had said goodbye to his fiancée, Alice, and to me. Dennis had often joked that he wanted "his boys" to celebrate his death by partying as though there would be no tomorrow. However, I certainly didn't feel like partying the Saturday morning of his funeral, even though I knew Dennis was rejoicing in heaven.

Classes had not started, and people were streaming in and out of the apartment throughout the day. Distracted, I didn't realize that Little Neesee, the girlfriend of one of my roommates, was walking toward me. With the gun pointed directly at her head, I unconsciously pulled the trigger. Then I froze as dark terror choked my breath.

I was in such a rush to leave Allentown that I had totally forgotten to check and see if the gun was loaded. I just assumed it was empty.

I was wrong. Seconds later I discovered that a bullet was snugly resting in the chamber of the gun. Little Neesee was still walking toward me, unharmed.

I rose from the chair, walked outside, and stood on the balcony, struggling to comprehend what had just happened. The hot, humid air made it hard to breathe as I blindly stared into the deep blue Carolina sky, slowly recognizing that a miracle had just occurred, but too numb to comprehend the Holy Spirit's intervening role. Something in my soul unraveled as the Spirit of God went to work, teaching me about His presence.

How the gun had failed to fire, I can't explain. Why it happened, God's grace.

Growing up, I was unaware of the Holy Spirit's presence. But as I look back over my life, I clearly see His hand protecting me, just as He did in apartment A7 on that unforgettable Saturday afternoon in 1972. When I reflect on where I was then, both physically and spiritually, and where God has brought me today, there is no doubt in my mind that the Holy Spirit has hovered over my life. The event with the gun in apartment A7 on Pilot Street was a stark reminder of how fragile life can be, but also explicit evidence of God teaching me about His love and constant presence in my life.

I never told anyone this story, and even now it seems incredible. Some people will say that the gun failing to fire was luck. I firmly believe there is no such thing as luck, because God our Father oversees all of creation through to the end of time. In one instant, my life could have changed and become defined by involuntary manslaughter, but as I was then, I am still now, protected by the Spirit of God.

This is my true story and testimony about God's love, mercy, and protection from the time of my childhood until this very day. It was written to help you discover your God-given spiritual identity and recognize that you are loved by your Creator more than you could ever imagine. This book is about relationship, not religion.

> "Jesus doesn't want to make us more religious. He wants to see us become more alive."
>
> Pastor Deron Spoo[1]

Just as with Enoch, a man who walked with God and then disappeared, as related in Genesis 5:21-24, this book is about a real and tangible relationship with our Creator. It is also about a relationship *within ourselves*, and an understanding of who we are in Christ and His Holy Spirit. It is about living life as it was designed by our Creator.

As His creation, you carry God's DNA in your heart and soul. He wired you to enjoy an intimate relationship with Him as you produce the fruit of the Spirit (see chapters 11-13). *Masterpiece* teaches readers like you how to intimately experience God. But, how do we begin to experience God more intimately? The way I learned to draw closer to God was through continuously reading the Bible, journaling, studying real-life stories (those of biblical characters, individuals I have known, and my own), praying, serving, and spiritual reflection. These methods will empower you to clearly recognize the voice of the Holy Spirit; and trust His leadership and protection in a world that places money, pride, possessions, sensuality, hurry, and self above God.

Masterpiece teaches principles from the Word of God that are illustrated by stories from the lives of those who lived out the truth of God's Word and were on their own journeys of transformation. More importantly, *Masterpiece* demonstrates the power that is transmitted through the Word of God and available to each of us when we acknowledge the *living* Word.

> *"For the word of God is alive and powerful. It is sharper than the sharpest two-edged sword, cutting between soul and spirit, between joint and marrow. It exposes our innermost thoughts and desires. Nothing in all creation is hidden from God. Everything is naked and exposed before his eyes, and he is the one to whom we are accountable."*

> *Hebrews 4:12–13*

This book is for people like you, who desire to know their spiritual purpose, but have struggled to find it. It is for people who are searching for joy and peace, want to win souls, and desire to build a closer, intimate walk with the Holy Spirit.

How often have those of us who grew up poor and loved the comfort and thrill of the streets, looked back and acknowledged situations that were crazy, but somehow we lived through them. Yet our loving God reached down and pulled many of us from the raging fires of hell, and He will continue to pursue us as long as we have breath.

And you might think, but why?

Because He loves us and created us for a purpose.

This book demonstrates that the Holy Spirit is closer than the sound of your breath and that He loves you more than you could ever imagine. As you read and take time to reflect, you will begin to see beyond the shadows into places where the Holy Spirit has been, and is now active in your life. I frequently refer to *soul* as the individual character, or person God has created each of us to be. At times, I will use *spirit* and *soul* interchangeably. "Spirit," or Holy Spirit however, is God, the essence and Creator of all life. As you grow in close intimacy with the Holy Spirit, your life will slowly transform into a day-by-day journey of peace, surrender, joy, and love as you fulfill your destiny as God's *Masterpiece*.

Chapter One

Purpose of the Holy Spirit

"No eye has seen, no ear has heard, and no mind has imagined what God has prepared for those who love him. But it was to us that God revealed these things by his Spirit. For his Spirit searches out everything and shows us God's deep secrets. No one can know a person's thoughts except that person's own spirit, and no one can know God's thoughts except God's own Spirit. And we have received God's Spirit (not the world's spirit), so we can know the wonderful things God has freely given us. When we tell you these things, we do not use words that come from human wisdom. Instead, we speak words given to us by the Spirit, using the Spirit's words to explain spiritual truths. But people who aren't spiritual can't receive these truths from God's Spirit. It all sounds foolish to them and they can't understand it, for only those who are spiritual can understand what the Spirit means. Those who are spiritual can evaluate all things, but they themselves cannot be evaluated by others. For, Who can know the LORD's thoughts? Who knows enough to teach him? But we understand these things, for we have the mind of Christ."

1 Corinthians 2:9–16

If you could receive the answer to *one* ultimate, life-changing question during your time on earth directly from God, what would it be? Identify one question that could revolutionize your life, and ensure your supreme success; a question that would ensure your ultimate happiness. What would *your question* to God be?

How to acquire wealth? Find true love? How to make a great name for yourself? How to be happy?

Since I am suggesting possible scenarios, I have obviously thought about my question. I would ask a question that would bring the greatest value to my life. As a person who has come to know God personally, but still struggles with a flawed human heart, I would ask God the Father the following question:

"How can I know *You* more intimately to fulfill *Your* purpose for my life?"

We must first understand that God longs for an intimate and tender Father-child relationship with each one of us. A bedrock faith emerges as we engage in conversation with Him through the work of the Holy Spirit. The faith and personal relationship that grow from our communion become the foundation that carries us even through deep grief and tragedy in our lives.

So, how do I learn to talk with the Creator of the universe *as my loving Father,* and hear Him talk with me? Is such a thing possible? If it is, how would it change my life?

In the opening verses of this chapter, the apostle Paul is speaking to the church at Corinth, which was located in a very sinful city. He talks about the purpose of the Holy Spirit and how He reveals the deep secrets of God to us, His children, if we put in the time and effort to listen.

This is how we learn to know God through His Spirit. "*For God is Spirit, so those who worship him must worship in spirit and in truth*" (John 4:24).

> **We must train ourselves to recognize His voice and hear the things He wants to share with us. This requires us to slow down, be still, humbly listen and discern His voice among the many competing voices.**

We must train ourselves to recognize His voice and hear the things He wants to share with us. This requires us to slow down, be still, humbly listen, and discern His voice among the many competing voices and messages directed at us in a world frantic to devour our souls.

Learning to See Beyond and Between

Spiritual disciplines such as slowing down, being still, humbly listening, and learning to recognize the quiet whispers of the Holy

Spirit run contrary to the culture of today's fast-paced, technologically addicted Western world. Contemporary culture demands that we interact with messages often contrary to God's Word. Technology also makes it easy to let others think for us through computers and Artificial Intelligence (AI). Learning to slow down and learning to see through the Spirit requires discipline. Discipline to recognize there is another way of seeing, and discipline to recognize the importance of your spirit. We can just ask Google, Chatbot, or any other technical platform for answers to our burning questions. In the words of Reverend Kirk Byron Jones:

> "Slow seeing, yielding a few extra seconds to things that we see on purpose or things that graciously catch our eyes, sets off the second stage of seeing more clearly: seeing with heart and mind wide open. This second stage of seeing more clearly is about opening ourselves up to the observations, questions, and conclusions inspired by those extra moments of looking. It does not mean that we spend all of our waking hours pondering the mundane. It does mean that we allow space for intervals of insight that may, on a smaller scale, provide momentary levity for living, or on a much larger scale, to provide the scaffolding for a new living paradigm, a new way of envisioning and interpreting the world."[2]

On Friday, February 29, 1952, my dad, James B. Morris Sr. (nicknamed Junior) and my mom, Dorothy Mae (Scott) Morris (nicknamed Dot), were expecting to take home their newborn son, James B. Morris Jr. Instead, at 1:00 a.m. Mom and Dad were notified that their baby boy had died from an intestinal obstruction known as meconium ileum. My brother died in the Sacred Heart Hospital located on Fourth and Liberty Streets in Allentown, Pennsylvania, at the age of three days. I often stared at the picture of a healthy-looking baby hanging on Pop's, my paternal grandfather's living room wall at 422 ½ East Court Street and wondered, how this bright-eyed baby could have died so suddenly.

I questioned the death of my big brother and desired to see his medical transcripts, but I never had the courage to take my parents back to untangle the residual pain surrounding one of the darkest times of their lives. I realized, that if James Jr. had survived, his chances of having a normal life might have been slim, at least according to the medical journals discussing children born with his assumed illness. But something failed to make sense to me about the death of the baby in the picture. How could he have died so abruptly, especially given that he appeared to have looked so healthy. To this day I still question whether my brother actually died because of health-related issues, however, I never investigated my beliefs and have surrendered my doubts and misgivings to God.

In order to function in the spiritual realm, we must learn to see between, beyond, beneath, and above our own thoughts. So many things happen in the spiritual realm that exceed our grasp. Why are we not able to comprehend them? One reason is that most of us live so engrossed in our own thoughts, perceptions, and emotions that we only see the physical world around us, and are oblivious to anything deeper. Another reason is the majority of us were never taught how to see and walk in the spiritual realm. However, we can learn.

Thriving Beyond the Odds

In May of 1952, three months after losing her first son, Mom became pregnant with her second child, but was told by her doctor to abort the fetus because of hemorrhaging that was threatening not only her life, but also the life of the baby as well. Mom was determined that nothing would keep her from carrying her baby to full term. She would not agree with the doctor's recommendation and spent the majority of her nine-month pregnancy bedridden.

Mom told me that Dad, my grandmothers, and Aunt Louise took turns helping her throughout the pregnancy. Aunt Louise, Mom's younger sister, was twenty years old and raising four daughters, all under the age of five. After I was born, Mom had difficulty doing simple things like feeding me, changing my diapers, and following simple nutritional regimens. I believe she had been traumatized at some point in her young life and struggled to live with her shame and false guilt. Yet Mom was a gifted singer and artist whose true talents, unfortunately, were never fully developed.

After I graduated from college and worked as a geriatric case worker, I realized that Mom had a learning disability. Yet somehow she had managed to deliver me on February 6, 1953 at the Sacred Heart Hospital.

> Much that is beyond our comprehension radar takes place between the Holy Spirit and those with whom He engages. In order to interact with Him in the spiritual process, we must learn to see between, beyond, beneath, and above our own thoughts.

My parents named me James B. Morris Jr. III. I never thought much about my name until I applied for a marriage license in Atlanta, Georgia, in 1977. The license supervisor asked me, how I could be both a junior and a third? Maria, my fiancée, also asked me how that could have been possible?

My immediate response was defensive: "Because that's the name my parents gave me." Then I got even more contentious and explained, "My brother died, so he was no longer alive; therefore, technically, I was now the junior. Since he lived briefly, I was also the third James B. Morris, making me a junior and a third at the same time." The explanation made perfect sense to me. But I did start wondering why my father was called Junior when he should have been senior based on me being a junior.

All I can say is . . . my parents did the best they could.

Love Over Perfection—Mom and Dad

Mom and Dad were both children of alcoholic and abusive fathers, James Scott and John Morris, respectively: "the Sons of Thunder." Thankfully, my parents found solace in their relationship with one another. They both experienced love and joy from their marriage, which lasted forty-three years . . . until the day Dad dropped dead from a stroke while mowing grass in the backyard, as Mom looked on in shock.

On July 24, 1994, at 6:00 p.m. on a Sunday afternoon, Mom called to simply say, "Dad is gone."

My response was, "Mom, where did Dad go?" Caught off guard, I thought the poor guy had finally gotten fed up with Mom's nagging, and had decided to pack up and leave home, three days short of his 71st birthday. I was in a quandary as to where he would have gone.

My sister-in-law, Verona, a critical care nurse who lived in Daytona Beach, Florida, "just happened" to be visiting relatives in Allentown and was with Mom in the hospital. She told me over the phone that Dad had died. The next morning I caught the first flight out of Chicago O'Hare to Newark Airport. I had spoken with Dad earlier that afternoon, our typical two-minute Sunday afternoon check-in. He seemed to be in a good mood.

Mom told me later that Dad had insisted on paying his life insurance policy that afternoon and made sure to drop off the envelope at the main post office at Fifth and Hamilton Streets. My parents never paid their bills on time and had a balance of $0.22 in their checking account at the time Dad died.

I smiled and shook my head when I saw their checking account balance. Mom and Dad never appeared to worry about anything; they were always trusting that God would somehow work things out. Thinking back, I can't in truth ever remember a time when things didn't work out.

My parents were able to work through their pain and dysfunctionality to provide a roof over my head and peaceful solitude for me while I was growing up. Our house was quiet . . . except for Mom, who woke up every morning at around 5:30 a.m., singing heartily in her deep alto voice, whether or not Dad and I were prepared to appreciate the song.

As I matured, I realized that my parents tried their best to give me what little they had, which amounted to consistent manifestations of their full, undeniable, and unconditional love. Although I was surrounded by crime and darkness beyond our doors, I was quietly protected by their love and the presence of the Holy Spirit at home. Growing up in Allentown at the junction of Fifth and Union Streets was a joyous experience that defied circumstances. In spite of the poverty, pain, and death that surrounded me, I can honestly say that I greatly enjoyed my childhood years.

But why wouldn't I? I did pretty much whatever I wanted to do. I never had a curfew, wore whatever clothes I wanted to wear, and was never expected to do my homework. I loved being with my friends Dennis, Shotgun, Cal, Greg, Toot, Teace, Monk, and Pipe, who also seemed to have had few to no restrictions. I guess that, if no one tells you that you are poor and life is rough, you don't necessarily recognize these realities, until later, through the lens of retrospection. I was truly blessed, despite my youthful indiscretions that I was never arrested, which I now perceive to have been a miracle in and of itself. To this day I firmly believe the Spirit of God kept me safe.

Mom and Dad were sometimes overtly mocked by people who often laughed at them and referred to them as Heckle (Mom) and Jekyll (Dad), the names of Looney Toon cartoon characters. Some thought my parents were strange because they always stayed to themselves. They lived in their own world and didn't care what anyone else thought about them. I adopted this philosophy from a very young age. Speck was one of the teenagers whose voice I heard while he stood on the corner of Fifth and Union Streets in front of the Franklin Bar, laughing with his friends, as the three of us walked by. He later spent time in prison for murder.

Mom worked as a domestic maid who cleaned the homes of Jewish families, and Dad worked odd jobs, sometimes two at a time cleaning office buildings and washing dishes until he was hired full-time as a truck driver for the City of Allentown Maintenance Department. This is the job from which he retired, and the one that brought stability to our home, another gift from God.

My Spiritual DNA

My parents separated themselves from our community and found solace in solitude. Somehow, the Holy Spirit gently led their reserved souls and provided them with His comfort and peace. I have long believed that, just as two people pass along their physical and mental attributes to their offspring, parents also pass along their spiritual attributes and spiritual DNA to their children. I believe I inherited my parents' spiritual DNA.

Dad was extremely introverted and never referred to me by name. He spoke in short statements whenever he decided to converse, which was rare. He had a quiet spirit and was a brilliant problem solver. He would assemble three-thousand-piece puzzles with minimal effort and enjoyed playing his guitar. In spite of his few words, I knew deep in my heart that he loved me.

Mom, however, talked incessantly and never met a stranger she didn't know. She had a beautiful alto singing voice and was a gifted artist who hid her work. She had a loving heart and was always trying to solve other people's problems. Mom always spoke on Dad's behalf. My parents both accepted Jesus as their Lord and Savior after I went away to NCCU.

God also desires spiritual offspring, and that was one of the reasons He separated the Israelites from the people around them, as told in the book of Exodus. We inherit the physical qualities of our parents, and, to a great degree, we can see those characteristics carried on in the physical qualities of their children. However, most of us are not taught to recognize the characteristics of the Holy Spirit, who dwells in our hearts. Some people have a soft nature, which is reflected in their character in the form of gentleness, kindness, and goodness. This fruit is birthed through the Holy Spirit (Galatians 5:22), which we will talk about in chapter 11. On the other hand, a covering (shielding or protection of the Holy Spirit) and boldness can be found in people with strong spiritual maturity.

Our character and soul are also often communicated through our voice and behavior. If we listen carefully, we can hear the Spirit in the tone, pitch, and expression of a person's voice, and we can see the Spirit in their demeanor. Our sincerity, humility, and passion are transmitted in both the way we speak and the way we live. It's easy to detect when a person either spews hatred or bitterness, or speaks love and compassion. Words are powerful and have a direct effect on our body, our mind, and our soul.

Dad never raised his voice, even when he was angry, but his spirit traveled through his words. If we listen attentively when a person speaks, without focusing on what we are going to say in response, we can discern a person's spirit in their words. Whether good or bad, their heart condition will be confirmed in our spirit by the Holy Spirit, if we truly listen.

I once saw Dad's Army discharge papers and learned that he had been deployed to Normandy, France, on D-day during World War II at the age of nineteen. He never talked about the war, or about anything else, for that matter. He deferred to Mom, and did almost everything she told him to do . . . provided it made sense to him. Dad was a highly intelligent man, while Mom was spoiled and extremely self-centered, often referring to herself in the third person. She once told me that she had suffered something like a nervous breakdown, but she never fully explained the circumstances.

I heard rumors that Mom had Dad arrested when I was a baby, but I was never told the full details. Then a month before he died, Dad gave me a hint of what happened, and Mom was furious that he shared the story with me, even though it was almost forty years later. (Mom had difficulty remembering dates.)

Despite their shortcomings, my parents both loved me with an undying love. Something good and powerful in my soul was gifted to me by my parents, inherited from their spiritual DNA. I am also convinced that I received a great deal of spiritual DNA from my paternal grandfather, John Baker Morris, or Pop. Humans are more than flesh and blood. We are spiritual beings, and until we acknowledge this reality, we will never become all God created us to be. Trees and plants grow from seeds sown in soil. The same is true of our hearts and souls that grow from the Word of God, Revelation 19:13.

Spiritual Genes Passed Down

After joining Yale New Haven Health System, I met Dr. Stephen Byrum who introduced me to the work of Dr. Robert S. Hartman, who was responsible for developing formal axiology, which is the study of value judgment. Dr. Hartman believed that children inherit their parents' spiritual DNA, just as they inherit their physical and mental characteristics. I first read his research in his esteemed manuscript, *One with God*, which is kept in the archives of the Hartman Institute.

Dr. Hartman was also one of the founders of the concept of profit sharing in the 1940s. He and his wife, Rita, were very close friends of Dr. Abraham Maslow and his wife, Bertha. Dr. Hartman was a colleague of Viktor Frankl and Paul Tillich. He was nominated for a Nobel Prize for his work on peace, but died suddenly in 1972 from a heart attack. He believed the spiritual attributes of parents are passed down genetically to their children, and if we think about our makeup as human beings, why would this belief be questioned? I was blessed to receive an appointment to sit on the board of trustees at the Robert S. Hartman Institute located on the campus of the University of Tennessee in Knoxville, Tennessee from 2016 to 2022.

In Genesis 46:28–29, as well as in the book of Joshua, we read that God separated the Hebrews in Goshen from the surrounding nations because He wanted holy offspring who would represent Him throughout the earth. God desired that godly men and women come together and produce godly children who would also follow the ways of the Lord. My parents had gentle spirits, and I believe I was the recipient, through them, of that same gentleness. The power of the Holy Spirit used my own gentle nature to protect me and keep me from straying too far from the narrow path in life.

> **We are spiritual beings, and until we acknowledge this reality, we will never become all God created us to be.**

I am convinced that Pop, my paternal grandfather, was summoned to the ministry at some point in his life, and for reasons I can only surmise, he turned his back on God. A diminutive man, Pop stood about 5' 4" and weighed approximately 130 pounds. He fought in France in World War I and was a very violent and dangerous man, especially when he was drinking. He carried a Cavalry Colt .45 pistol neatly tucked into the back of his pants, which concealed a dark, shiny wooden handle that contained six etched notches in its grooves, an indication that he killed six people. Yet Pop taught me to pray when I was four and introduced my spirit to the things of God.

While Pop grounded me in the practice of prayer and faith in God, his struggle with alcohol prevented him from developing many of the qualities we often associate with spiritual mentors. The men who worked at the Union Street Boys' Club, reinforced the importance of living a life of service and demonstrating a spirit of compassion. These men walked beside me and other young men at the Union Street Boys' Club and modeled how to grow and walk in confidence.

We do well to surround ourselves with spiritually mature people who love God and live according to His Word. Great mentors exemplify patience and exude joy, even when everything around them is hectic and chaotic. They allow us to be transparent about our guilt or shame and help us renew our spirit. If you can't locate a mentor, ask the Holy Spirit to help you find one. Jesus taught and mentored his twelve disciples and His followers for three years.

Taking time to read the Word of God regularly is a critical first step in understanding our spiritual pedigree. As we get into the habit of doing this, we come to know men and women in scripture and see how God moved in their lives. When you read the Bible cover to cover and let His Word penetrate your soul and not just your mind, God speaks to you through the work of the Holy Spirit. Learning to hear the Spirit takes practice and discipline. This is why it is important, whenever possible, to find spiritual mentors to walk beside us as we mature in the Spirit. The Holy Spirit will do the rest. As the evangelist Billy Graham reflected:

> "George Muller, (the great founder of the Bristol Orphanage in the last century) once said, the vigor of our Spiritual Life will be in exact proportion to the place held by the Bible in our life and thoughts . . . I have read the Bible through one hundred times, and always with increasing delight. Each time it seems like a new book to me. Great has been the blessing for consecutive, diligent, daily study. I look upon it as a lost day when I have not had a good time over the Word of God."[3]

Pop Baker

Dad and my grandmother, Nanna B, were often the recipients of Pop's fury. Nanna B was a soft-spoken, gentle, humble woman who loved God. I never knew her family because they disassociated from her after she married Pop. I witnessed one violent fight when I was five years old while visiting my grandparents' home. I was sitting at the kitchen table at 820 Lawrence Street at around 5:30 one Saturday evening, listening to Harry Belafonte singing *Dao* over radio station WAEB while watching cockroaches frolic across the table.

When suddenly, my attention was drawn to Nanna B, who viciously smashed a heavy porcelain plate over Pop's forehead. Blood spewed from a gaping wound and splattered all over the tiny kitchen floor and table. I sat and stared at the blood, while my grandparents continued to violently argue, as though their grandson wasn't even there, taking in every detail. Pop grabbed a dishrag and pressed it against his forehead, telling me to get my jacket, and we quickly left.

I grieved my unfinished dinner and the abrupt end of the cockroach show as Pop Baker walked me the six blocks home. He continued to press the rag against his head to slow the flow of blood. I didn't say a word and walked quietly beside him as we made our way together down the dark, silent sidewalks of Lawrence Street.

Then, for some strange reason, Pop stopped at Mr. Bosket's barber shop at the corner of Fifth and Willow Streets.

Why in God's name would Pop stop at the barbershop when blood is dripping from his head? I wondered. His actions made no sense to me.

When Mr. Bosket saw Pop's wound, he panicked and pleaded with him to go immediately to the hospital. Pop dropped me off at my house at 458 Union Street, and I never heard another word about the incident.

I was one person who witnessed Pop's goodness and kindness. He treasured his only grandchild and was the only person who ever encouraged me to go to college. Although he only had a fourth-grade education, he was a prolific reader and one of the most educated individuals I have ever known. In spite of his shortcomings, my grandfather not only introduced me to the things of God, but helped me to value learning and education from an early age.

32

Violence and vulgarity spewed from Pop's mouth when he was drunk, while kindness and love flowed unconditionally from him to me when he was sober. I learned valuable lessons from watching my grandfather interact with others. He genuinely listened to and respected all people, no matter who they were. I am convinced that God had called Pop Baker to the ministry, but the call of the streets was more compelling to his spirit. That same call enticed me for most of my younger years.

On July 1, 1960, Dad found Nanna B lying at the bottom of her kitchen steps with a broken neck. She was rushed to Allentown Hospital and died three days later, at the age of fifty-four, on July 4, 1960, from cardiac tamponade caused by blunt trauma. There was no question that my grandparents had been fighting, and this would be their final battle.

I can't imagine how agonizing it must have been for Dad to find his mother lying at the bottom of the narrow wooden steps, crumpled, and dying. Only God knows how long she had lain there alone. Pop never expressed any visible remorse about Nanna B's death.

On a sunny July 4th morning, I sat on the stairwell landing with Mom and Dad and listened as my other nanna explained to me that Nanna B had died and gone to heaven.

Protecting Presence

Eventually I realized that the Holy Spirit allowed me to be repeatedly exposed to worldly violence and abuse as a child, but not to the point at which the abuse destroyed my body, mind, and soul. He sheltered me.

> "Though the Lord gave you adversity for food and suffering for drink, he will still be with you to teach you. You will see your teacher with your own eyes. Your own ears will hear him. Right behind you a voice will say, 'This is the way you should go,' whether to the right or to the left."
>
> Isaiah 30:20–21

I know without a doubt that the Spirit's presence protected my body and mind from internalizing the horrors that shadowed my young life. I never told anyone that I was sexually assaulted. I finally shared this with Mom and later with Pastor Gary, the senior pastor at North Shore Assembly of God in Skokie, Illinois, at that time when I was in my early thirties. It took a lot of courage for me to talk about what had happened. Mom's response caught me off guard, and it hurt for a moment. She didn't show me the emotional support I so desired. Looking back, I don't believe she knew how.

Instead of offering comfort, she asked me whether *he*, the perpetrator, had hurt me. She didn't think to ask me questions about what happened. If she had, she would have learned that my primary abuser was an older girl who lived next door to Pop, not a male, as Mom assumed.

I eventually understood that Mom gave me the best support she could offer. I realized that she was still coping with her own internal trauma. She more than likely didn't have the strength to ask me what had happened, or deal with my revelation beyond her initial assumption.

Years later, I heard a rumor that the girl who raped me was burned alive in prison to keep her from testifying against a prostitution ring. I know in my heart that she was a tender, kind soul who was searching for love. Unfortunately, she had grown up in deplorable circumstances. It was also rumored that her older brother died of HIV/Aids and that one of her younger brothers was convicted of murder. I never held bitterness toward her in any way.

As I grew older, I realized that the Holy Spirit was with me long before I took my first breath. He was with me long before I was a four-year-old child, wandering the streets unsupervised from early morning until late in the evenings because my parents had to work, or were distracted by their own silent challenges.

> *"You made all the delicate, inner parts of my body and knit me together in my mother's womb."*
>
> *Psalm 139:13*

The Holy Spirit protected me from the rampant death and destruction that exist in many urban communities across this country, including Allentown. I was protected because God ordained my protection, and I was His child. God has a purpose for every one of us. Even when we experience atrocities, He shields us from the full force of the horror the enemy directs our way. We are also given prayer as a source of power for engaging the Holy Spirit in our defense.

In prayer, we can tell the Spirit what we need, and listen as He comforts, teaches, and guides us. And when we don't know what to say, He speaks on our behalf: *"The Holy Spirit helps us in our weakness. For example, we don't know what God wants us to pray for. But the Holy Spirit prays for us with groanings that cannot be expressed in words"* (Romans 8:26).

Prayer is critical. Prayer is powerful. Prayer is unstoppable when it is combined with the Word of God. We know this because Jesus prayed.

The Holy Spirit, Our Teacher

I encourage young believers not to get overwhelmed by trying to fully comprehend the Word of God on their own. If we pray and ask the Holy Spirit, He will bring godly mentors and teachers to us, or He will personally instruct us. We will recognize potential mentors by their fruit, their godly character, and actions. Consider what type of person a potential mentor should be (their character and reputation), and what they do (priorities and service), as you wait quietly upon the Holy Spirit to direct a mentor to you. Their faith and actions should reflect Christlike behaviors, such as a powerful love for all people, and for the Word of God.

At times we all must walk by faith and, in a laser-focused manner, rely upon the Word of God and the Holy Spirit to sustain us supernaturally. When you face such seasons of life, the following actions can help expedite your spiritual growth:

- Take time to read and let the Word sit in your heart and soul through silence, solitude, and reflection
- Memorize verses that speak directly to your soul
- Write down your questions and ask the Holy Spirit to enlighten you

♦ Pray for wisdom
♦ Meditate on the Word and apply it to your life on a daily basis
♦ Spend daily time with God in prayer, solitude, and journal your progress
♦ Listen for the voice of the Spirit throughout your day

Eventually, you will see changes in your thinking and attitude. This process takes time and discipline, but that is okay. God loves you, and He won't abandon you. You are getting to know Him, and He is delighted.

Spending time in the Word of God requires us to slow down and discipline our bodies and minds to focus on our souls, as we humble ourselves before the Spirit. At the end of our lives, our bodies will return to dust and our souls will surrender to the things of the Spirit. Wasting opportunities to deepen our relationship with God on this side of heaven is our greatest loss, and it breaks God's heart. His deepest longing is to be in an intimate, living relationship with you, and with all of His children.

Unfortunately, many Christians abdicate the privilege of deepening their relationship with the Spirit of God and jeopardize their spiritual health by relying on other people to spoon-feed them the Word. Listening to sermons, podcasts, and reading books as our primary source of spiritual development is important but could impede our spiritual growth. While these approaches can enrich our faith, the most powerful force available to believers for spiritual wisdom and growth comes from our personal interaction with the Holy Spirit through reading God's Word and hearing directly from Him. All too often, we spend little to no time beyond Sunday morning in church to meditate on and apply God's Word to our lives; rather, we need to continually listen for His voice to guide us.

God has equipped us to be taught directly by His Spirit, but this will happen only if we humbly place ourselves under His authority. We must learn to sit, be still, absorb, and reflect upon what His Spirit reveals to us. Additionally, spending only twelve minutes a day enables us to read the Bible cover to cover in one year and absorb the full scope of God's Word. There is no other source in the world more powerful and transformative for both believers and those who do not know God.

After reading each of the following verses, allow some time to reflect on the meaning before proceeding to the next verse:

"Ask me and I will tell you remarkable secrets you do not know about things to come."

Jeremiah 33:3

"If you love me, obey my commandments. And I will ask the Father, and he will give you another Advocate, who will never leave you. He is the Holy Spirit, who leads into all truth. The world cannot receive him, because it isn't looking for him and doesn't recognize him. But you know him, because he lives with you now and later will be in you."

John 14:15–17

"But when the Father sends the Advocate as my representative— that is, the Holy Spirit—he will teach you everything and will remind you of everything I have told you."

John 14:26

"There is so much more I want to tell you, but you can't bear it now. When the Spirit of truth comes, he will guide you into all truth. He will not speak on his own but will tell you what he has heard. He will tell you about the future."

John 16:12–13

"The Spirit is God's guarantee that he will give us the inheritance he promised and that he has purchased us to be his own people."

Ephesians 1:14

"I pray that from his glorious, unlimited resources he will empower you with inner strength through his Spirit."

Ephesians 3:16

The Holy Spirit fulfills many purposes in our lives. He comforts us, teaches us, protects us, guides us, inspires us, fills us, empowers us, leads us, and points us to Jesus. Jesus said that He would not leave us as orphans, but would instead leave us under the protection of the Holy Spirit.

Unfortunately, we miss out on this wonderful relationship with the Holy Spirit because we spend so little time getting to know Him.

Fruit of the Spirit-Led Life

When we pray using scripture, the Word of God becomes deeply ingrained in our hearts, the seeds of the Spirit take root, and our branches grow stronger, eventually bearing fruit. The Word of God is a powerful source in stabilizing our souls through the Holy Spirit.

> *"Blessed are those who trust in the LORD and have made the LORD their hope and confidence. They are like trees planted along a riverbank, with roots that reach deep into the water. Such trees are not bothered by the heat or worried by long months of drought. Their leaves stay green, and they never stop producing fruit."*

> *Jeremiah 17:7–8*

I am living proof that God can take nothing and make it into something. Although I am not famous, by most standards I have done well. As pointed out earlier, I have been blessed to have worked in companies like Allstate Insurance Company, Ernst & Young, Computer Sciences Corporation (CSC), Merck & Company, Trinity Health, and Yale New Haven Health. I retired from Yale New Haven Health as a vice president. I was able to earn my masters, juris doctor, and doctor of philosophy degrees while working full-time. No one else in my immediate family had ever gone to college. I can tell you without a doubt, that all of my achievements have been the direct result of the Holy Spirit's influence in and through my life, including forty-six years of marriage to my wife, Maria. I could not have accomplished any of these things in my own strength.

I have learned that, when we intentionally cultivate our souls, we become more spiritually attuned and aware of the presence and work of the Holy Spirit. He has always been by my side, even when I wasn't aware of it. I have learned that the Word of God was planted in my heart from the beginning of my life, and that the Holy Spirit can manifest Himself in the lives of His children even when we are unaware of His presence. These truths have anchored my spirit and have kept me on course throughout my life.

More importantly, when we sow the Word of God in our hearts, by the power of the Holy Spirit the seed grows, and His work creates a powerful dynamic that transforms our lives.

Consider

- What do you believe about the Bible?
- Have you ever read the Bible from Genesis through Revelation? If so, how did this discipline affect you? If not, what has kept you from doing so?
- What do you know about the Holy Spirit, factually or experientially?

Chapter Two

Planting of the Holy Spirit

"Go and get your husband,' Jesus told her. 'I don't have a
husband,' the woman replied. Jesus said, 'You're right! You don't
have a husband—for you have had five husbands, and you aren't
even married to the man you're living with now. You certainly
spoke the truth!"

John 4:16–18

The Gospel of John, chapter four, opens with a scene of Jesus engaging in a culturally shocking meeting with a Samaritan woman. The Samaritans were despised by the Jews, and women were given little to no recognition or social standing in Jewish society. Additionally, the woman in this scene admitted to living in a sinful relationship. Jesus' disciples were in shock when they arrived to find Him speaking with her. Yet Jesus went out of His way to make time to talk to the Samaritan woman in a highly public location.

Barrier-Breaking Love

We can feel Jesus' love for this lost soul, and we also see her desperate desire to be loved. Of course, Jesus knew this about her and that is why He was there.

The Holy Spirit is not something or someone who can be comprehended by intellect, rationale, or science. He is God, and can only be understood in the perspective of His appointed role in the godhead, and with God's people. Believe me when I tell you that once someone experiences the touch of God through His Spirit, they will never be the same.

Let us look more closely at the Samaritan woman in John 4:4, whom Jesus met at the well outside the village of Sychar. This precious woman deliberately went to the well when no one else would be there because she was a social outcast. She certainly wasn't expecting to find the Jewish Messiah waiting for her! Jesus asked her for a drink, and she was shocked that a Jewish man would risk his reputation by speaking to her, much less asking her to give him water that she had drawn.

Jesus wasn't concerned about the opinions of critics. He had kingdom work to do.

"Go and get your husband," Jesus instructed her.

"I don't have a husband," the woman replied, looking away in shame.

Unleashing the Spirit

Jesus responded, compassion emanating from His tone: *"You're right! You don't have a husband, for you have had five husbands, and you aren't even married to the man you're living with now. You certainly spoke the truth"* (John 4:17–18).

His words and actions touched the woman's heart. She didn't realize all of this at the time, but the reality was that a Jewish man took the time to travel out of his way to find her at the well and speak to her. Jesus went on to tell her that he knew the details of her life and still had come to forgive her. He was not ashamed to stand in the same physical space as she. This Jesus, the Messiah, loved her in spite of her many sins. His Spirit reached beyond her sin and shame, speaking hope to her soul, and life to her spirit.

The Samaritan woman suddenly realized that Jesus, the Son of God, loved her in spite of her sins and the life she was living. He didn't judge her.

Jesus goes on to say in John 4:23–24, *"But the time is coming—indeed it's here now—when true worshipers will worship the Father in spirit and in truth. The Father is looking for those who will worship him that way. For God is Spirit, so those who worship him must worship in spirit and in truth."*

Jesus disclosed to her, and through her to us, who God is. God is spirit, and those who worship Him must worship Him in spirit and in truth.

The combination of spirit and truth *is* the Word of God (John 17:17). This means that we must release our thoughts in submission to the Word as it speaks to our hearts and souls.

We find in verse 28 that the woman left her jar beside the well and ran back to the village to tell everyone she had met the Messiah.

Surprisingly, they all came to see this self-proclaimed Messiah. It is important that we remember that the woman in this story was considered immoral and ungodly. She was more than likely ostracized by the people in the community. But if we look at biblical genealogy, a Canaanite prostitute named Rahab, a Moabite named Ruth, and a woman named Bathsheba were all recorded as being members of Jesus' lineage (Matthew 1:3). God uses us despite our past. When He forgives us, He no longer remembers our sins.

Miraculously, the Samaritan woman was so transformed by the love of Jesus that she left her jar, which was a valuable possession, and ran into the village to proclaim her discovery. She convinced busy people who were working in the middle of the day to leave what they were doing and run to the countryside to see a stranger. When had the people in the Samaritan woman's village ever before respected or responded to a word she had spoken? Jesus stayed with them for two days.

> **We must release our thoughts in submission to the Word as it speaks to our hearts and souls.**

Those of us who are touched by the Holy Spirit are so filled with His power and love that His Spirit is unleashed; it flows into our being and touches our essence, our world, and those around us in ways that nothing on earth can duplicate. This is how the Spirit empowers us to connect with others. But this unleashing of the Holy Spirit requires faith, surrender, humility, and spiritual discernment.

Intimacy with Jesus

Jesus creates intimacy with the people He meets. He shows us love, regardless of our circumstances. He loves us unconditionally, as we are. Once He embraces us, He proceeds to heal us, takes away our pain, and restores us to who He created us to be.

The Creator of our soul speaks to us through means that are woven into our design. He communicates to us in ways that reverberate in the fiber of our being. However, we must stop our busyness and learn to be still. According to Reverend Kirk Byron Jones:

"Hurry is a serious threat to the deepening spiritual life available to us all in all walks of life, not just called religious people. The gifts of stillness cannot be realized with our present fixation on hurry. We cannot give ourselves permission to be still as long as we are addicted to hurry. Hurry is a spiritual issue.

As we slow ourselves, we become better able to perceive and receive the blessings of stillness for deepening our relationship to God. Stillness helps us to engage two important movements where God is concerned: discerning God and receiving God."[4]

When the power of the Spirit courses though our bodies, it affects those around us in ways that nothing on earth can replicate. Those who have been filled with the Spirit understand and recognize how they can be directly used by the Spirit. We must learn to be comfortable with silence so we can hear and experience the presence and power of the Holy Spirit.

We find very few places in scripture where Jesus reveals who He is, yet in John 4:26 He tells the Samaritan woman outright that He is the Messiah. Jesus was so moved by this woman's heart that He entrusted her with His spiritual identity, which filled her with such an overflowing of His Spirit's love, that she ran back to the village to share the good news with people who most likely despised her. What an image of God's overflowing grace!

> **Because the Samaritan woman had been in Jesus' presence, she was overflowing with His power and love so strongly that they could feel it, and the Samaritans believed her. This is the power the Holy Spirit gives to those who are open to His voice.**

Nonetheless, the people ran to see the man she had encountered, as His Spirit flowed from her and touched them. The

Spirit overflowed from the temple of her body, as described in 2 Corinthians 4:7: "*We now have this light shining in our hearts, but we ourselves are like fragile clay jars containing this great treasure.*"

Because the woman had been in Jesus' presence and was overflowing with His power and love so strongly that they could feel it, the Samaritans believed her. This is the power the Holy Spirit gives to those who are open to His voice. Just as we can feel when someone physically touches us and says something that affects our emotions, we react in in the same way in our spirit when someone does or says something that is either dark and evil, or joyous and Spirit-filled.

Learning to Yield

The Holy Spirit can also flow uninhibited through us as we yield to Him and desire His indwelling. One way to yield is to develop the habit of reading the Word daily and allowing it to sit in, simmer through, and saturate your soul. When we plant the Word of God in our hearts and feed it like a growing seed, it continually produces spiritual insight. If we intellectualize this process, as did the Pharisees and Sadducees in the New Testament, we will never experience the power inherent in the Word. Practice by reading, reflecting on, and reviewing the Word's influence on your thinking and actions. Keeping a journal can be helpful in this process.

Growing up, I knew women like the Samaritan woman and their families. On the outside they often appeared cold, belligerent, and angry; but on the inside they were vulnerable, scared, hurting, and often alone; still, they were loving people.

It is important to take the time to understand hurting people, as Jesus did at the well. Who is Jesus? God's Son, who loves us and knows our hearts. We feel safe only when we open our hearts to those we trust. The Holy Spirit knows our hearts, and we are inherently safe with Him. Before we can feel safe, we must come to know and trust Him.

The Neighborhood

Pop was a man of the streets who was viewed as a drunkard. He was older than Daddy G, my maternal grandfather, and lived

44

at 820 Lawrence Street, located under the 8th Street Bridge in Allentown, Pennsylvania. This bridge is now called the *"Bridge of Despair"* because people have used it to jump to their deaths.

When I turned five years old we moved to 458 Union Street. Before that time we lived in the unit above Pop Baker and Nanna B. Most of the people in that neighborhood were low-income families. Migrant workers and others who were transient often moved in and out of the neigh-borhood throughout the warmer months. Unfortunately, Pop and Nanna B were poor and consid-

> They often gave with a smile that reflected their generous hearts. I believe this happens in communities where heartache is part of life and the Spirit of God is stirring.

ered lower class on the economic scale. However, the Scotts, Daddy G and Nanna, my maternal grandparents, were middle class, as Daddy G worked at the Bethlehem Steel Mill, a job that provided him with a steady salary, nice clothes, a very nice house, a new Cadillac, and a garage.

Nanna belonged to several social organizations, including the Order of the Eastern Star and St. James AME Zion Church, where the respected women in the community provided services to those in need. The Scotts had beautiful hardwood floors, a finished basement, hot water, and a furnace that warmed their entire four-story home at 460 Union Street. Pop and Nanna B, in contrast, had a two-unit home heated by a coal stove and no hot water or flushing toilet. As a result, I lived in poverty from birth up to the age of five, when we moved to 458 Union Street and Dad had a steady job.

Aunt Louise had four pretty daughters, including a set of twins. My first cousins were highly favored by Daddy G and were always dressed in beautiful outfits. As babies, the twins were considered for an advertising opportunity with Gerber Baby Foods, but because of my Aunt Louise's fear of what could happen if they were to be the recipients of notoriety, the deal never materialized.

I, on the other hand, was fortunate if I received a bath once a month. My clothes were bought at thrift stores, usually two sizes too large so I could eventually grow into them. I usually appeared clean enough to get by in public. But looking back, I wonder how bad I must have smelled, especially in the summer when I slept in the same clothes for who-knows-how-long? I was, all in all, a happy kid who was loved by his mom and dad. Their love had an immeasurable influence on my life and to some degree protected me from evil.

As I grew older, I realized that many of the other people who lived under the bridge were poor, but I often saw them share what little they had with those in need. They usually gave with a smile that reflected their generous hearts. I believe this happens in communities where heartache is part of life, and the Spirit of God is stirring. Conversely, those who have plenty often appear to hoard their possessions and try to impress those around them. They take what they can get, work to benefit themselves, and ease their pain and suffering with materialism that, in reality, only increases their insatiable hunger for more.

In the Sermon on the Mount in Matthew, chapter five Jesus talks about the poor in spirit and tells us in verse one that He blesses them. He talks about those who mourn in verse four, and who tend to suffer more than those who are poor? Jesus also talks about those who hunger and thirst for righteousness, the people who came running from the Samaritan village . . . and those who lived under the 8th Street Bridge. They felt the Holy Spirit flowing from Jesus, who was filled to overflowing with the Spirit from before the beginning of creation.

So, who is the Holy Spirit? He is God the Father, He is God the Son, and He is God the Holy Spirit, as delineated in Matthew 28:19, where Jesus instructs His disciples to go and make disciples of all the nations, baptizing them in the name of the Father, the Son, and the Holy Spirit. Many people find this passage confusing, and most believers are hard pressed to explain it. How can God be three in one?

Think about this: I can be a father, a son, a husband, a cousin, a friend, a vice president, a trustee member, and so on, all at the same time. You can be a mother, a daughter, a wife, a sister, a lawyer, a friend and a coworker, all at the same time. Although the identities of the members of the triune God entail more than their respective roles, they are one. We have a tendency to separate the persons when we would be better off focusing on their respective function and character within the integrated godhead. This focus might help our finite minds to appreciate and trust the magnitude of one God acting as three distinct, yet unseparated persons manifesting as God in their unique and distinct roles.

Sin, Shame, and Separation

An important purpose of the Holy Spirit is to teach God's children to see life through the lens of the Word of God and to live under His guidance. The Holy Spirit's job, in part, is to guide us back to the intimate fellowship we as humans once enjoyed with God in the Garden of Eden. As recorded in Genesis 3:7, that relationship was broken when Adam and Eve ate the forbidden fruit: *"At that moment their eyes were opened and they suddenly felt shame at their nakedness. So, they sewed fig leaves together to cover themselves."*

In verse eight we are told *"they hid themselves from God,"* and heard His call to them: *"Where are you?"* Their physical eyes were opened, but they hid from God because their spiritual eyes had been blinded by their disobedience. Sin separated them, and all humanity from their Creator.

God actively sought them out, but Adam and Eve lost their ability both to discern God and His Word through "spiritual eyes" and to see Him in His true form. They were no longer able to see God in His Glory or to be present with Him. Remember that God said, *"I am Spirit and Truth, and those who worship Him must worship in spirit and truth."* (John 4:4).

We became attached to the created and not the Creator, which placed us at enmity with God. At that point, humanity lost the infilling of the Holy Spirit and our intimate relationship with the Father. We needed a Savior to restore our severed standing with the Father and return us to the intimacy of the garden. Sin separates us from God because our eyes and our focus fall away from Him onto ourselves and the things we believe we can gain from this world.

Jesus reminded His disciples in the book of John that He was leaving, but would one day return. He also made a promise that the

Holy Spirit would never leave us. He further stated in John 14:26, *"When the Father sends the Advocate as my representative—that is, the Holy Spirit—he will teach you everything and will remind you of everything I have told you."*

The Holy Spirit is God, and He is a person, not simply a role in the godhead as we will see in later chapters. We can know God and have intimate fellowship with Him through our spirit. It is impossible for us as finite creatures to fully understand God, but we can know Him and have a real relationship with Him, just as we have relationships with the people we love.

But that means, as with the Samaritan woman at the well, that you and I must be open, willing to listen to the Spirit, and be obedient in doing as He says.

Multiple levels of spiritual maturity are represented in Jesus'

> **You and I must be open, willing to listen to the Spirit, and be obedient in doing as He says.**

parable of the seeds. As believers, we require wisdom, spiritual maturity, and discernment to understand and grow through these levels. This parable represents the Word of God in us, our spiritual maturity, and power in the Spirit as we become more like Jesus, bearing fruit for the kingdom. It illustrates what happens when the Holy Spirit penetrates and permeates our hearts.

Parable of the Seeds

> *"If you can't understand the meaning of this parable, how will you understand all the other parables? The farmer plants seed by taking God's word to others. The seed that fell on the footpath represents those who hear the message, only to have Satan come at once and take it away. The seed on the rocky soil represents those who hear the message and immediately receive it with joy. But since they don't have deep roots, they don't last long. They fall away as soon as they have problems or are persecuted for believing God's word. The seed that fell among the thorns represents others who hear God's word, but all too quickly the message is crowded out by the worries of this life, the lure of wealth, and*

the desire for other things, so no fruit is produced. And the seed that fell on good soil represents those who hear and accept God's word and produce a harvest of thirty, sixty, or even a hundred times as much as had been planted!"

Mark 4:13–20

Seed on the Footpath—Mark 4:15

The *first sowing* represents those who hear the Word of God, but Satan comes at once and snatches the Word away. The spirit of those in the first sowing are separated at the outset from following God, and they sustain no interest in God's Word because of their greater attraction to materialism, physical pleasures, and darkness.

The people who respond to the first sowing are children of Satan, and we can discern who they are by the fruit they bear. They are wicked and filled with hatred. We can perceive their hearts by their fruit (or the absence of positive fruit), as described in Galatians 5:20. They are of the flesh, meaning they live for fulfillment of their human desires and care only about themselves. Their gods are pride and self, and they are driven by pleasure and possessions. If we look carefully at their lives, we see they are selfish, and their hearts are cold to godly interests. Many people who respond to the first sowing might tell you they are godly and reverent, but unfortunately, they will hear Jesus say, "Depart from me, for I never knew you." I believe that Judas, King Ahab, Jezebel, and others like them in the Bible were such people.

We can see darkness on the faces of people who are on the footpath. They rarely, if ever, smile from the heart or laugh. They exhibit no joy but focus instead on hostility, quarreling, jealousy, outbursts of anger, dissention, and similar behaviors as listed in Galatians 5:19–20. This dark fruit emanates from their hearts, and mature Christians can often detect the evil in their eyes and actions.

Those of the first sowing are devoid of love, and they pursue things that bring them temporary pleasure, wealth, and power. They are cruel, deceitful, and void of compassion and empathy, and their hatred abounds for God's work and His children.

The children of Satan focus on materialism and the attractions of this world. They pursue power to use for themselves. While they may talk about God, the fruit of the Spirit cannot be observed in their lives. Unless they repent and turn back to God, death and darkness will follow them . . . and often their families.

> *"When you follow the desires of your sinful nature, the results are very clear: sexual immorality, impurity, lustful pleasures, idolatry, sorcery, hostility, quarreling, jealousy, outbursts of anger, selfish ambition, dissension, division, envy, drunkenness, wild parties, and other sins like these. Let me tell you again, as I have before, that anyone living that sort of life will not inherit the Kingdom of God."*
>
> Galatians 5:19–21

Seed on the Rocky Soil—Mark 4:16-17

The *second sowing* represents people who are immediately joyful when they receive the Word, but their passion soon fades away, and they eventually return to their old way of life. Although they are well intentioned, they often remain attached to old friends and continue to walk the same old paths. Their hunger for the Word is short lived. The attraction of the world is too strong, and they turn their backs on God and return to their old ways of life. As the apostle Peter so graphically reminds us, *"They prove the truth of this proverb: A dog returns to its vomit"* (2 Peter 2:22).

It was hard for me to remain focused on God when I lacked friendship and companionship with other believers. This happened to the children of Israel in the book of Judges. They wanted to do what they saw other people and nations doing. By the time we get to the end of the book, we see everyone in Israel doing as they saw fit, with God as a distant memory. *"In those days, Israel had no king; all the people did whatever seemed right in their own eyes,"* (Judges 21:25).

The types of people we surround ourselves with are key to helping us maintain our faith walk. No matter how many times we mess up, God will take us back! This is the reason Christ died on the cross. God knew we had wandering hearts like lost sheep, and *still* He loves us.

I had a strong attraction to hanging out and partying until two or three o'clock in the morning. When I was fourteen, Mom told me that if Satan had a party in hell, I would be the first one at the door. She also told me that when I was two years old, she and Dad would take me uptown, and as soon as I heard music, no matter where I was, I would break out dancing.

Save yourself first, by God's grace; then go back to throw your friends a lifeine with the help of the Holy Spirit.

By the time I was a teenager and was staying out all night, I thought I was living the so-called good life. The good life eventually gets old because it is not fulfilling, and it can't sustain a person's soul. God doesn't plot a path to nowhere for you or me. We might have to cut old friends loose, but when we come to a place of spiritual strength, we are in a position to help them.

Save yourself first, by God's grace; then go back to throw your friends a lifeline with the help of the Holy Spirit. The streets have a tempting allure, and the evil one is real, and roams those streets, and he is looking to devour whomever he may!

People in the second sowing are like sheep being led to slaughter. They are easily influenced by those they believe are powerful, because they long to be loved. People are susceptible to being influenced, and gravitate to those who show them kindness and attention. Since they are fearful, lonely, and desperate, they will follow almost anyone who conveys a thread of hope.

I believe that King Saul and King Solomon were such people. They had intimate walks with God, but eventually lost their way . . . and with it their close fellowship with God. They both had a desire to follow God, but became distracted by earthly desires. King Saul eventually committed suicide, and King Solomon worshiped demons after turning his back on God.

> *"Solomon did what was evil in the LORD's sight; he refused to follow the LORD completely, as his father, David, had done."*
>
> *1 Kings 11:6*

Seed in the World and the Word—Mark 4:18-19

The *third sowing* represents many people in the church today. These individuals straddle both the world and the Word, while trying to have it all. Their beliefs are a mix of the world's philosophies blended with the Word of God. They serve in the church but are torn about the things of this world because they have their feet in both worlds. Their lives are inconsistent, and they ride the fence in terms of their stand on many things. They may appear to the outside world to have it all together, but those who are spiritually discerning see evidence of inconsistencies in their spiritual talk and walk. A good example of this can be found in Revelation when the Angel is speaking with the Church in Sardis:

> *"I know all the things you do, and that you have a reputation for being alive—but you are dead. Wake up! Strengthen what little remains, for even what is left is almost dead. I find that your actions do not meet the requirements of my God. Go back to what you heard and believed at first; hold to it firmly. Repent and turn to me again. If you don't wake up, I will come to you suddenly, as unexpected as a thief. Yet there are some in the church in Sardis who have not soiled their clothes with evil. They will walk with me in white, for they are worthy."*
>
> *Revelation 3:1–4*

Mature believers can observe the pain in these Christians' eyes and sense their struggle and the sadness in their souls. Many Christians who walk in this path feel unhappy, yet they do their best to portray to others that they don't struggle. They are unsettled and often unproductive because they work in their own strength, while trying to demonstrate holiness.

These Christians display immaturity, although many have been walking with the Lord for twenty, thirty, or more years.

> *"You have been believers so long now that you ought to be teaching others. Instead, you need someone to teach you again the basic things about God's word. You are like babies who need milk and cannot eat solid food. For someone who lives on milk is still an infant and doesn't know how to do what is right. Solid food is for those who are mature, who through training have the skill to recognize the difference between right and wrong."*
>
> *Hebrews 5:12–14*

Spiritual maturity is not a matter of how long a person has been a believer in Jesus. It is a matter of how intimately they know Him through the sanctifying power of the Holy Spirit.

I consider people from scripture like Reuben, Jonah, and Saul of Tarsus (before his radical conversion) to be in this category of the third sowing. While their intentions might be good, their efforts are feeble and misguided without the Spirit. People in this category can do more harm than good to the church and sometimes behave like spoiled brats. Unfortunately, these men and women often drive new believers to flee the church because of their hypocrisy. They have salvation, but produce little to no fruit.

Seed on Good Soil–Mark 4:20

However, the *fourth seed* that fell on good soil represents those who are totally committed to the Word of God, are driven to service, and attuned to His voice as they walk in the Spirit. Depending upon their level of maturity, they may produce a harvest of thirty, sixty, or a hundredfold of that which was sown; we will talk about this later. It is important to note that, while many believers produce fruit that may only be five or tenfold, these believers *are* still producing fruit for the kingdom. Those who have a stronger Spirit outpouring are those who are more closely aligned with the Holy Spirit. This principle was also true with Jesus and his disciples. Peter, James, and John had a deep, intimate relationship with Jesus as can be seen in their New Testament writings. They still had ups and downs until they were fully immersed in the Holy Spirit as found in the book of Acts. These three disciples who were closest to Jesus were also with Him on the Mount of Transfiguration, where they saw Him in all of His glory. Nevertheless the other disciples, with the exception of Judas, still bore fruit for the kingdom.

Each of us is blessed with different gifts, and we should never be envious of our spiritual siblings. We should look at their giftings and nurture our brothers and sisters when we see the opportunity, or help them when the Holy Spirit gives them greater assignments, rejoicing in *all* opportunities to advance God's kingdom.

If one part of Christ's body suffers, all the parts suffer with it, and if one part is honored, all the parts are honored (1 Corinthians 12:26). People like Paul, Stephen, David, Abraham, Joseph, Deborah, and many other men and women in the Bible are included in the category of seed that fell on good soil. Not only did these men and women serve God wholeheartedly, but they also experienced the unspeakable joy that comes when we walk in the fullness of the Spirit. I have witnessed this in missionaries from Afghanistan, Liberia, India, Kenya, the Ukraine, and other parts of the world who understood what Jesus meant when he told the Samaritan woman about the living water in John 4:13–14. May we aspire to be among them.

When we use our gifts to produce the fruit of the Spirit, joy springs to life in the souls of those who serve, and those who are served. *"Taste and see that the LORD is good. Oh, the joys of those who take refuge in Him"* (Psalm 34:8).

What are you waiting for?

Consider

♦ Do you know anyone who is filled with the Holy Spirit? What do you see in them that makes you think they are filled with the Holy Spirit?
♦ What have you observed about the Holy Spirit thus far?
♦ What do you think the Holy Spirit desires for you?

Chapter Three

The Person of the Holy Spirit

*"I will send you the Advocate—the Spirit of truth. He will come
to you from the Father and will testify all about me."*

John 15:26

In the previous chapter we noted that the Holy Spirit penetrates
our heart and soul, the seat of our emotions and being. In this
chapter we will focus on the person of the Holy Spirit, a *person* sent
by Jesus so that His followers would not be alone in this world. We
will start by looking at scriptures that give evidence that the Holy
Spirit shares in the characteristics of God and is, therefore, someone we can talk to, depend on, and trust in any situation.

Speaking to Us, Instructing Us

*"The Holy Spirit said to Philip, Go over and walk along beside
the carriage."*

Acts 8:29

We see the Holy Spirit speaking directly to Philip and telling him
to go to the chariot of the Ethiopian Eunuch. The Holy Spirit gives
Philip specific instructions about what to do. Because the Holy
Spirit was in a relationship with Philip, He could speak directly to
him. Philip could hear and understand Him and could, therefore,
decide whether or not to be obedient.

*"When the Father sends the Advocate as my representative—that
is, the Holy Spirit—he will teach you everything and will remind
you of everything I have told you."*

John 14:26

Jesus referred to the Holy Spirit as an advocate who acts as His representative, giving instructions that would teach, or remind the disciples of what He said. It is clear from scripture that Jesus and the Holy Spirit are one, and that the Holy Spirit will continue the work Jesus had started, and serve in that role until Jesus returns.

> *"There is so much more I want to tell you, but you can't bear it now. When the Spirit of truth comes, he will guide you into all truth. He will not speak on his own but will tell you what he has heard. He will tell you about the future. He will bring me glory by telling you whatever he receives from me."*
>
> *John 16:12–14*

It is clear from Scripture that Jesus and the Holy Spirit are one and that the Holy Spirit will continue the work that Jesus had started and serve in that role until Jesus returns.

The Holy Spirit guides the disciples and conveys information and knowledge from Jesus to them. This becomes evident in the Book of Acts when the Holy Spirit descends on the disciples and those who are with them awaiting the Holy Spirit, as instructed by Jesus.

> *"Next Paul and Silas traveled through the area of Phrygia and Galatia, because the Holy Spirit had prevented them from preaching the word in the province of Asia at that time. Then coming to the borders of Mysia, they headed north for the province of Bithynia, but again the Spirit of Jesus did not allow them to go there. So instead, they went on through Mysia to the seaport of Troas."*
>
> *Acts 16:6–8*

We can see the Holy Spirit preventing Paul and Silas from entering Asia and redirecting their work. He is in direct communication, and they are responding to His directives.

> *"Do not bring sorrow to God's Holy Spirit by the way you live."*
>
> *Ephesians 4:30*

Because He is a person, the Holy Spirit can be hurt and grieved by the things we do. He has emotions that can cause Him sadness. These, again, are behaviors manifested by people who care about other people. The Holy Spirit loves us in the same way that Jesus and God the Father love us.

I reference here the New Living Translation Bible, where there are specific mentions of the Holy Spirit in both the Old Testament and New Testament. The Holy Spirit possesses attributes of a human being, and we should think of Him as a person. However, we must not forget that He is also God. The power and majesty of the Holy Spirit are beyond our comprehension, but He is always available to us, 24/7. He hovered over the waters in Genesis 1:2 as God created the heavens and the earth, but He also filled Jesus and fills believers, while at the same time He can reside in the womb.

> *"The Spirit and the bride say, 'Come.' Let anyone who hears this say, 'Come.' Let anyone who is thirsty come. Let anyone who desires drink freely from the water of life."*
>
> *Revelation 22:17*

The Role of the Holy Spirit

The purpose of the Holy Spirit is to protect and keep His children safe and to fill them so they will overflow with His presence. The Holy Spirit was present in Genesis and also in Revelation. He appears throughout the entire Bible, but is more visibly active in the New Testament after Jesus' ascension into heaven. There are not as many direct references to the Holy Spirit in the Old Testament, but it is evident that the Spirit led and filled men and women from the beginning to the end of scripture.

> *"If you love me, obey my commandments. And I will ask the Father, and he will give you another Advocate, who will never leave you. He is the Holy Spirit, who leads into all truth. The world cannot receive him, because it isn't looking for him and doesn't recognize him. But you know him, because he lives with you now and later will be in you; No, I will not abandon you as orphans I will come to you."*
>
> *John 14:15–18*

We know that Jesus was filled and led by the Holy Spirit. His desire is that His children be led and filled by the same Spirit who is in the Father and the Son. I believe that the Spirit hovers over His children before we invite Him into our hearts. He knew us before we were born, so why would He abandon us until such time as we are saved? He patiently and lovingly stands nearby.

We can have a personal relationship with the Holy Spirit, just as we have relationships with people every day. This requires that we look at the world through spiritual eyes and listen with our hearts, which is counter to what we see as normative in this world. As we spend time in the Word of God, in prayer, and in meditation, our awareness of the presence of the Holy Spirit grows stronger.

When we discipline ourselves to read the Word of God, the Holy Spirit speaks directly to our spirit and awakens our spiritually intuitive abilities. Constant absorption of the Word attunes our hearts and spirits to the voice of the Holy Spirit, the author of the Word of God.

> *"The gatekeeper opens the gate for him, and the sheep recognize his voice and come to him. He calls his own sheep by name and leads them out. After he has gathered his own flock, he walks ahead of them, and they follow him because they know his voice. They won't follow a stranger; they will run from him because they don't know his voice."*

John 10:3–5

As we read and meditate daily on the Word of God, the Holy Spirit brings insights to our hearts and intuitions. This enhances our ability to communicate with God through the Spirit. There is no quick formula, or trick for experiencing the Holy Spirit. This discipline requires time, commitment, surrender, and faith.

The Spirit in the Fire

In October of 1961, I was in Allen Park hanging out on a cool, brisk Saturday evening at around seven o'clock. It was already dark, and Greg was playing with matches and setting dry leaves and newspaper on fire. This was the first time I had ever seen anyone playing with matches. I was so fascinated by the fire that I got the bright idea of a no-cost way to improve my bedroom. During my walk home, I decided to remove the threads and torn fabric that hung from the bottom of my second-hand bed. As soon as I got home, I found some matches and went straight to my bedroom to try my experiment. I was so excited that I didn't tell my parents about my grandiose idea. I would surprise them.

My eight-year-old mind was unable to comprehend the horror that instantly followed. No sooner had I lit a match and held it to a tendril of fabric beneath my box spring, when out of nowhere, my dilapidated, second-hand bed burst into ravenous flames emitting rolling waves of dark, suffocating smoke. I jerked back and stared in absolute horror.

Our house was in deplorable condition and one of the worst on our row of homes. We lived next door to my maternal grandparents at 460 Union Street on the left, and Uncle Frank's (Aunt Louise's husband) sister, Dolly at 456 ½ Union Street on the right.

Our three-story home included a dingy, damp walk-out basement. The roof leaked so badly that Dad had to skillfully arrange buckets and containers in the attic to catch the rain. Huge brown water spots stained the walls of my bedroom, which was located on the back side of the house. The linoleum on the floors was rotted, and the exposed wood was scarred and splintered. At night I often listened to mice prancing through the walls.

An old coal stove located in the basement vainly attempted to heat our house in the winter, but when it got dreadfully cold I often slept with my clothes on to stay warm. Although my grandparents lived next door, I can never remember them or any other relatives other than Nanna ever coming to visit us, even at Christmas. I have no memories of any of my grandparents ever visiting, except the morning when Nanna told me that Nanna B had died.

The houses in my neighborhood were narrow row homes neatly built, one next to the other. In the early 1960s there were no such things as smoke detectors, or fire alarms, to warn people that their homes were ablaze. Unfortunately, there were only two ways out of our row homes, either down the narrow steps to the living room and out through the front door, or by jumping out of the bedroom window to a thirty-to-forty-foot drop onto a surface of hard-packed dirt, weeds, and rocks.

Our home was furnished with dilapidated, second-hand junk. Mom said the furniture was antique, but I can tell you it was obviously someone else's junk, bought from a store named Schlichers on Hamilton Street that was always furnished with all kinds of well-used stuff.

Our house was a tinder box waiting to ignite. The Allentown Redevelopment Authority eventually demolished our entire community in 1968 after deadly riots took place across urban America. Their decision displaced thousands of people in my neighborhood. When I travel home, I am sadly reminded that my old Union Street neighborhood and family home no longer exist.

Four streets encompassed my neighborhood block. Facing north on the main street, Union Street, were approximately twenty row houses. Facing west on Fifth Street, not including Franklin's Bar on the corner with rooms above the hotel, another five homes lined the street. Willow Street ran behind our house facing south, with approximately fifteen other row homes nestled along it. The east side was marked by Penn Street, where Crowder Jr. Company, an electrical engineering building, was located. These streets marked the parameters of many of my childhood memories.

I bolted down the stairs to warn Mom and Dad there was a fire in my room and grabbed my winter coat on the way to the basement coal bin, where I planned to hide until I could make my escape to the train tracks and run away. Why I didn't keep heading down the street to escape at that moment, I don't know. I guess the reality of what I caused had not fully sunken in, or maybe the Holy Spirit led me to the coal bin to save me. This, I believe, is the true answer.

My grandfathers both shared a history of running away from home at early ages. Daddy G ran away at the age of nine and was raised in a brothel in South Carolina. Pop left home and lived in West Virginia, where he ended up serving time in prison. He never mentioned his early years, except to tell me that he once had sex with a woman behind a judge's bench in a West Virginia court-room, while he served time in jail. One of my older peers taught me to survive by stealing and hustling, so I was confident that I could find a way to survive. For as far back as I could remember, I always managed to have a few dollars in my pocket.

By God's grace, the same power of the Holy Spirit that pro-tected Dad on the beaches of Normandy, helped him discard my flaming box spring out of my broken bedroom window that had been nailed shut for years to help keep the cold air out. Somehow my dear dad managed to drag the flaming mattress down the steps and out of the house before anything else could catch on fire. Yes, I realized as an adult that the Holy Spirit helped Dad do these things to save our family . . . and, most likely, our neighborhood. I cannot imagine what Dad felt when he entered a room that was engulfed with flames and smoke. Only God knows!

Nanna caught me as I made my escape out of the basement through the coal chute that opened to face Union Street. I was attempting to make my way to the train tracks, where I could catch the next train heading to who-knew-where? I did not intend to set my bed on fire. All I wanted to do was to make my room a little neater. I was determined to get away, and my first inclination was to catch a train and leave home.

God saved my parents from losing their second son on that cool and dark October night in 1961. Needless to say, Nanna caught me and everyone in the neighborhood heard me screaming for dear life, pleading with Dad, and then with Mom to have mercy on my derriere. I was convinced that Dad was trying to kill me as he spanked, no, as he beat the feeling out of my buttocks. Mom and Nanna were casually seated on the couch watching, as though they were at the Colonial Movie Theater on Fifth and Hamilton Streets watching a show. The only thing they needed was a box of popcorn.

But even in darkness I cannot hide from you.

It might sound silly, but no one had ever told me not to play with matches. I was a compliant kid who did what I was told and never talked back. I tended to be quiet and observant and never got caught doing bad things. That didn't mean that I didn't do bad things, just that I was good at not getting caught. Nanna said I was sneaky, and, looking back, I don't think I could disagree.

I guess my parents assumed that a somewhat intelligent eight-year-old would know better than to set his bed on fire. Especially an eight-year-old who spent most of his life exploring the streets of the neighborhood for the better part of four years. It was a miracle that our old house did not go up in flames.

After spanking me for the very first time, Dad suddenly started crying uncontrollably. Actually, he started to howl, a deep-from-the-gut cry that spewed from the depths of his soul. It was loud and awful.

I am not sure what Mom and Nanna thought, but I was confused. Dad had just worn himself out by spanking me nearly to death, and now he was crying as though he was the one who had been spanked. What was going on?

The look on Mom and Nanna's faces told me they were feeling sorry for Dad. They both turned to me, shaking their heads and saying, "Now look what you did!" I knew I set my rotten, deplorable bed on fire. How was I to blame for making Dad cry like a baby? I was confused (and sore).

I realized much later in life that it was impossible to know how many people would likely have died that night, if Dad hadn't quickly removed the flaming bed from my bedroom. A lot of elderly people in my neighborhood would not have escaped from their homes. Although I never intended to burn my bed, I acknowledged that I *did* intentionally set it on fire. Such are the mysteries haunting an eight-year-old boy's mind.

But, how was I now responsible for making a grown man cry? Why did my father break into tears? When I look back from the perspective of an adult, I see my father weeping in gratitude for the child and family he had nearly lost. For a neighborhood that could have gone up in flames . . . And I see him overcome with memories from the war. I clearly see and understand that the Holy Spirit intervened, not only on my behalf and for my family and neighbors, but for my father's wounded heart.

My Father's Tears

That spanking was the first and only time my father had ever put his physical hands on me to punish me. It was also the only time I ever remember seeing Dad shed a tear. I can't even remember seeing him cry at the funerals of Pop or Nanna B. I have since wondered whether he cried because he envisioned the death and destruction that was averted by his quick action; or was it because he was forced to inflict physical punishment on me, his son, for the very first time?

I believe that Dad had been physically abused by his father when he was drunk. Did spanking me trigger old memories? Or did he realize I planned to run away? The agony he no doubt felt as he spanked me must have stirred the recollection of pain he endured as a child. I can only imagine the trauma Dad experienced growing up.

Mom told me that as a child, Dad had often slept on the roof because the fighting between Pop and Nanna B was so horrible. She also told me that Nanna B would wait for Dad in high school at the end of the school day to walk him home. She had promised God that if her son returned home from the war, she would go to church every Sunday for the rest of her life.

She kept her promise.

By the grace of God and the work of the Holy Spirit, I am where I am today. When I think about Dad's childhood, and the

> **Somehow, my father learned to deal with death and dying in ways that only the Holly Spirit could show him.**

horrors he certainly faced during World War II, I am overwhelmed over the recall of all he did for me. He and Mom gave me a peaceful, loving home that was a haven from the world beyond our doors.

I have often thought about my father as an introverted, abused 19-year-old on D-Day in Normandy, and what he must have faced as over 150,000 troops descended onto the shores of France in the bloodiest battle in World War II. Somehow, my father forced himself to cope with death and dying in ways that only the Holy Spirit could have shown him. Whenever I envision this portion of Dad's life, I am overwhelmed with sadness.

As I sat on the front porch early the next morning near the burned mattress lying on the ground in front of the house, Mr. Jackson passed by and asked if there was a fire, which I thought was odd. If you see a burned mattress lying in front of a house, don't you assume there had been a fire? Just as I was pondering Mr. Jackson's bewildering question, who should come walking down Union Street at 9:00 a.m. on Sunday morning?

None other than Dora Smith, Uncle Frank's niece whom I admired and feared with childhood awe. Astoundingly, she marched right up on the porch, sat down, put her arms around me, and laughed as she told me she heard that Dad had beaten my butt (my word, not hers) like a bass drum. How could Dora have known I was spanked the night before? She lived at Fifth and Lawrence Streets, almost two blocks away. People in our neighborhood were obviously very nosey and only too happy to spread everyone else's business.

I revered Dora. She was my heroine; tall, gorgeous, and reminiscent of a Greek goddess. She was a queen! I once saw her kick the monkey snot out of Pernell on the corner of Fifth and Union Streets in broad daylight on a hot summer Saturday afternoon. Pernell was a teenager, much older than I. He came from a tough family with some members who were rumored to have been involved with illegal drugs and prostitution. When Dora finished whipping Pernell, she got up and looked menacingly at the boys and men standing curbside watching her, as though to ask, "Who's next?"

Dora had taken the time to sit on the porch and put her arms around me. I felt majestic, like the king of Union Street, even though she had gotten a good laugh out of my misery.

Somehow, on that chilly fall Sunday morning, the Holy Spirit used Dora Smith to reassure me that He loved me, and was near, and that everything would be all right. Dora went to be with the Lord in October of 2016, and I was honored to say a few words at her funeral. When I spoke at my Aunt Louise's funeral, I mentioned that Dad, Aunt Louise, Curtis Cole, and Dora were the only people in my life I had ever feared.

After Aunt Louise's funeral, Dora asked me why I called her out in my aunt's funeral service. I explained to her it was out of my admiration that I spoke about her, and that I respected her as I did very few people in my life. In 2008 I traveled to Cape Town, South Africa, for a global workshop and was asked to speak about people I admired. I spoke about Pop and Dora.

Finding God in the Wilderness

On the Monday evening after the fire, Mom and Dad took me to the Union Street Boys' Club at 6:15 p.m., just before it opened. The club was located at Fourth and Union Streets, a place where I would eventually spend the better part of ten years of my life. The Boys' Club provided me with the discipline I needed as an inquisitive, energetic young boy. The men who ran the club had a great influence on my life. They committed themselves to caring for and nurturing the minds of the boys who lived in the community. Nick, Hertzog, Finnegan, Fritz, Jim, and Carl were men who cared about the lives of poor young boys who lived on and around Union Street, regardless of their circumstances, faith, or race.

Oftentimes, we visualize God as a holy deity who sits high above the heavens and the earth, and looks down on humanity from a complacent distance. Yet He tells us in Matthew 10:29 that not a single sparrow can fall to the ground without His knowing. Because the Spirit of the Lord is in us and around us, He knows our circumstances intimately. In fact, He knew our future circumstances before we ever came into existence.

> The moments when we feel we are sitting in the wilderness alone are often the times we hear God speak. When we're totally surrendered, with no place to go and no one to help us, God is able to use us.

We see how intimately God knows us as exemplified in the story of Hagar in Genesis 21:19–20. Hagar was alone, running from Sarah, sitting in the desert with nowhere to go. With no food or water, Hagar feared for the death of her son, Ishmael. When God opened her eyes, she saw a well full of water. She quickly filled her container and gave her boy a drink. God was with Ishmael as he grew up in the wilderness.

The moments when we feel we are in the wilderness alone, are often the times we hear God speak. When we are totally surrendered, with no place to go, and no one to help us, we cry out for rescue. This is when the Holy Spirit is most able to teach us and use us. As God tells us in Isaiah 57:15, *"The high and lofty one who lives in eternity, the Holy One, says this: 'I live in the high and holy place with those whose spirits are contrite and humble. I restore the crushed spirit of the humble and revive the courage of those with repentant hearts.'"*

God knew I had no evil intentions when I set my bed on fire, but I understood that I had to be disciplined because I did something wrong, despite having had no malice in my heart. Many people in my crowded neighborhood might have been killed, if not for the intervention of the Holy Spirit and Dad. Sin often works this way. We act in ignorance or in haste, without talking to the Spirit of God, and we and others in our way may pay the price, sometimes for generations to come.

God uses circumstances to remind us of His love. Strangely enough, not one person spoke a single word to me after the fire about the destruction that could have resulted from my reckless behavior. However, I felt as though the Holy Spirit said in my heart, "Let Me show you how I can protect you, even when you are totally outside My will."

You might protest, "That makes no sense. How can God convey a concept like that to a child at such an early stage in life?"

We must understand that God speaks to His children in different ways: through dreams, visions, directly, through others, through donkeys (think of the Old Testament Balaam), through nature, through circumstances, through His work, and through our hearts with messages directly from the Holy Spirit. Somehow, my tender spirit understood even when God was teaching me. God spoke directly to Samuel when he was only a little boy, 1 Samuel 3. What it was He was conveying I didn't understand at the time. However, I did recognize that something very bad could have happened on that October evening and that God did not allow it to happen.

Dad spanked me for the very first time on the night of the fire, and I knew I deserved to be punished. My spirit also knew that no matter what happened, he still loved me. We do not need to use our minds to communicate with God because we are also spirit. Remember that the unborn John the Baptist leaped in his mother's womb when he heard Mary's voice, Luke 1:41.

The Spirit of God brings life to our being. All of nature is filled with the essence of God; this is the reason we see the seasons come and go, the stars and moon shine at night, and the sun blaze during the day. God's Spirit is the essence of low and high tide, the beginning and end of each new day. When we turn our attention from self to God, we begin to commune with Him in unspeakable, meaningful ways that transcend speech.

When I sat on the front porch of 458 Union Street on the morning after the fire, something deep in my soul told me that God still loved me. Sometimes, that revelation doesn't come right away. Sometimes, our spirit will comprehend things that our mind cannot conceive. There are times when we need to allow our spirit to just be, without trying to logically understand. The key is to reflect, to avoid being critical of ourselves, and to listen with an open heart and soul. Something as simple as stopping to acknowledge the Holy Spirit in the moment allows us to grow in intimacy with Him.

> *"Listen to me, O family of Jacob, Israel my chosen one! I alone am God, the First and the Last. It was my hand that laid the foundations of the earth, my right hand that spread out the heavens above. When I call out the stars, they all appear in order."*

Isaiah 48:12–13

> *"Look up into the heavens. Who created all the stars? He brings them out like an army, one after another, calling each by its name. Because of his great power and incomparable strength, not a single one is missing."*

Isaiah 40:26

Why is it hard for us to relinquish our will and allow the Creator of our souls to have full reign in our lives? The answer is *"Pride."*

We believe that we lose our identity if we are not in control. Unless we die to self, you and I will never experience the essence of who we are and the fullness of the Holy Spirit indwelling us.

The Holy Spirit is with us to help us. He can also protect us from the evil one and mold us into the creation that God designed us to be. God wants so much for His children, but we must be willing to give up our desires, and trust the One who designed us, before the creation of the world. All too often we live imprisoned by what we believe *we* cannot do, because we do not trust the One who created the heavens and the earth.

The enemy's scheme is to keep us looking at our feet and choosing our steps based on what we see, think, and feel, even while we tell ourselves how worthless we are. Instead, we are called to look up and survey the cosmos to see what is possible for God's children who trust their Father, and turn their eyes, ears, and hearts to the heavens to hear His voice

> *"No eye has seen, no ear has heard, and no mind has imagined what God has prepared for those who love him. But it was to us that God revealed these things by his Spirit. For his Spirit searches out everything and shows us God's deep secrets."*
>
> *1 Corinthians 2:9–10*

When I reflect on the fire, without a doubt I see the presence of God with me in the form of the Holy Spirit. The fire was real. The house should have been consumed by the flames and burned to the ground, along with many other tinder-dry homes on our block. Lives could have been lost.

God, the Holy Spirit was in that place! The house didn't burn. Our neighborhood remained intact. Lives were *not* lost. I did *not* run away, but remained at home, and as an adult I am stepping into God's purpose.

My sisters and brothers, know that God's desire is to have an intimate relationship with each one of us. Listen to the voice of the Spirit. He's speaking to *you*. Stop and take the time to listen!

Consider

- With whom do you speak when you need encouragement?
- What dreams and aspirations lie deep in your heart?
- Can you think of a time when the Holy Spirit was clearly present in your life?

Chapter Four

The Power of the Holy Spirit

*"Once when he was eating with them, Jesus commanded them,
'Do not leave Jerusalem until the Father sends you the gift he
promised, as I told you before. John baptized with water, but in
just a few days you will be baptized with the Holy Spirit.' So
when the apostles were with Jesus, they kept asking him, 'Lord,
has the time come for you to free Israel and restore our kingdom?'
He replied, 'The Father alone has the authority to set those dates
and times, and they are not for you to know. But you will receive
power when the Holy Spirit comes upon you. And you will be
my witnesses, telling people about me everywhere—in Jerusalem,
throughout Judea, in Samaria, and to the ends of the earth."*

Acts 1:4–8

We see in Acts, chapter one that Jesus is speaking with the disciples and has informed them that God will send them a gift, who is the Holy Spirit. When I was a child growing up, I was always excited to receive gifts because they brought me joy. Now imagine being told that you will receive a gift from God. Jesus goes on to say that His gift would endow power. According to Merriam-Webster's Dictionary, the word power means, "the ability to act or produce an effect." Power is all about possessing control, authority, or influence over things or other people. Jesus says that those who receive the gift of the Holy Spirit from God will be *endowed with power*.

But power for what purpose?

Holiness Requires Reverence

We see the Holy Spirit's power activated immediately in Peter and John as they visited the Temple:

> *"Peter and John went to the Temple one afternoon to take part in the three o'clock prayer service. As they approached the Temple, a man lame from birth was being carried in. Each day he was put beside the Temple gate, the one called the Beautiful Gate, so he could beg from the people going into the Temple. When he saw Peter and John about to enter, he asked them for some money. Peter and John looked at him intently, and Peter said, 'Look at us!' The lame man looked at them eagerly, expecting some money. But Peter said, 'I don't have any silver or gold for you. But I'll give you what I have. In the name of Jesus Christ, the Nazarene, get up and walk!' Then Peter took the lame man by the right hand and helped him up. And as he did, the man's feet and ankles were instantly healed and strengthened. He jumped up, stood on his feet, and began to walk! Then, walking, leaping, and praising God, he went into the Temple with them."*

> **For God's temple is holy, and you are the temple.**

Acts 3:1–8

God's holiness resides within His Word.

> *"The Word became human and made his home among us."*

John 1:14

Jesus is the Word.

> *"Don't you realize that all of you together are the temple of God and that the Spirit of God lives in you? God will destroy anyone who destroys this temple. For God's temple is holy, and you are that temple."*

1 Corinthians 3:15–17

> *"More and more people believed and were brought to the Lord— crowds of both men and women. As a result of the apostles'*

*work, sick people were brought out into the streets on beds and
mats so that Peter's shadow might fall across some of them as
he went by. Crowds came from the villages around Jerusalem,
bringing their sick and those possessed by evil spirits, and they
were all healed."*

Acts 5:14–16

*"When they came up out of the water, the Spirit of the Lord
snatched Philip away. The eunuch never saw him again but
went on his way rejoicing. Meanwhile, Philip found himself
farther north at the town of Azotus. He preached the Good
News there and in every town along the way until he came to
Caesarea."*

Acts 8:39–40

How is it that some Christians regularly demonstrate the power of
the Holy Spirit, while the majority seem to bear little to no evidence
of God's Spirit? Furthermore, why do some people produce much
fruit, while most produce negative outcomes, turmoil, and sadness?
Unfortunately, many and perhaps most believers in the church are
filled with self and spend little to no time thinking about or communicating with the Holy Spirit. Therefore, we go about life in our own
strength, doing things our own way. Things of God are an after-
thought, a Sunday morning habit, or an interruption to our schedule,
and we wander through life miserable, unhappy, and unproductive.

Frankly, being filled with the Holy Spirit in and of itself is not
the goal for the true believer. The process of activating the Spirit's
work in us is similar to the way lights work in a lamp, or keys engage
the engine in a car. Until the switch is turned on, the power goes
nowhere. The power of the Holy Spirit must be activated by God.
But *we* must first turn on the key to activate the power.

Filling of the Holy Spirit in the Old Testament

There are instances in the Old Testament where we see a direct
infilling of the Holy Spirit:

*"When the people of Israel cried out to the Lord for help, the
Lord raised up a rescuer to save them. His name was Othniel,*

*the son of Caleb's younger brother, Kenaz. The Spirit of the
Lord came upon him, and he became Israel's judge."*

Judges 3:9–10

*"At that moment the Spirit of the LORD came powerfully upon
him, and Samson ripped the lion's jaws apart with his bare
hands."*

Judges 14:6

*"The Spirit of the LORD came powerfully upon David from that
day on."*

1 Samuel 16:13

*"Stand up, son of man," said the voice. "I want to speak with you."
The Spirit came into me as he spoke, and he set me on my feet."*

Ezekiel 2:1–2

The presence of the Holy Spirit is observed in approximately sixty-five separate occurrences in the Old Testament (New Living Translation). However, because of the power of sin, the Holy Spirit was restricted from resting upon people in massive numbers and from remaining in some people because of their inability to walk with God in a sustained manner. Nevertheless, there were men, women, and children who walked with God (Enoch, Samuel, Elijah, Elisha, Huldah, and David immediately come to mind, although there are others as well).

*"Moses went out and reported the LORD's words to the people.
He gathered the seventy elders and stationed them around the
Tabernacle. And the LORD came down in the cloud and spoke to
Moses. Then he gave the seventy elders the same Spirit that was
upon Moses. And when the Spirit rested upon them, they prophe-
sied. But this never happened again."*

Numbers 11:24–25

The Holy Spirit in the New Testament

The presence of the Holy Spirit is evident in the Old Testament, but it is nowhere as widespread and powerfully seen as in the New

Testament, especially in the book of Acts. There we see clearly that the blood of Christ made it possible for the indwelling Spirit to take root and produce fruit when people accepted Jesus as the Messiah, Savior, and Lord of their lives.

Engaging the Holy Spirit

In July of 1997, I accepted a position at Merck Pharmaceutical Company as the Director of Global Organization Development in the Business and Organization Consulting (BOC) Group, a department in the Corporate Human Resource Division. On July 7th, during the orientation meeting, I first learned from one of the new junior employees that I would be responsible for the global implementation of a companywide performance management system for 60,000 employees, in 65 countries, speaking sixteen different languages, for a company responsible for producing revenues of more than $24B. Jack, a newly promoted consultant, told me about my new assignment in the orientation session and indicated that he would be working directly for me. Can you imagine finding out about your primary job responsibilities during an orientation session from one of your staff members?

Our house was on the market, and my family was in the process of moving into temporary housing in Skillman, New Jersey. My wife, Maria, had stayed behind in Illinois with my son, Zach and my daughter, Marissa to get things packed and moved. To add to my concerns, I heard a rumor that the previous director who I was replacing had been "let go" in May. I was brand new to pharmaceuticals, did not have any experience in implementing global programs, and knew very little about performance management systems. In addition, the new performance management system included a three-point leadership rating that would impact the salaries of senior leaders across the company. For many senior executives and scientists, this would be the first time in their careers they would be told their leadership skills were poor. It was too late, however, for me to reconsider going back to my old job in Illinois.

Jack, who was twenty years younger than I, had little experience in the corporate world, and was my only resource. Fortunately for me, Jack was a young man with both strong faith and strong business maturity. I was later informed that the program was to be implemented by the end of November, and that the consulting firm involved in the initial stages of planning and implementation design was fired, and no longer permitted to come onto the premises. I didn't mention any of this information to Maria.

At the outset, Jack and I identified HR peers from across the company who worked in Europe, the Middle East, Africa, Asia, the Americas, manufacturing, research, legal, finance, HR, and Merck-Medco. We engaged these directors to work as our partners on the creation of an implementation plan. I had no choice but to trust and treat Jack as my peer, and he did bring a remarkable level of maturity and wisdom. In addition to all of the other challenges, my boss informed me that two of the senior HR directors were opposed to me presenting the strategy of the performance management system, and leadership model, to the HR department during our global HR meeting in September. Nevertheless, I was given permission to make the presentation and align my HR colleagues across the globe on the rollout strategy.

At this point I was reading through the Bible twice a year, but I realized I needed greater strength and wisdom, and increased my reading to three times a year. Jack and I were responsible for presenting our strategy to each of the division presidents, and the divisions were split between the two of us. My HR colleagues joined Jack and me in making the presentations.

My first meeting was with the manufacturing division, which was a tough, no-nonsense group. I presented to the president and to all of the global manufacturing vice presidents. The leaders were direct and to the point, and at the end of the meeting the division president provided us with more resources and support than any of the other divisions in the entire company.

Jack and I were forced to rely totally on the Holy Spirit to fulfill our responsibilities. His power helped us navigate through what would otherwise have been an impossible situation. In mid-November we delivered a performance management system with leadership ratings to 60,000 employees, in 65 countries, and sixteen different languages with a paltry budget of $1.2MM. The performance management system brought a major cultural change and should have encountered a lot of resistance, but it didn't.

Have you ever experienced "lucky coincidences" and wondered whether God was at work behind the scenes?

The changes were embraced with little resistance because we included four nonnegotiable elements from the Chief Executive Officer (CEO), Ray Gilmartin, at the outset. These elements were a powerful addition to the process. The most astonishing factor is that I had no prior experience leading a large-scale global implementation. If I had taken the time at the outset to stop and think about the magnitude of this project, I would have panicked and failed. I was forced to trust Jack, as well as my own experience and knowledge, and to allow the Holy Spirit to lead. The program was recognized as a best practice by the U.S. General Accounting Office (GAO) in 2000 and the American Society of Training and Development (ASTD), at whose national conferences I made presentations about the program and its implementation.

We were able to complete the rollout in November and did it within budget. Amazingly, we worked long hours and won the support of the HR executive team. Impressive for two new employees who had no global experience, minimal performance management knowledge, and little pharmaceutical expertise.

I eventually told my boss that I had retained the services of the previously banished consulting firm, and he told me he had known all along. Through this project I recognized that the Holy Spirit is not limited. His presence has been as powerful in my personal journey, as well as in my professional journey. He is the same yesterday, today, and forever. As I reflect, I can see how the power of the Holy Spirit led and guided this project.

I learned so much about business and navigating corporate politics from this very difficult experience, but realized that many of the lessons I learned earlier in life had also served me well, as Jack and I maneuvered through what could have been a disastrous situation. Because I focused on the Holy Spirit, I was not distracted by the many things that could have gone wrong. Jack and I developed a strategy, and we allowed the Holy Spirit to execute that strategy. I never doubted that we would implement this program. It also helped that I had a praying partner who was filled with the Holy Spirit. My time at Merck produced some of the best experiences in my professional career. The culture was exceptional, and the people were tremendous. Thank you, Holy Spirit.

When I reflect back on my life, I trace numerous experiences like this, situations in which the Holy Spirit protected me in the streets and later in the corporate hallways. I could choose to assert that these were instances of luck or good karma, but I believe with regard to the situation at Merck, that the Holy Spirit guarded me from the time I sat in orientation until I left seven years later . . . and that the same is true of so many other events.

Have you ever looked back at moments in your life when you know, if only in hindsight, that God's grace spared you? Where you sensed, either at the time or later on, His Spirit at work in your rescue? For us to recognize God's work and His presence, we must first know His voice. It is imperative for God's children to take in the Word of God like nutritious food in order to be able to digest the wisdom and power of His messages to us.

> *"Now I am coming to you. I told them many things while I was with them in this world so they would be filled with my joy. I have given them your word. And the world hates them because they do not belong to the world, just as I do not belong to the world. I'm not asking you to take them out of the world, but to keep them safe from the evil one. They do not belong to this world any more than I do. Make them holy by your truth; teach them your word, which is truth. Just as you sent me into the world, I am sending them into the world. And I give myself as a holy sacrifice for them so they can be made holy by your truth."*
>
> *John 17:13–19*

Promised Presence

God is holy, and His presence cannot endure sin. However, we can catch a glimpse of a profound spiritual exchange as we see

God engaging in an intimate face-to-face, spirit-to-spirit conversation with Moses:

> *One day Moses said to the LORD, "You have been telling me,*
> *'Take these people up to the Promised Land. But you haven't*
> *told me whom you will send with me. You have told me, I*
> *know you by name, and I look favorably on you. If it is true*
> *that you look favorably on me, let me know your ways so I may*
> *understand you more fully and continue to enjoy your favor. And*
> *remember that this nation is your very own people." The LORD*
> *replied, "I will personally go with you, Moses, and I will*
> *give you rest—everything will be fine for you." Then Moses*
> *said, "If you don't personally go with us, don't make us leave*
> *this place. How will anyone know that you look favorably on*
> *me—on me and on your people—if you don't go with us? For*
> *your presence among us sets your people and me apart from all*
> *other people on the earth." The LORD replied to Moses, "I will*
> *indeed do what you have asked, for I look favorably on you,*
> *and I know you by name."*
>
> *Exodus 33:12–17*

God heard Moses and sent His presence to the people through him so he could lead the congregation forward. Moses established a deep intimacy with God. You and I have the same opportunity to become intimate with God as Moses did. Listen to another discussion between God and Moses, when Moses was not very happy with the Israelites, and he asked God to kill him on the spot:

> *"Where am I supposed to get meat for all these people? They*
> *keep whining to me, saying, "Give us meat to eat!" I can't carry*
> *all these people by myself! The load is far too heavy! If this is*
> *how you intend to treat me, just go ahead and kill me. Do me a*
> *favor and spare me this misery!"*
>
> *Numbers 11:13–15*

We see a progression in Moses' relationship with God from their first dialogue on Mt. Sinai. Moses is now having more intimate discussions with God. In fact, we see Moses getting a little testy with God. A far cry from the timid Moses who God approached in the desert (Exodus 4:10). We know that God poured out His Spirit on the seventy elders to give Moses relief, but He still worked through Moses to lead the people.

Sometimes the burdens of this world become so overwhelming that we cannot carry them alone. Moses reached that point. However, we must understand that, in our moments of pain and frustration, we need more of the Holy Spirit and less of ourselves. The ongoing relationship between Moses and the Spirit allowed him to be intimate with God.

Filled with the Spirit

In the beginning of the New Testament, only two men and two women were identified as being filled with the Holy Spirit: Jesus and John the Baptist, both of whom were filled before birth, and their mothers, Mary and Elizabeth. Through Jesus' sacrifice and resurrection, the Holy Spirit was available to many. If we revisit the spiritual DNA conversation, we can see that God chose Mary, a virgin, to bear His Son. We also see that John the Baptist was born of the union of a high priest named Zechariah and his wife, Elizabeth, a virgin and cousin of Mary. Only special people were filled with the Spirit. Our spiritual DNA is important to God. That is why we required a perfect sacrifice, His own Son to die in our place on the cross. It was not until the book of Acts where we read of various and diverse people being filled with the Holy Spirit, as well as an outpouring of the Holy Spirit on *all* believers, including Gentiles. As we see in the Old Testament, God does make exceptions. God saw a quality in Moses that enabled him to be used mightily. God desires to use us right where we are.

> *"Moses was very humble—more humble than any other person on earth."*
>
> *Numbers 12:3*

As a result of emptying himself of his pride and selfish ego, Moses was able to be filled by God. He allowed God to both fill him and use him, even though he had murdered an Egyptian.

When the presence of God is brought to bear in our lives, powerful and wonderful things happen. As we will see in the scripture quote to follow, whenever God's presence is evident, nothing in creation can hinder Him.

> *"Next in rank among the Three was Eleazar son of Dodai, a descendant of Ahoah. Once Eleazar and David stood together against the Philistines when the entire Israelite army had fled. He killed Philistines until his hand was too tired to lift his sword, and the LORD gave him a great victory that day. The rest of the army did not return until it was time to collect the plunder! Next in rank was Shammah son of Agee from Harar. One time the Philistines gathered at Lehi and attacked the Israelites in a field full of lentils. The Israelite army fled, but Shammah held his ground in the middle of the field and beat back the Philistines. So the LORD brought about a great victory."*
>
> *2 Samuel 23:9–12*

I love the stories of David's mighty men because they are examples of men who were filled with the Holy Spirit, men whom God through his Spirit was able to use mightily. Although scripture does not specifically state that these men were filled with the Spirit, remember that *David chose* them to be included in his inner circle of mighty men. Each

It is impossible to fully comprehend with our natural minds the vast resources available to us through God's presence.

of these men had extraordinary fighting skills, and they were not intimidated by anyone. They were committed to God and to the things of God, and we see them perform with supernatural power in the book of 2 Samuel. They fought side-by-side with a man who once slew a giant with a sling shot.

In the Old Testament the power of the Holy Spirit is often identified with military battles. There are also passages in which healing, raising of the dead, and the multiplying of food are evident, especially under the ministries of Elijah and Elisha. The major and minor prophets also exhibited the presence and power of the Holy Spirit.

Other historical examples of Spirit filling from the Old Testament includes: Jashobeam the Hacmonite used his spear to kill eight hundred enemy warriors in a single battle (2 Samuel 23:8), and Abishai once killed three hundred enemy warriors in a similar manner (2 Samuel 23:18). Shadrach, Meshach, and Abednego were able to step out of a raging fire, unscathed (Daniel 4:27).

However, it isn't until we move to the New Testament that we see the power of the Holy Spirit fully activated. Note that, once we are filled with the presence of the Holy Spirit, we take that presence with us wherever we go. In essence, we as believers carry the presence of God inside ourselves. I believe that we become temples of the living God at birth. The decision to be filled is one that each of us must make.

The Spirit is God's deposit of His presence in His children (Ephesians 1:14); this transition for believers occurred on the day of Pentecost, after Jesus had been resurrected. Paul talks about the power that is available to those of us who believe. It is impossible to fully comprehend with our natural minds the vast resources available to us through God's presence.

> *"I also pray that you will understand the incredible greatness of God's power for us who believe him. This is the same mighty power that raised Christ from the dead and seated him in the place of honor at God's right hand in the heavenly realms."*
>
> *Ephesians 1:19–20*

God's presence was limited in us due to the Old Testament primacy of the Law, which none of us could possibly have kept, but that restriction was done away with when Christ died to transcend the Law.

> *"I tell you the truth, anyone who believes in me will do the same works I have done, and even greater works, because I am going to be with the Father. You can ask for anything in my name, and I will do it, so that the Son can bring glory to the Father. Yes, ask me for anything in my name, and I will do it!"*
>
> *John 14:12–14*

Jesus' death on the cross made it possible for us to renew our relationship with the Father. This gives us a power that is indescribable. The presence of God goes with us and enables us to do wonderful things for the Father when we are obedient.

Are you aware that God says we can ask for *anything* in His name, and He will do it? We do well to bear in mind that only those who walk in close harmony with the Spirit are granted this power. We must be completely emptied of self in order to be filled with His presence. Only one source of water can fill God's vessels.

Often the Lord had to rebuke the disciples for their pride and exhort them to humility. It was all to no avail. Even on the last night of His earthly life at the table of the Holy Supper, there was strife among them as to which of them was the greatest.

> *"The disciples began to ask each other which of them would ever do such a thing. Then they began to argue among themselves about who would be the greatest among them."*
>
> *Luke 22:23–24*

Andrew Murray stated:

> "The outward teaching of the outward Christ, whatever other influences it may have exercised, was not sufficient to redeem them from the power of indwelling sin. This could be achieved only by the indwelling Christ. Only when Jesus descended into them by the Holy Spirit did they undergo a complete change. They received Him in His heavenly humility and subjection to the Father and in His self-sacrifice for others. Henceforth all was changed. From that moment on, they were animated by the Spirit of the meek and lowly Jesus. Many Christians keep their minds occupied only with the external Christ on the cross. They wait for the blessing of His teaching and His working without understanding that the blessing of Pentecost brings Him into us. This is why they make so little progress in sanctification. Christ Himself is made unto us sanctification."[5]

Dying to Self

"The seed that fell on good soil represents those who hear and accept God's word and produce a harvest of thirty, sixty, or even a hundred times as much as had been planted!"

Mark 4:20

Are you ready to bear fruit? Unless we die to self, we cannot become empty, and available vessels into which the Holy Spirit can pour Himself. If we reflect on our past and see where, and how God has sustained us, we will see His presence at work throughout our lives. He has always been with us, if only we will take the time to look, reflect, and acknowledge the evidence. His presence and power have been exercised through each of us, even at times in our most difficult situations.

"Jesus looked at them intently and said, 'Humanly speaking, it is impossible. But not with God. Everything is possible with God.'"

Mark 10:27

When we learn to pray in the Spirit and with the Word of God in our heart, the "impossible" in our estimation becomes possible.

Looking for God in the Storms

Unfortunately, we often move from one problem to the next with little regard for what we have experienced or accomplished. We do not take the time to reflect upon and acknowledge the work of the Spirit. This is one reason many people remain in a tailspin throughout their lives, repeating the same mistakes. I recommend reading Viktor Frankl's book *Man's Search for Meaning* to see God's presence sustaining Viktor through four different Nazi concentration camps. God is with us in the midst of our most violent storms, even when we don't see Him.

Psalm 45:7 tells us that God is sovereign and that He, not blind "luck," both knows and controls all things. The reality that God created all things can be a tough concept to embrace because both good and evil exist in the world; we need to bear in mind at all times that God is neither the source nor the author of evil. Full reliance on the Holy Spirit is essential for God's children because He protects those who trust Him, even when we cannot see Him.

The more we read the Bible as one book, cover to cover, the more the Word will saturate our spirit and speak directly to our hearts and souls.

God is able to make old things new and bad things good, but He expects us to participate in the process. Practice being quiet. Learn to sit, breathe calmly, and be still. Meditate on the Word of God and listen for the voice of the Spirit. The more we read the Bible as one book, cover to cover, the more the Word will saturate our spirit, and speak directly to our hearts and souls.

Allowing the Holy Spirit to teach us requires commitment and discipline. We must make time to meditate on the Word, and let it rest in our spirit. Be patient, we won't understand everything we read immediately. Some things will make sense only later when the context is right, and God desires for them to make sense. Timing is the work of the Holy Spirit.

Many Christians today walk in the flesh and are bearing little to no kingdom fruit, although their minds may tell them that they are. Only when we are directed and filled by the Holy Spirit can we make an eternal impact for the kingdom of God.

Consider

♦ Do you recognize that the Holy Spirit knows everything there is to know about you and He still loves you unconditionally? Meditate on this truth.

♦ Identify one thing you have accomplished that you are most proud of. Why are you proud of this accomplishment? What did it take for you to accomplish it?

Chapter Five

Personal Relationship with the Holy Spirit

"The king of Aram had great admiration for Naaman, the commander of his army, because through him the LORD had given Aram great victories. But though Naaman was a mighty warrior, he suffered from leprosy.

At this time Aramean raiders had invaded the land of Israel, and among their captives was a young girl who had been given to Naaman's wife as a maid. One day the girl said to her mistress, 'I wish my master would go to see the prophet in Samaria. He would heal him of his leprosy.'"

2 Kings 5:1–3

Second Kings, chapter five tells a remarkable story, but we may not have noticed some of the subtle details that provide a surprising context.

God Shows Up in Unexpected Places—Through Us

The king of Aram greatly admired the commander of his army, Naaman, because Naaman had won great victories for the king. But Naaman suffered from leprosy, a disease that carried great social stigma. The Aramean army had invaded Israel and brought back a young girl as a slave, and she was given to Naaman's wife as a maid. One day the girl suggested to Naaman's wife that Naaman go and see the prophet Elisha for healing. Elisha heard about the request and recommended that the king send Naaman to see him. Let us pause and fast-forward for a moment to expand our context.

Approximately four hundred years later, Jesus was at home in Nazareth preaching in the synagogue where He had grown up. Referring to the story of Naaman's healing, He said:

> *"Certainly there were many needy widows in Israel in Elijah's time, when the heavens were closed for three and a half years, and a severe famine devastated the land. Yet Elijah was not sent to any of them. He was sent instead to a foreigner—a widow of Zarephath in the land of Sidon. And many in Israel had leprosy in the time of the prophet Elisha, but the only one healed was Naaman, a Syrian."*

Luke 4:25–26

Amazingly, this unnamed servant girl with boldness (we might call it *chutzpah*) went to Naaman's wife and recommended that Naaman visit Elisha for healing.

Remember, Jesus had just reminded His listeners that *no one* in Israel had been healed from leprosy prior to the time of Naaman, with the single exception of Moses' sister, Miriam, hundreds of years earlier, as related in the book of Exodus. Still, a young girl torn from her family and living in captivity passionately believed that a miracle would take place that no one else, then living had ever witnessed. This child's faith was so extraordinary that Jesus used this story as an example to those scoffing Him. Although we don't know her name, God knew her and used her to display His glory.

A faith-filled, Spirit-led child displayed confidence in God for the unseen and the unknown, and was used to predict an extraordinary miracle. All because she listened to and obeyed the voice of God's Spirit.

Why, we might well ask, would this young girl, who had every reason to be bitter, angry, and resentful toward her master and mistress, have wanted to help Naaman experience the power of the Holy Spirit? She was *certain* that Elisha was *the one person* who could heal Naaman *through the power of God*. This child possessed holy boldness, compassion, and the confidence to approach Naaman's wife, and recommend that her husband travel to see Elisha. She brought forth fruit, as compelled by the Holy Spirit and her profound faith.

86

How did *this* girl, who may well have been barely a teen, have known about Elisha's healing powers when he had not yet healed anyone of leprosy? *This nameless servant knew because she had a personal relationship with the Holy Spirit,* which she demonstrated while performing her daily duties as a handmaiden to Naaman's wife. She lived out the identical qualities that Joseph had demonstrated as a slave while he was living in the home of Potiphar, as told in Genesis 38. And we can assume when Naaman returned home fully healed, this young girl was given other opportunities to talk about God's power, the Holy Spirit, and her personal faith.

This insight helps us to understand the power of this story. A faith-filled, Spirit-led child displayed confidence in God for the unseen and the unknown, and was used to predict an extraordinary miracle. All because she listened to and obeyed the voice of God's Spirit.

Love Through the Holy Spirit

It is important for us to pause and think about the remarkable child in this story. She had been wrenched from her family, likely under terrifying and violent circumstances, and placed in involuntary servitude. Yet she responded to the injustice against her by showing love for her captors and faith in God that matched that of Moses. Through the Holy Spirit's power, Naaman's wife, his servants, and the king of Aram were convinced to encourage Naaman to visit Elisha based on the advice of a young, female Hebrew slave.

> In the midst of her own horrible circumstances, this young servant girl blessed those who should have been her enemies.

In the midst of her own horrible circumstances, this young servant girl *blessed those who should have been her enemies.* Abraham was credited as a man of great faith, but this child stands beside him for her faith in God to do the seemingly impossible. And with faith comes hope.

God endowed this servant girl with a faith and hope that allowed her to *live in the power of the Holy Spirit.* She possessed faith so powerful, that she convinced Naaman's wife to tell her husband, a general, to go to the king and get permission to see the prophet Elisha.

Her relationship with the Spirit enabled her to speak to Naaman's wife with holy confidence. *Instead of focusing on her own needs, this child served others.*

Hebrews 11:1–2 tell us that faith shows us the reality of what we hope for; it is the evidence of realities we cannot see. Noah built an ark without seeing rain. Abraham moved his family without knowing where he was going. David believed God when He proclaimed that David would be king, even when he was being pursued by the then king, Saul. The Holy Spirit directs us to trust what He plants in our hearts and whispers to our souls. When *we listen and obey,* we are enabled to do great things through God's Spirit.

There is power in faith, and even more power in hope. Still, the greatest of the Spirit's gifts is love, which enables us to walk in boldness, knowing that whatever God says, He will do. When the people of God realize that His Word is real and reliable, we *change the world, both within and around us.*

Cultivating Our Seeds

Pop began to encourage me to go to college when I was still very young. Although he possessed only a fourth-grade education, he planted a seed of encouragement in me to pursue higher education. Somehow, deep in my soul, I knew I would do so. No one in my immediate family talked about college, and it wasn't a concept I heard about from either side of my family, or from within my circle of friends. Only a few of the young men in our neighborhood did enroll, but almost all of them returned home shortly, thereafter.

One young man, nicknamed Red was recruited to play basketball at the University of Cincinnati, while another young man by the name of Oscar Robinson, who would go on to became an NBA Hall of Famer, was also on the team. Red didn't stay at school for long, but returned to Allentown after a short stint in Cincinnati.

Charles was a first-team all-state wrestler in Pennsylvania and was recruited to Oklahoma University, . . . though he, too, soon dropped out. Big Bob was recruited by South Carolina State University to play football, but returned home before the end of the first year.

The only male I knew who attended college for any period of time was Robert, who attended St. Augustine College in Raleigh, North Carolina. Although most of the older guys I knew did not pursue college, many of them looked out for me and encouraged me as I was growing up. They meant well and gave me the best advice they had to offer, as well as their support when we played basketball at Allen Park. When I completed my freshman year of high school, I started to hang out with some of the older guys.

I played football, basketball, wrestled, and ran track in high school but never committed to any one sport. I was a decent athlete, but I started drinking with my friends on the corner of Penn and Union Streets in junior high school. Some people thought I would play Division I Football, and I believed this might have been a strong possibility for me, however, both of my knees were badly damaged.

My dream of Division I Football, and with it college, quickly disappeared.

The Call of My DNA

I was a good student up until junior high school, when hanging out became my first love. By the time I reached ninth grade, my grades were a disaster, and I really didn't care. What I *did* care about was playing football and partying. One Saturday night in the summer of 1967, I was walking home from a YMCA dance at approximately 11:30 p.m. with Tease and Toot, when my right knee suddenly buckled. I don't remember much, but recall that I ended up in the hospital and required emergency surgery the next morning for my first knee operation. Tragically (or not, given the ramifications of this injury for my future path), I had torn my right anterior cruciate ligament (ACL).

> There is power in faith—and even more power in hope. Still, the greatest of the Spirit giftings is love, which enables us to walk in boldness, knowing that whatever God says, He will do. When the people of God realize that His Word is real and reliable, we change the world, both within and around us.

On the Friday night after I was discharged from the hospital, I went to a party in Easton, Pennsylvania, twenty miles away with Dennis and some of my "boys." Driving back to Allentown on Highway 22, Dennis and his older brother, Big Al, decided to switch seats while cranking down the highway in a 1957 brown and black Chevy, three-speed with 350 horsepower named "Tippin In," a car that Big Al and Dennis had built. We could have all been killed as we sped down Highway 22 at about ninety miles per hour—seat belts were not required in 1967. I didn't get home until about 4:00 a.m. the next morning, crutches and all, feeling no pain. My parents were waiting. They had no idea where I had been.

Big Al dropped me off at the corner of Penn and Union Streets, and I hobbled home on my crutches, as though my injury was no big deal. When I arrived, Mom asked where I had been, and I told her at a party in Easton.

A New Beginning

After the nationwide riots in 1968, my entire neighborhood was displaced and relocated through a redevelopment effort by the city. We were forced to sell our home to the city, and leave my neighborhood, and move to the southwest side of Allentown. Mom and Dad moved as far away from Union Street as they possibly could, without leaving the Allentown city limits. The family next door immediately moved out after we moved in.

In spite of my parents' lack of involvement in my academic activities, they made the huge decision to transfer me from Louis E. Dieruff High School to William Allen High School in my junior year, in the hope that I would improve my D+ grade point average and salvage my life. Dieruff was on the east side of town, where all my friends and the other kids in the neighborhood attended. I had been with them since kindergarten.

At the time, William Allen located on the more affluent west side, had a very large Jewish student body, . . . and was academically one of the best high schools in the country. There were close to seven-hundred and seventy students in my senior class, and only four of us were Black. Rumor had it that close to one hundred students in my class ended up attending Ivy League Schools after graduation.

Unfortunately, I received no guidance or help from my counselors and didn't apply to college until February of my senior year. I applied to North Carolina Central University, North Carolina A&T, and South Carolina State University, all HBCU (Historical Black Colleges and Universities), and schools with great football programs.

I happened to see NCCU on television playing in the Pelican Bowl in December and decided at that time to attend. The defensive coordinator, Robert Herbert "Stonewall" Jackson, had lived in Allentown and was one of the first HBCU football players drafted into the NFL by the New York Giants in the sixteenth round of the 1950 NFL draft.

I was rejected by North Carolina A&T. South Carolina State University didn't even bother to respond. Thankfully, however, NCCU sent me a letter of acceptance. I was happy to be accepted because they had a tremendous football program . . . and a ratio of fifteen females to one male. God was good! (Pardon my then, immature male theology.)

It didn't take long for me to decide to focus my attention on my favorite subjects, consisting of partying and hanging out. Besides, I couldn't pursue a career in football with two bad knees, and preferred to enjoy my time exploring new experiences and gaining new knowledge.

The Holy Spirit, Our Rescuer

I was drunk only twice in my life, once in my junior year of high school the night before taking my SATs, and once in college during my freshman year. I started drinking beer when I was in eighth grade and never drank anything stronger than Colt 45 or Boone's Farm wine. I vividly remember hanging out of the back window of what I believe to have been a faded, canary-yellow, 1960 Pontiac with six freshmen jammed inside as we drove from Durham, North Carolina, to Greensboro for a rival football game between the NCCU Eagles and the North Carolina A&T Aggies.

The car had a broken muffler that sounded like a tank, and four tires with little or no tread. The vehicle was in bad shape, to say the least, but to a college freshman it was a limousine. It was proudly owned by Big Nasty and required expert automotive skills to drive. Big Nasty was about 6' 3" in height and scrunched his enormous frame into the seat while driving. He sat with his left shoulder against the door because the driver's seat was broken. The top half of the right side of the seat leaned perilously into the back seat, but the bottom half remained somehow mysteriously attached.

I was seated behind Big Nasty and spent most of the 54-mile drive from Durham to Greensboro vomiting out of the back window. Earlier that evening I experimented with a mixture of Boone's Farm wine, Mogen David 20/20 (otherwise known as Mad Dog 20/20), Southern Comfort, and a little weed to top it off. Why I decided to be so stupid, God only knows, but it didn't take long for the afterburners to kick in. I was miserable and wanted to die.

The plan that night was to attend the NCCU, North Carolina A&T football game and then party after the game. We somehow ended up in the hotel room of an older man who was dating Sharon, the ex-girlfriend of Killer, who was one of the six freshmen in the car (occupied by Big Nasty, Killer, Luby, Dip, Mike, and me). Sharon also happened to be in the room where we had been invited for the pregame warm-up. The people in the room were all sitting around, drinking and smoking weed, and I was feeling beyond miserable. I had vomited everything in my stomach and was experiencing dry heaves.

I desperately wanted to go back to the dorm and sleep for the rest of the year, but was trying my best to look cool, while choking down my gags. Sharon's boyfriend insulted Killer, and for some reason, likely related to alcohol, I jumped up to defend Killer. The boyfriend pushed me, and I fell backward, while threatening that, "No one pushes me around and gets away with it," which must have sounded quite humorous since I was hardly able to stand.

Killer, who was holding a hawk-billed knife that appeared out of nowhere, suddenly lunged at Sharon's boyfriend. In an instant, Big Nasty and Dap (I'm not sure how Dap, the roommate of Dip, happened to be in the hotel room) grabbed Killer's arm midair at the same time, and both were able to restrain him before the knife hit its mark.

Killer was enraged and was bent on ending that man's life. How in God's name Dap and Big Nasty prevented Killer from doing the unimaginable could only have been accomplished by the power of the Holy Spirit.

Needless to say, we never made it to the game.

That was the last time I was drunk. I promised myself I would never allow myself to be in a situation where I could lose total control of my mental and physical faculties and become totally unaware of what was taking place around me. Because the presence and power of the Holy Spirit flooded the hotel room that dark night, we were all spared deadly, and at the least, life-changing consequences.

> **The Spirtit of God works in unique ways, but we must train our eyes and hearts to recognize them.**

It is not until we examine our past that we see the Spirit of God hovering over us, just as He hovered over the waters in Genesis 1:3. In the same way He hovered over the young servant girl and demonstrated His presence and God's power in Naaman's healing. The Spirit of God works in unique ways, but we must train our eyes and hearts to see and recognize His presence. He is even present in angry brawls and in those times when we act foolishly.

The Holy Spirit spoke to the Israelite servant girl, who responded by speaking to Naaman's wife about Elisha's healing power. Naaman's wife recommended that her servant speak directly to Naaman, which the girl did. He also received a letter from King Aram, who sent the letter to King Joram, whose fear reached Elisha's ears. The Holy Spirit stirred Elisha's heart and strengthened the conviction of Naaman's servants. They encouraged Naaman to get into the water to be healed, a nuance of the situation that would be mentioned by Jesus in his hometown of Nazareth as a testimony of faith.

One child's faith influenced world leaders she would never meet, and glorified the power of God for centuries into the future . . .

and, ultimately, into eternity. All because she listened, trusted, and acted in childlike faith to the leading of the Holy Spirit.

Our Defender, Shield, Solace

I continually marvel at how God kept me from being consumed by the violence and darkness that surrounded me in my early years. When I was growing up there were frequent neighborhood deaths that triggered sad reminders of the horrors that surrounded me and many of my young peers. I distinctly remember the day in March 1958 when Cal's brother, Cecil drowned. At five years old, I stood along the muddy and flooded Little Lehigh River watching scuba divers search for his small body, and I vividly retain that image to this day.

Then there was the time when the Garber Horne Elementary School first graders were at recess and heard that a fire had broken out on Fifth Street; we all raced from the playground five blocks to the fire. Tragically, Kenny, who was a toddler, died from smoke inhalation. Or the time when little Arnold was hit and killed by a car. I remember watching Nanna, my maternal grandmother on the morning she was preparing to go to the hospital, never to return home. Mom told me that she had suffered a massive stroke, ostensibly caused by family drama, at the age of 55. I attended the funeral of Nanna B at the age of six after she died from a broken neck at the age of fifty-four. Or when I saw Barry's dad's picture on the front page of the *Morning Call* after he shot and killed his wife in 1965.

Violence, alcoholism, prostitution, gambling, and drugs were not uncommon influences when I was growing up as an inner-city youth. My maternal grandfather was a numbers runner who was involved with illegal gambling. Desperation creates violence, and violence foments trauma, especially in the lives of children who grow up in urban America. Violence in turn produces fear, anxiety, destructive coping mechanisms, and other negative consequences in a child's development.

The Adverse Childhood Experience (ACE) Study is based on ongoing collaborative research between the Centers for Disease Control and Prevention in Atlanta, Georgia, and Kaiser

Permanente in San Diego, California; it links childhood trauma to long-term negative health and social consequences. The initial phase of the study was conducted at Kaiser Permanente from 1995 to 1997. More than 17,000 participants completed a standardized physical examination. The study continues to examine the medical status of the baseline participants. According to Dr. Robert Anda:

> "The ACE Study findings suggest that certain experiences are major risk factors for the leading causes of illness and death as well as poor quality of life in the United States. It is critical to understand how some of the worst health and social problems in our nation can arise because of adverse childhood experiences. Realizing these connections is likely to improve efforts toward prevention and recovery."[6]

ACE Study major findings include the following:

Adverse childhood experiences are common. Almost two-thirds of the study's participants reported at least one ACE, and more than one in five reported three or more. The short-term and long-term outcomes of these childhood exposures include a multitude of health and social problems.

♦ The ACE Study Score is based upon a total count of the number of ACEs reported by respondents. The ACE Score is used to assess the amount of stress experienced during childhood and has demonstrated that, as the number of ACEs increase, the risk for the following health problems also increases in a strong and graded fashion:
♦ Alcoholism and alcohol abuse | Risk for intimate partner violence
♦ Chronic obstructive pulmonary disease COPD | Multiple sexual partners
♦ Depression | Sexually transmitted disease
♦ Fetal death | Smoking
♦ Health-related quality of life | Suicide attempts
♦ Illicit drug use | Unintended pregnancies
♦ Ischemic heart disease (IHD) | Early initiation of smoking
♦ Liver disease | Early initiation of sexual activity
♦ Adolescent pregnancy
(See http:/www.cdc.gov/violenceprevention/acestudy/ for additional information.)

The ill effects of trauma are often passed through generations, negatively affecting bodies, minds, and souls, unless their influence is offset by the Word of God and the Holy Spirit. In cases of severe trauma, trauma-specific treatment is almost always needed to curtail lifelong adverse effects caused by changes in the brain due to chemical and hormonal reactions.

"I lavish unfailing love to a thousand generations. I forgive iniquity, rebellion, and sin. But I do not excuse the guilty. I lay the sins of the parents upon their children and grandchildren; the entire family is affected—even children in the third and fourth generations."

Exodus 34:7

Because I was exposed to the streets at a young age, I have an affinity for hanging out with people who I believe are authentic. I still feel pulled to hang out with street people, who are often more genuine, more transparent, and more willing to share what little they have. I have seen more compassion among the poor, than I have seen among those who are well off.

Jesus was drawn to the tax collectors, prostitutes and common "street people" of His day. He saw their true essence and respect for each other, and they were usually more receptive to His teaching than the religious and aristocratic elite. I believed this when I was growing up, and I still believe it is true in most cases today. A remnant of people who are evil and wicked will always be among us. However, people living in lower-income neighborhoods want the same things that people in higher-income neighborhoods want: a nice

God wanted to stretch his (Naaman's) faith and humble his heart until he attained the same faith, humility, and heart of service as the servant girl. This is the effect God wants us to have on others when we yield to the Holy Spirit.

home, a good job, a safe place to raise their families, opportunities for their children, chances to be successful, and respect.

Exposure to hardship, abuse, and trauma at the early developmental stages of a child's life can create debilitating consequences for inner-city children as they mature and grow into adulthood. Their environment negatively impacts their physical, mental, and spiritual development. The power of the Holy Spirit protected me.

The presence of the Holy Spirit is everywhere, but His power is not always activated by those in His presence. Many had leprosy in the days of Naaman the Syrian, but he, a non-Jew, was notably the only one healed.

- ◆ The first act of power was exercised by a servant girl who believed that all things were possible for those who believe. She learned, perhaps from her mother and father, that God is real. She also chose to forgive and serve her master and mistress through the power of the Spirit.
- ◆ The girl's Spirit-led humility, forgiveness, and grace convinced Naaman's wife of her servant's trustworthiness. The child apparently spoke openly about her faith, and Naaman's wife learned to trust her enough to urge the girl to talk to Naaman about her suggestion that he seek out Elisha.
- ◆ The Spirit's power was persuasive, and Naaman decided to go to the king of Syria and solicit a letter of reference to take to the king of Israel. The power of the Holy Spirit was activated in the heart of Naaman as he stepped out in faith believing that God could indeed heal him. Naaman was so convinced that he traveled with his entourage at personal risk to the king of Israel with his letter of permission. The king of Israel had no idea that Elisha was capable of healing Naaman. However, God made His plan known to Elisha, who sent a servant to instruct Naaman to go to the Jordan River and wash himself.

However, the prospect of washing in the dirty Jordan River insulted Naaman's preconceived ideas of how a great general like himself should be healed. This is not to mention that he was indignant and highly insulted when Elisha did not take the time to personally honor his presence. Naaman, the great general, felt that he deserved respect and honor. God wanted to stretch this man's faith, and humble his heart until he attained the same faith, humility, and heart of service as the servant girl. This is the same effect God wants us to have on others when we yield to the Holy Spirit.

Naaman came to a powerful realization after he experienced a meltdown and refused to dip into the Jordan River. Naaman's servants must have loved him enough to challenge him when he was in a rage. They, as well as the servant girl, put their lives in jeopardy by challenging this great general, who was their master.

Why would they have risked their lives? Because they possessed a heart of love, and they knew and cared about their Syrian general. Even in the midst of his rage.

The power and faith demonstrated by the young Hebrew servant was a demonstration of God's power, expressed through the Holy Spirit, and of her personal relationship with the Holy Spirit. Naaman went back to Elisha and proclaimed there was no other God in all the earth like the God of Elisha. Not only did Naaman realize and acknowledge this, but the people with him that day were changed by what they witnessed.

But the question remains, How could the servant girl have known that Elisha could heal Naaman? A few thoughts come to mind. Quite likely she either heard Elisha speak, or she heard her parents or someone else close to her talking about the power of the man, or she was internally directed by the Holy Spirit. Scripture is silent on this, so we can only speculate.

> *"For the word of God is alive and powerful. It is sharper than the sharpest two-edged sword, cutting between soul and spirit, between joint and marrow. It exposes our innermost thoughts and desires. Nothing in all creation is hidden from God. Everything is naked and exposed before his eyes, and he is the one to whom we are accountable."*
>
> *Hebrews 4:12–13*

Whether in the context of hearing Elisha or hearing *about* him, she was connected to the Spirit of God, and serves as an example of being obedient when prompted by the Holy Spirit.

> *"It is the same with my word. I send it out, and it always produces fruit. It will accomplish all I want it to, and it will prosper everywhere I send it."*
>
> *Isaiah 55:11*

The Word of God is supernatural and carries the power to change all things. I believe the Word was securely planted in this girl's heart. She was content where God placed her, and despite her less than desirable circumstances, she was radiant with the power and presence of God. What other reason would she and the Syrian servants have implored Naaman to wash in the Jordan River? And why did this powerful general travel to a distant land to receive healing that no one, in his time had ever witnessed or heard of before?

Divine power activates in us when our faith engages through action. It is one thing to believe, but another to proceed. This girl's actions powerfully demonstrate the work of the Holy Spirit in a surrendered life.

> **The Word of God is supernatural and carries the power to change all things.**

Faith without action is dead. This young servant believed and acted out of confident faith. She heard and knew the voice of the Holy Spirit and was led by the Spirit, which is a critical lesson for us today. It is also important that, as we activate our faith, we surround ourselves with other God-fearing people, and set aside time each day to sit quietly before the Holy Spirit.

When I was only four, the Word of God was planted in my soul when Pop Baker taught me a prayer that I prayed daily for almost twenty years, regardless of my mental, physical, or spiritual condition. The words were simple: *"Father, Father, I will find you. Trying to be true. He will let me serve You as the angels do. Amen."* This prayer grounded me and helped me focus on the power of God from an early age.

While the prayer refers to the Father, it also talks about the One served by the angels, Jesus. I prayed that prayer every night until I got married at the age of twenty-four.

I accepted the Lord when I was thirteen while attending a Youth for Christ Convention at the Philadelphia Convention Center. I was invited to participate through a summer program sponsored by Grace Episcopal Church at Fifth and Linden Streets. College students would come from New York City during the summer and work with kids like me from the inner city. They took about twenty-five teenaged boys from the neighborhood to the Philadelphia

Convention Center. We stopped at the Philadelphia Museum prior to going to the center and were quite rowdy. To this day I remain shocked that the Philadelphia Museum security team did not evict us from the premises.

My parents had no idea I was in Philadelphia, sixty miles from home, but I was often absent without explanation. Not surprisingly, young people were called to go forward to accept Christ at the Convention Center, and Cal and I did so in the summer of 1966. The Spirit of God prompted me to respond and my legs propelled me forward. This was the most important decision I made in my lifetime, and my salvation was real.

There are times when the Holy Spirit directly intercedes in our lives. Often those moments will not be obvious. However, when we reflect on times of disappointment, success, close calls, mysteries, heartaches, blessings, seemingly inexplicable "chance" moments and meetings, plus countless other overlooked divine interventions in our lives; we will see the hand of the Holy Spirit at work again and again.

Mom's prayers were answered. She knew that her wayward son was on the road to destruction. If I had gone to Atlanta single, the chances of my long-term survival (both physically and spiritually) would have been slim to none. By placing a godly woman in my life who was both smart and gorgeous, God knew I would be properly directed.

God, through the Holy Spirit, continued drawing me into deeper relationship with Him as my will was consumed by His love. My journey of knowing and loving Him more deeply is not yet done.

What about you?

Consider

- ♦ What is your opinion about Naaman's servant girl? How would you describe her relationship with the Holy Spirit?
- ♦ Has your perspective on the Holy Spirit changed? If yes, how has it changed?
- ♦ I encourage you to get into the practice of journaling your thoughts and experiences on a regular basis and reflecting on them to observe the Holy Spirit's hand on your life.
- ♦ See Appendix B, Learning From our Highs and Lows.

Chapter Six

The Patience of the Holy Spirit

"When Joseph was taken to Egypt by the Ishmaelite traders, he was purchased by Potiphar, an Egyptian officer. Potiphar was captain of the guard for Pharaoh, the king of Egypt.

The LORD was with Joseph, so he succeeded in everything he did as he served in the home of his Egyptian master. Potiphar noticed this and realized that the LORD was with Joseph, giving him success in everything he did. This pleased Potiphar, so he soon made Joseph his personal attendant. He put him in charge of his entire household and everything he owned. From the day Joseph was put in charge of his master's household and property, the LORD began to bless Potiphar's household for Joseph's sake. All his household affairs ran smoothly, and his crops and livestock flourished. So Potiphar gave Joseph complete administrative responsibility over everything he owned. With Joseph there, he didn't worry about a thing—except what kind of food to eat!"

Genesis 39:1–6

In the above passage we meet another Old Testament teenager, a seventeen-year-old boy named Joseph who had been forcibly removed from his Hebrew family when his brothers sold him as a slave for twenty pieces of silver. Joseph was shackled in chains and forced to walk approximately two hundred miles across the blazing desert to the country of Egypt, where Egyptian Arabic, or Masry was spoken.

Imagine a seventeen-year-old spoiled brat who was his father's favorite child trudging through scorching sand to face life as a slave.

What do you imagine might have been going through his mind? He had just been sold by his ten older brothers and ripped away from his comfortable life. What were your priorities when *you* were seventeen? What was *your* level of maturity?

Have you ever known, or heard about a young person who, through a tragic experience, suddenly found vision and purpose? Keep this in mind as you read about Joseph and what he endured, and how he responded. Hopefully, you will see more clearly how the Spirit of God intervened in this teen's life and turned great tragedy into an astounding, history-changing triumph.

The Spirit's Presence in Injustice

Joseph was brutalized by his angry, jealous brothers, and was unjustly accused of attempted rape by Potiphar's wife, and was thrown into prison. These circumstances might sound like a good reason for a bad attitude. In spite of his devastating situation, Joseph responded with unexpected focus on God, not on the unjust treatment he was enduring. During his imprisonment, a sense of clarity and single-mindedness kept him from being destroyed physically, emotionally, and spiritually because the Holy Spirit was in control of his life. Read about Joseph's imprisoned life in Genesis chapters 37–40.

There are times when God removes His children from pleasant circumstances to places that are harsh and difficult in order to prepare us for kingdom work.

As Joseph kept his eyes on godly goals, he was able to access the presence of the Holy Spirit and deepen that relationship despite his circumstances. He quickly learned to access the Word of God and hold it close to his heart. The only person he could talk to in Egypt was the Holy Spirit. If we doubt the presence of the Holy Spirit in Joseph's situation, how do we explain Joseph's success and influence on Potiphar, the prison warden, and Pharoah? Joseph activated the Word of God through the Holy Spirit and gained favor in the eyes of his enemies.

Joseph was forced to adjust to an entirely new way of life and had to learn a new language. He lost his freedom, lived as a slave, and did not know anyone in Egypt. He had to build relationships and demonstrate faith in what seemed like a hopeless situation. Everything he knew and relied upon was gone . . . except for God. Yet Joseph worked his way up the ranks, which meant doing whatever tasks he was given as unto the Lord. We can assume that, as a newly enslaved person, Joseph was given menial and difficult jobs, but eventually, he found favor and was promoted.

All of this required enormous tenacity, character, resilience, determination, faith, hope, and trust. Joseph, who was a pampered rich kid, had to forgive his brothers for selling him as a slave into Egypt. Joseph was able to accomplish this *only because he was filled with the love, joy, peace, and patience of the Holy Spirit*. We can imagine that Joseph talked often with the Spirit before he was enslaved, while still exercising basic authority over his own life, *but circumstances now forced him to listen to, and obey the voice of the Holy Spirit*. He had two choices, either give up, or look up.

If we practice listening, we will learn to discern the Holy Spirit's voice. God sometimes moves His children from pleasant places to harsh, dry deserts to prepare us for kingdom work. We are in good company and will do well in our hard times if we keep in mind that David, Joseph, Moses, Jacob, the servant girl, and even Jesus experienced deserts.

Eventually, Joseph was removed from his menial jobs and given a role that brought him to Potiphar's attention. The little things Joseph did with quality and integrity got him noticed. He solved problems, overcame an enormous learning curve, endured trials, managed frustrations, and showed himself trustworthy. But most importantly, *he managed with the Holy Spirit's help to release the pain and bitterness of his past so he could be filled to bear fruit moving forward.* Joseph relinquished his anger regarding his brothers' vicious act and learned to lean on the Holy Spirit. He also let go of the life of wealth and prosperity he had enjoyed with his father and, instead, committed to excellence in all he did for his master in Egypt by relying on the Holy Spirit. Joseph was eventually promoted to the second highest position in Egypt, and saved his entire family, including his brothers and their families from starvation and death.

The Girding of the Holy Spirit

Mom often left me in the care of babysitters while she and Dad worked during the day. When I was four years old, I spent the summer with a babysitter, Mrs. Fisher, who lived in a big house on the corner of Lehigh and Lawrence Streets. Mrs. Fisher was close to eighty years old and was not in the best of health the summer she was hired by Mom to take care of me. I didn't have much interaction with her, other than when I arrived in the morning, and when she gave me lunch at noon.

Many mornings I sat on the patio, cold and shivering, waiting until the sun came out and the air warmed up. One day an older boy who was about twelve years old called me into his house, and told me to stand behind a big chair and pull my pants down. He began to fondle me while I stood there, not knowing what he was doing. He told me I was never to tell anyone what he had done, and for some reason I am still uncertain of, I never did. I am sure that this experience affected me in some manner, but the Holy Spirit prevented it from damaging my overall development as a child.

The next summer when I turned five, Mom left me to stay with Pop at 820 Lawrence Street. I only saw Pop in the morning when I woke up, and sometimes at night around 10:00 p.m. when it was time to go to bed. The family next door had six children, and one was a girl who was much older than me. One day she instructed me to go to bed with her and sexually assaulted me. I had no idea what was going on. I just knew, once again, that I was never to tell anyone what happened.

Joseph and many other people who go through difficult times are often able to be girded (fortified and built up) solely through the Holy Spirit. But there are times when professional clinical assistance or therapy are needed to help us work through our mental and emotional suffering.

I didn't realize how much these incidents affected me, as I was so young when they happened. Deep inside, I knew these actions were wrong, but I never talked to anyone about them. Yet the Spirit of God protected my mind and my soul. I attended Sunday school, but was not grounded in the Word of God. The only scriptural contexts I had were the children's Bible stories I had heard, and the prayer Pop had taught me.

I am aware that child sexual abuse can have lasting effects on its victims. By the grace of God, the protection of the Holy Spirit, the prayers Mom prayed, my exposure to Sunday school, and my simple daily prayer, the emotional trauma of

> When we listen with our souls, we will hear the voice of the Holy Spirit.

those evil assaults was minimized. The Holy Spirit guarded my heart and mind as I worked to make sense of the abuse that was inflicted upon me. It is only through the work of the Holy Spirit that I did not suffer long-term mental disturbances that often affect young children in these situations as described in the ACE Study. Yes, I did experience some mental and emotional trauma, but, thanks to God, I retained healthy control over my emotions.

Solace in Creation

God allows us to endure hardship to help us grow the fruit of His Spirit. Joseph and many other people who go through difficult times are able to be fortified and built up solely through the Holy Spirit. There are times when professional clinical assistance or therapy are needed to help us work through our mental and emotional trauma.

When I was staying with Pop during the summers, I would often wander to Fountain Park and lie in the grass, spending hours resting in the soft, green, protective expanse while gazing at the brilliant white clouds as they passed overhead. Contemplating each wonder as though it were a piece of art, I watched as they glided overhead. Captivated, I examined each cloud for unique differences. No two were the same. I witnessed the limitless beauty of God's creation in the majesty of the clouds. The Holy Spirit was by my side, pointing out to my expanding mind the magnitude of God's glory.

When we learn to be quiet in the presence of nature as we watch and listen, our spirit becomes sensitive to the voice of God's Spirit as He speaks through His creation. When God speaks we must learn to listen. Animals and plants recognize His Spirit, but many of us human beings have lost our ability to hear God's voice through His Spirit. When we learn to listen with our soul, we will clearly hear the voice of the Holy Spirit in all living things.

> *"But the one who enters through the gate is the shepherd of the sheep. The gatekeeper opens the gate for him, and the sheep recognize his voice and come to him. He calls his own sheep by name and leads them out. After he has gathered his own flock, he walks ahead of them, and they follow him because they know his voice. They won't follow a stranger; they will run from him because they don't know his voice."*
>
> *John 10:2–5*

Interestingly, in the above verse the physical appearance of the shepherd isn't mentioned; instead, the verse emphasizes his voice. The sheep *hear* it, and develop a relationship through the shepherd's voice, not his physical attributes. Shepherd and sheep are in tune with the spirit and not just the body.

As we abide in the peace and patience of the Spirit, our faith and wisdom evolve.

Another of my favorite pastimes as a child was to sit by the waterfalls at Fountain Park and listen to the sound of the water. The sound and presence of water have always produced a soothing effect on my soul. The peace magnified in the depths of my spirit was beyond description. The water would calm my soul, quiet my heart, and instill within me peace. A picture of those waterfalls hangs today in my office, and it is also the background image on my cellphone. My idea of a vacation is to sit near the ocean and do nothing but read, rest, and listen to the waves.

Fountain Park was the one place where the Holy Spirit taught me to discern His nature and build a relationship between us. It was also the place where He placed His protective shield around me to hide me from the evil and wickedness that were so pervasive. Despite the social and spiritual challenges I faced as a child, the Spirit hovered over me and kept my mind and spirit intact. This is what the Father did for Jesus when the Son carried His cross to Calvary, suffered, and gave His life as a sacrifice. As we abide in the peace and patience of the Spirit, our faith and wisdom evolve.

I was horrified to learn that in the late 1980s the Eighth Street Bridge, under which the Little Lehigh River flows, and from which I could gaze on the river from my perch on the falls, later became known as the *"Bridge of Despair"* after more than eighty people committed suicide by jumping to their deaths. The same bridge that stood as a beacon of hope for me during the days when I lived under its expanse, is now a place where people choose to end their lives. How heartrending that a place that could elicit and sustain so much hope, could also inspire so much death and destruction?

Using beautiful clouds, lush green grass, and rippling water, the Holy Spirit filled my childhood soul with His presence. Despite the horrendous things that happened to me, the Lord protected my heart, my mind, and my soul. I found the presence of God through His Spirit in the clouds, the waterfalls, the grass, the prayer, the kindness of friends, neighbors, and the scripture I heard, which gave me the assurance that God was always with me. I needed only to look and listen.

Awareness of God's presence is not limited to our senses or mind alone. He can speak to us through our hearts and souls. Patience teaches us to attune to Him with our spirit in addition to our mind and five senses. Learning to see God's presence in people, nature, and circumstances is key to developing intimacy with the Holy Spirit. I sense the Spirit of God as I observe the trees, the birds, the weather, and other aspects of nature. Truly, the earth and its beauty are the Lord's.

However, the world and sin make every attempt to deaden our hearts and souls by quenching the Spirit's stirrings, especially through technology and media. It is vital to both our hearts and souls that we learn to practice stillness in body, mind, and soul and turn off the pervasive noise around us. The lure of technology and our constant "need" to be connected to computers and gadgets, unrelentingly drains our spirits and drowns out the voice of God, the source of our faith, and deadens our souls.

Seconds after my birth, breath flooded my body. With that first sip of life comes power, peace, and protection that seals those who belong to the Lord. Even though I did not accept the Lord until I was thirteen, the Lord sealed my heart at the time of my birth. Although I was a fairly compliant child, I also was a product of the streets and of my physical and mental DNA. I had learned early on to steal and could lie like a dirty politician. But even in my sin, the Lord loved me.

A spirit of joy filled me as a child, even when times were bad. The same seed of faith that drove Joseph, Moses, Naaman's servant girl, and others, stirred in me. God knew me before I was conceived in the womb, and today I am connected to God in prayer, through reading His Word, and in constant conversation with His Spirit, who is always speaking to me.

Pablo's Heart

I often reminisce about early childhood friends. Pablo was one of the kindest kids in the neighborhood once you got to know him. There was also the Pablo who fought Mr. Coyle in front of the sixth grade class, pulling the ends of the man's tie to choke him as he struggled to get away from his teacher's grip. Then there was the Pablo who stabbed a young woman to death while he was high on drugs.

I saw Pablo the summer after he was released from prison. As we stood in the gas station lot, he told me he was planning to go back to school. I could see the pain in his eyes and the remorse in his heart for having committed murder, and I didn't know what to say.

Unfortunately, I wasn't spiritually mature enough at the time to ask him how he was doing and give him an opportunity to express his pain. The Pablo I knew didn't kill that young woman. His pain and suffering, along with the effects of the drugs coursing through his veins killed her. Through spiritual eyes, I saw his heart, but I also recognized his grief and pain as I stared into his haunted, lonely eyes, knowing I couldn't help him.

Later, I heard that Pablo hung himself and I was deeply saddened.

Many of the kids I grew up with were considered low achievers by the school system, and dropped out of school by tenth grade. However, it was very clear to me that many of them were very

108

smart, but didn't get the proper academic resources they needed. I sometimes regret my inability to share the gospel with Pablo on the day I saw him at the gas station on the corner of Sixth and Walnut Streets. I still pray that the God who is the same yesterday, today, and forever (Hebrews 13:8) will show mercy on my dear friend's soul. I still pray that He knew Jesus.

One of my close friends, Junebug (Bug for short), sold drugs and eventually died from stomach cancer. He was from a large family and did not grow up under the best of circumstances. He was as smart as any kid who attended William Allen High School, but he lacked the support and encouragement he needed. I lost track of him for many years and eventually learned that Bug was living in Orlando and had been homeless for a period of time.

> A spirit of joy filled me . . . even when times were bad. The same seed of faith that drove Joseph, Moses, Naaman's servant girl, and others, stirred in me.

Concerned, I flew to Florida. He told me he visited an Orlando hospital emergency room when he was suffering with stomach cancer. Since he was homeless, the staff assumed he was looking for drugs. Undeterred, he went to the library, researched his condition, and convinced the next doctor he saw that he did, indeed, have a medical problem. Although Bug didn't go to college, he had a brilliant mind. By the time he received treatment, it was too late. Bug was admitted to hospice on three separate occasions, but God enabled him to be released twice before he eventually died from the cancer.

> God's patience is beyond remarkable . . .Every day He eradicates the new sin of all His children and purifies us anew!

Sadly, Bug also told me of the times when he attempted to attend church, but was turned away from the building because of his unsanitary condition. His sister, ReeRee sent me his journal from his last months in hospice; to my relief, I found that the entries demonstrated his intimate, trusting relationship with the Holy Spirit.

I spoke at Bug's funeral, and after the service family members, friends, and I took his ashes to a nearby river to scatter them over the water. We tried desperately to open the lid of the urn, but no matter how hard we tried, we could not get it to budge. One of his sisters was forced to take his ashes home on a plane to Indiana. I later told the story of my friendship with Junebug and our futile efforts to scatter his ashes over the river during my induction into a professional fraternity. At that point in my presentation, someone in the audience yelled out that Bug probably couldn't swim and refused to allow the contents of the urn to be thrown into the water. I thought about that and smiled. It certainly sounded like Junebug.

Many of the guys I knew growing up spent time in prison, however, most of them were good people. Others who managed to escape the lure of the streets, lived far less promising lives than God had planned for them. Only one of my closest friends, Cal, graduated from college with a master's degree, and only one other, Big Al, never divorced but remained married to his wife, LaVerne. Only God's grace spared me and empowered me to flourish wherever He has placed me. His patience has been beyond remarkable, and not because I was better than anyone else. God knows I am still a wretched soul, and only His mercy and grace have brought me where I am today.

Even more amazing is that He eradicates the sins of all His children and purifies us anew each and every day!

God's Unexpected, Unmerited Grace

In the fall of my senior year of college, I decided to throw a party with my roommate, Otis. It was a Tuesday night, and the party started at about 10:00 p.m. At least 120 people were crammed into our tiny two-bedroom abode at 410 Pilot Street, apartment D7. My bedroom and my roommate's bedroom were both packed with people getting high and drinking alcohol. The living room and kitchen were filled with people I had never seen before. I made sure to tell the next-door neighbors that we planned to have the party, since they had three little girls. Whitney, the oldest of the three, had found a large plastic bag of "tea" while playing in the complex the day before. Her mother brought me the bag to examine its content.

I told her that I would be elated to take the bag of "tea", actually, about 2 ½ ounces of marijuana, off her hands. A drug bust had recently taken place in our complex, and someone had apparently discarded some of the evidence.

Fortunately, six-year-old Whitney had the foresight to take the "tea" home to her mother. Whitney's dad, a Vietnam veteran, came over later to examine the bag of "tea". I asked him whether he wanted any, and he just smiled and said, "No thanks."

During the more than two years that Otis and I had been roommates, we never had a party. But finding the bag of "tea" seemed at the time a reason for great celebration, even if it was a school night. We announced the party that morning, and, lo and behold, people showed up.

Lots of people.

Our place was packed beyond capacity and was probably a fire hazard. A guy named Stacey from Reading, Pennsylvania, which was located thirty miles south of Allentown showed up. He had grown up with Keith, another friend who lived in Allentown. The news had apparently traveled fast and far.

The most surprising thing occurred the evening *after* the party. At about 6:00 p.m., I heard a knock on the door. When I opened it, to my surprise stood a plain-clothes detective who showed me his badge and smiled, while four unmarked cars waited in the parking lot. All eyes were fixed on me as I spoke with the detective. He explained that he had received a report about a disturbance in the apartment and was there to investigate.

Fortunately, no one was in the apartment except my girlfriend, Rita, Otis' girlfriend, Kathy, and me. Our tiny apartment was impeccably clean, and the detective looked into the living room, where Rita and Kathy stood and both said hello.

While the detective was talking with me, he noticed

> But the Spirit of God living in us protects us, even when we don't realize it. The Lord promises to never leave nor forsake us, in good times or in bad. He is our refuge, our ever-present shield in times of trouble.

Mom's tall artificial plants sitting against the wall in the living room and "smiled" as he walked over to feel their texture. I didn't realize the plants looked like marijuana. They were in plain sight, so the detective was legally able to enter our apartment. He walked over to the plants and disappointedly rubbed the leaves of harmless, plastic greenery. He frowned, turned around, and walked out of the apartment without saying a word.

I later found out that an informant told the police about the party, and somehow the detectives got the day of the event mixed up. Even though the party was illegal, the Holy Spirit still protected this ignorant, immature lamb. Thank You, Holy Spirit, for saving me from myself! Again!

In my heart, I always desired to do what was right. However, our fleshly sin nature often wars against the things of the Spirit. The desire to do good was ingrained in my heart, yet my flesh foolishly fought against the things of God. The Spirit of God living in us protects us, even when we don't realize it. The Lord promises to never leave nor forsake us, in good times or in bad times. He is our refuge, our ever-present shield in times of trouble.

> *"So the trouble is not with the law, for it is spiritual and good. The trouble is with me, for I am all too human, a slave to sin. I don't really understand myself, for I want to do what is right, but I don't do it. Instead, I do what is wrong, this shows that I agree that the law is good. So I am not the one doing wrong, it is sin living in me that does it."*
>
> *Romans 7:14–17*

I know my story may not resonate with many of you, because you have led obedient lives, and were not surrounded by the temptations and snares that existed for those of us who grew up in the inner city. Allentown is the third largest city in Pennsylvania, and I can't imagine how reckless I might have become if I had grown up in larger cities like Philadelphia and Pittsburgh.

My heart goes out to my brothers and sisters who live in major urban areas across America, who don't understand the importance of having a personal relationship with the Holy Spirit. Unless you have lived in a major city, it is hard to understand the pain, hopelessness, and trauma that confront families and individuals in urban centers. Living day-to-day without hope can starve our souls. Fortunately, however, many families refuse to allow hope to die. You can see determination in the hearts of parents who work, day in and day out, to make better lives for their children. They serve as examples to us all, as the Holy Spirit watches over them.

The gospel of Jesus Christ is not always proclaimed in churches with reliance on the power that resides in the Word of God. Evidence of this is found in the seven churches in the book of Revelation. Why were the churches of Smyrna and Philadelphia the only two churches that were not directed to repent? And why was the church of Philadelphia the only church that was raptured (Revelation 3:4)? The answer to both questions is that the Holy Spirit was active and fully alive in both churches, and partially active in the other five churches. His presence radiated particularly in the Church of Philadelphia.

At the time the book of Revelation was written, enormous evil and perversion existed within the church, and God was holding His church accountable.

When we look at the Church today, we must ask: how have biblical teachings and guidelines regarding sin in our churches changed from the time of the early church to the present? To begin with, levels of hate and dissension certainly seem to have intensified. America has become an increasingly divided nation, while the church, for the most part, has looked on from the sidelines and fought to protect its self-interests. In some instances, the church in America is more segregated than the communities it serves. In the words of A. W. Tozer:

> "It is literally true that some churches are dead. The Holy Spirit has gone out of them, and all you have left are "the remains." You have the potential of the church, but you do not have the church, just as you have in a dead man the potential of a living man, but you do not have a living man. He can't talk, he can't taste, he can't touch, he can't feel, he can't smell, he can't see, he can't hear—because he is dead!"[7]

God help the shepherds of the church who are not caring for their flocks by failing to teach them the power, preeminence, and practical mandate of God's love letter to us. And God help churches who do not read or follow the Word of God. However, that is another topic for another time, and another book. Instead, we must continue, as was stated earlier, to seek the guidance of the Holy Spirit in all we think, say, and do.

Consider

♦ What do you fear most? Why do you fear it?
♦ Do you attend a church or worship with a body of believers where the Word of God is taught and the Holy Spirit is present?

Chapter Seven

Peace of the Holy Spirit

"Put away your sword," Jesus told [Peter]. 'Those who use the sword will die by the sword. Don't you realize that I could ask my Father for thousands of angels to protect us, and he would send them instantly? But if I did, how would the Scriptures be fulfilled that describe what must happen now?' Then Jesus said to the crowd, 'Am I some dangerous revolutionary, that you come with swords and clubs to arrest me? Why didn't you arrest me in the Temple? I was there teaching every day. But this is all happening to fulfill the words of the prophets as recorded in the Scriptures.' At that point, all the disciples deserted him and fled."

Matthew 26:52–56

Peace is the third fruit of the Spirit listed in Galatians 5:22. We need peace the most when everything around us is in chaos and we don't know what to do or where to go. In those moments we feel cornered. Yes, we need peace at *all* times, but we need it most when all hell breaks loose, and darkness and evil seem to be prevailing.

We have all felt the panic

> So how do we stay calm when everyone around us is . . . acting out of panic? We must remain connected to the vine . . . by anchoring ourselves in the Word of God.

of these moments, perhaps especially during the recent pandemic.

The Source of Peace

It is not surprising that Jesus demonstrated the importance of peace as He was surrounded by His captors in the Garden of

Gethsemane, as told in Matthew 26. His disciples all deserted Him, yet He maintained a sense of calm and reminded those who came to arrest Him that He possessed the power to call legions of angels to rescue Him. Jesus was at peace, despite knowing that His death was imminent. He is our example.

How do we stay calm when everyone around us is losing control and acting out of panic? We must remain connected to the vine. And how do we do that? By continually anchoring ourselves in the Word of God and acknowledging the Spirit's presence.

> *"When the servant of the man of God got up early the next morning and went outside, there were troops, horses, and chariots everywhere. 'Oh, sir, what will we do now?' the young man cried to Elisha. 'Don't be afraid!' Elisha told him. 'For there are more on our side than on theirs!' Then Elisha prayed, 'O LORD, open his eyes and let him see!' The LORD opened the young man's eyes, and when he looked up, he saw that the hillside around Elisha was filled with horses and chariots of fire. As the Aramean army advanced toward him, Elisha prayed, 'O LORD, please make them blind.' So the LORD struck them with blindness as Elisha had asked."*
>
> *2 Kings 6:15–18*

In this passage, we find the prophet Elisha surrounded by soldiers who were sent by the king of Syria to take him captive. God gave Elisha the power to know everything the king of Syria spoke, even within the confines of his castle. Elisha heard the very words the king spoke and told them to the king of Israel. Hearing of this, the king of Syria sent his troops to capture Elisha. But the Holy Spirit filled Elisha, and he was able to use the power of the Spirit to open the spiritual eyes of his servant, and at the same time capture the Syrian army by blinding them. How was it possible that Elisha was able to maintain personal peace in a seemingly hopeless situation and trust the power of the Holy Spirit?

This kind of peace-filled confidence in what appears to be a hopeless circumstance happens only when someone has an intimate relationship with the Holy Spirit, through the power of the

Word of God. As Jesus stated, *"I must abide in you and you in me"* (John 15:5). This is the starting point.

Intimacy Equals Relationship

Living with someone doesn't mean we know that person. How many times have we heard stories about people who spent decades living together and yet did not know one another? Intimacy must precede peace. Elisha knew how to pray, and the Lord heard and responded to his prayers. Having God's peace means having God's attention. Once we have God's attention, we have access to His power. That means we know how to properly access the power God makes available to us.

Consider the men who were given the talents in Matthew 25:14–28. Two servants used their talents to gain additional talents, but the servant who hid the one talent lost it, and was cast into outer darkness. This seems like a horrible price to pay for protecting his talent, but God had given him something to be used and developed. God holds his shepherds to a higher standard than he does other people.

When we waste the gifts God gives us, we disregard His goodness and purpose for us. In this case, God, the owner of the talent, informed the servant of what he would be receiving and implicitly notified him in advance of his responsibility. It appears that the servant with the one talent had a relationship with the owner, based on the fact that he knew what type of man he was. He discerned the negative side of his master's heart because he couldn't see past the evil in his own heart.

However, the other two servants learned from the master and applied the positive abilities they saw him demonstrate. They also had a level of intimacy with the master, which might be one reason he gave them more than the servant who received the one

> When we come to know the Holy Spirit, we also know His ways because we learn to see and know His heart. His peace becomes part of our nature and directs and guides us because we know His voice as He leads us in the path we are to take.

talent. They were able to connect to the positive, loving side of their master's heart and emulate that same ability in order to produce fruit.

These two servants, knowing the heart of the master and learning from him, were willing to take risks. I imagine that they may have prayed for insight. They were able to replicate the actions of their master and apply their talents with the confidence that they would be successful in getting results. Unlike the servant with the one talent who was driven by fear, they were motivated by faith.

When we come to know the Holy Spirit, we also appreciate His ways because we learn to see and recognize His heart. His peace becomes part of our nature and directs, and guides us because we follow His voice as He leads us in the path we are to take.

The two productive servants were guided by the voice of the Holy Spirit. They knew what to do and where to go. If the third servant had only prayed and taken a step forward, the Holy Spirit would have given him peace to trust and obey. It is critical that we spend time daily with the Holy Spirit in order to become intimate with Him; one of the ways to do this is by reading the Word of God. Another way is by praying and listening quietly as a component of praying. Meditating on what we read, controlling our thoughts, and focusing on our breathing, instead of allowing distractions to consume our thoughts, are good ways to practice stillness. Getting alone and away from the noise and distractions of this world is another helpful practice. It is important to assess where and with whom we spend the majority of our time, whether people or devices.

Have no doubt that the storms are coming, even though peace *can* come to us in the midst of storms. The time to learn about God's peace is not during the storm. Instead, it is in solitude sought out in daily life where we gain experience, love, and comfort as we lean on the Holy Spirit. In our ongoing, day-to-day trials, we can witness God's hand and gain sure and steady confidence of His presence in our lives. Learning to be still in the desert teaches us how to be still in the storm.

Many of God's greatest leaders spent time in the desert learning how to hear and trust His voice. Think about Job, Joseph, Moses, the children of Israel, David, Paul, and yes, Jesus Himself. In parched, arid deserts where all we see is desolation, we learn to listen for the voice of the Holy Spirit. Deserts are our preparation for the storms, providing us an opportunity to be alone with God, receiving instructions and moving forward in faith and hope when we hear His voice. Storms are the context in which we move forward and obey the discernible voice of God.

A. W. Tozer wrote:

> "It is part of my belief that God wants to get us to a place where we would still be happy if we had only Him! We don't need God and something else. God does give us Himself and lets us have other things too, but there is that inner loneliness until we reach the place where it is only God that we desire. Most of us are too social to be lonely. When we feel lonely, we rush to the telephone and call Mrs. Yakkety. So we use up thirty minutes and the buns are burned in the oven. With many, it is talk, talk, talk, and we rush about looking for social fellowship because we cannot stand being alone. If you follow on to know the Lord, there comes a place in your Christian life when Mrs. Yakkety will be a pest instead of being a consolation. She won't be able to help you. It is loneliness for God—you will want God so badly you will be miserable. This means you are getting close, friend. You are near the kingdom, and if you will only keep on, you will meet God. God will take you in and fill you, and He will do it in His own blessed and wonderful way."[8]

The Day They Pulled the Rug

On Thursday, October 26, 2006, at 1:00 p.m., I was called into the office of the Senior Vice President of HR. She sat with the VP of HR as they informed me that my job was eliminated. I anticipated this move and started interviewing months in advance. I traveled to Chicago just the day before to interview with Mercer. However, the finality of this event turned out to be the onset of one of the toughest spiritual chapters of my life.

I was lured to my job because of the title, and the fact that Trinity Health as an organization prayed before meetings and provided a very nice salary and pension plan, not to mention full relocation, which had been extremely attractive at that time. The CEO, Judy was a wonderful woman, and Bill, the SVP who hired me, was a man of faith. He also shared his feelings on the importance of bringing God into the workplace. The offer was attractive enough to convince me to leave Merck.

> My age, race, education, experience, and spiritual maturity were major obstacles in this job search. I knew that racism was alive and well, but confronting agism so suddenly and widely brought a stark new reality to my job search.

I once promised the Lord that I would never take a job for the money. Well, my decision to work for Trinity would be the one time I had abandoned my promise. Circumstances had made it appear as though God's hands were all over the job, and besides it was a faith-based organization where staff members prayed before meetings. I thought this was a phenomenal opportunity and, in my mind, a clear indication that the organization was the perfect place for me. Unfortunately, many things happened during the two-year span after I was hired, including an unexpected change in CEOs and the dismissal of my previous boss. However, my greatest concern after losing my job was that I was stuck in Michigan at the height of the collapse of the auto industry. My age, race, education, experience, and spiritual maturity became major obstacles in my job search. I knew that racism was alive and well, but confronting agism so suddenly, and unexpectedly brought a stark new reality to my job search. In the majority of the jobs I interviewed, I believe that I was more qualified and more experienced than the person who managed the position.

During the next 1 ½ years I learned what it was like to rely totally on the Holy Spirit for my spiritual, emotional, and practical survival. However, I was overly confident that I would quickly find a job, as I had done in all of my career transitions in the past. My initial confidence during this dark time rested totally in myself, my experience, and my education.

As it turned out, I realized I was in the middle of a deep spiritual battle, and I didn't know anyone I could ask for spiritual guidance. I needed to move beyond the words of the Bible to experience the Spirit behind the Word. I needed assurance that God was truly present. I needed the companionship of someone who would take time, feel my pain, and be with me through my battle. I found myself back in Fountain Park, lying in the grass looking up to the sky, waiting and hoping for the Holy Spirit to show Himself present in my situation. I had never before felt so alone. Unemployment felt like leprosy. Taking away a person's ability to earn a living can feel like a death sentence.

In the past, whenever I decided to change jobs, I always had two to three job offers from which to choose. I was skilled and educated. But this time was different, and it took me a grueling year and a half of grinding effort, without anyone to help me . . . except the Holy Spirit. I had a wife, a son who was a senior in high school and ready to head off to Stanford University in Palo Alto, California, a daughter in middle school, and a mother who was dependent on me for emotional support.

I was most concerned about my son, Zachery, making the adjustment with the move from New Jersey to Michigan. He was an extreme introvert, just like me. Making friends did not come easily for him. I wrongly assumed that Marissa, my baby girl, would have the easier time adjusting. Unfortunately, she was the one who suffered the most from the repercussions of the move to Michigan, even though the job looked as if it was sent straight from God. I had to maintain, or at times feign an optimistic spirit so my family would not lose hope, and my hope had to come from a dependable and deep well.

I contacted hundreds of companies, participated in over forty interview visits, and traveled to fifteen states during those one and a half years; when it seemed as though no one else understood or cared about the depths of my struggle. I sought the advice of one of the pastors at Northville Assembly of God about ways to communicate to my children the news that I lost my job. I took his advice and told them outright what happened. I should have consulted the Holy Spirit instead.

In hindsight, I realize that I should not have immediately told my children about my job loss. Instead, I should have prayed and asked the Holy Spirit how to handle my decision. My children were both worried, but my daughter, Marissa, started suffering from debilitating migraines. Her first attack took place during a service at church. I didn't realize the intensity of the spiritual war taking place in my household. Can you imagine your daughter going to church and being forced to leave because of an intense migraine for the first time in her life?

My wife, Maria, told me about a time when she and Marissa were in the grocery store and one of the members of our church saw them carrying two small bags of groceries as they were leaving. As he eyed the bags, he jokingly commented on how hard it must be for them since I was out of a job. Those kinds of responses were painful, but as the spiritual leader in my home, I worked to hide my emotions and claim God's promises.

Sympathy wasn't always available to my family, but Maria's youngest sister, Verona, was one of the few people who offered not only constant prayers, but also offered financial support if needed. One former Merck employee, Philisia, offered to give me her bonus. Her offer refreshed my spirit, but I knew she needed the money as much as I did, and gratefully declined her offer.

I started reading through the Word of God at least once a year in 1986, and then increased to twice a year in 1995. During this desert period, I was compelled to accelerate reading the Word and journaling about the impact of scripture reading in my life. There were days when I was not able to get out of bed because I was in deep depression. All I wanted to do was to remain in bed and sleep. During these faith-stretching months in 2007, I began reading the Bible cover to cover on a monthly basis and found a peace that rejuvenated my soul. The only month I missed reading in 2007 was the month of September.

I had no one, and nothing except the Holy Spirit to hold onto. Reading the Bible gave me a reassurance that all of our circumstances would work out for good. Maria and I spent more time praying together, even though I could see the stress and worry on her face. I felt peace whenever I read the Bible . . . and continue to feel that peace whenever I spend an hour or more with the Holy Spirit in His Word.

One afternoon as I was heading to an interview, I got a call from Scotty Smith, the HR director of a manufacturing company. He called to tell me that there had been a change in plans and that he was canceling the interview. In the middle of that conversation, Maria called to say that she had a flat tire while driving Zach and Marissa, in reality, all four tires on her car needed to be replaced immediately. It was in times like these that I learned to stop and plead for the Holy Spirit to strengthen me.

Not surprisingly, I never heard from that company again. But stress and strain were escalating, and the effects of unemployment were becoming unbearable. Our finances were dwindling, and there was no one I could call for help. All I could do was to pray and read the Word of God.

I eventually got an interview for a director level position at a major bank in Charlotte, North Carolina. Based on the telephone interview, I knew without question that the job would be mine. It had been one of my best telephone interviews and my confidence was sky high. However, when I met the VP to whom I would report, the look on her face immediately told me she had not expected to see me. My voice during phone interviews, along with my educational background, often caused potential employers to assume I was of a certain race, so when they met me in person and realized I was African American, shock set in.

When this woman saw me, she became visibly shaken. After she had composed herself, she asked me whether I knew the VP of Organization Development, who happened to be a woman of color. I did my homework and knew who she was. But, how was I supposed to know the VP of Organization Development, who lived in Charlotte when I lived in Michigan? It was a small world, but definitely not that small. As you may have guessed, I did not get the job. I continued getting rejection, after rejection, after rejection. Here I was, on the back end of my career, and I couldn't get a job to carry me through to retirement. What discouraged me the most was that almost every interview was for a position I could easily fill, but for some reason opposition seemed even more intense for those roles.

One blessing that came from this desert experience was that I received support through an outplacement firm called Right Management and was assigned a great coach, named Scott. During this time I met another believer named Al, who had been displaced from his job at General Motors after a thirty-year career. He was a godsend. Al encouraged me daily, and often prayed with me during a time in my life when I was experiencing enormous rejection from friends I had been certain would support me through the painful ordeal of losing my job. Other than Al and Maria, I had no spiritual support, apart from leaning on the Holy Spirit.

Some of my greatest disappointments came from the responses of individuals in my church and in the larger Body of Christ. Until we experience the significant pain of job loss, we don't realize how much of our identity is tied up in our work. I often felt so embarrassed about having lost my job. Four other lives were counting on me for provision. Although the guilt I was experiencing was false, negative emotions still clouded my mind.

The more I read the Word of God, the closer I felt to the Holy Spirit, and the more His comfort and assurance saturated my heart. Although I had never been through anything like this before, I began to feel a sense of peace that things would be okay. I recalled the times from my early years when God worked miracles and sustained me, and I believed He would do it again. Although my rational mind told me that my logic didn't make sense, my heart assured me that God would not abandon me.

> Although the guilt I was experiencing was false, negative emotions still clouded my thoughts . . . But the more I read the Word of God, the closer I felt to the Holy Spirit, and the more His comfortand assurance saturated my heart.

One Step at a Time

Many of my earlier challenges in life prepared me to trust in the Holy Spirit. Although I was depressed at times, my spirit was lifted by reading scripture, reflecting on past accomplishments, listening to, and trusting the Holy Spirit. Some things in life are hard to put into words, but are known in our spirit. The Holy Spirit reassured me as I remembered the many times when God held me and spared me, and the countless promises of His faithfulness in His Word. Sometimes just getting up and going into the outplacement center was a step of faith that kept my spirit moving forward, but somehow, God always gave me the faith and the confidence for the next step. I literally learned to live one day at a time.

My soul was reminded of the time when God had not allowed our house to catch on fire when my mattress was burning, or the time I was stopped by police in Philadelphia and was not arrested for driving on the wrong side of the street while possessing illegal marijuana, or the time God provided me with a job at the Agency on Aging when I was one of the youngest and least experienced candidates applying for the position; when God spared Marissa as the doctor fell asleep while monitoring Maria's labor contractions, and the umbilical cord was wrapped around Marissa's neck twice as she ingested meconium in her mother's womb. My soul was stirred by countless memories of God watching over me. Maintaining a heart that is open to reflection and thankfulness, is crucial to finding lasting peace.

Then, early one August morning, I was lying in bed asleep, feeling like the loser in a back-alley brawl. Maria woke me and told me that Pastor Brooks was on the phone, calling to ask if I could deliver a sermon to our congregation at Northville Assembly of God in September.

Somehow, my soul was revived and lifted me from my bed, as though I had been offered a priceless treasure. Immediately rejuvenated, I decided to speak about a young man named Joseph, who was violently taken from his home and forced to rely upon the Holy Spirit to see him through a horrific, unjust ordeal.

Joseph spoke to my heart because I knew him personally.

Calm and Confidence

That Sunday morning on September 9, 2007, as I finished the sermon, I was grateful to look over the congregation and see Bill in the assembly, as well as my good friend in the spirit, Sib, who had driven to Michigan from Chicago. At the end of the sermon, the altar was filled with people who were asking for prayer and for the infilling of the Holy Spirit. My relationship with the Holy Spirit moved to a whole new level. For the past eleven months I had come to rely on the Word of God more than ever before. My soul was revived, which enabled me to continue moving through the rest of the year in search of employment.

The Holy Spirit uplifted me as His peace revived my spirit. A new sense of calm and confidence assured me that God would work everything out after eleven long months, even with seven more months of rejection in front of me.

By God's grace, the darkness that shrouded my life during 2007 and into 2008 was not strong enough to blot out the peace given to me by the Holy Spirit. During and after those months, I came to rely upon the power of the Spirit to move me through personal, as well as professional challenges and carry the burdens of my family.

Zach started his freshman year at Stanford in September 2007 and had a tough time adjusting to life in Palo Alto, California. I was often on the phone with him into the wee hours of the morning, talking and praying him through his difficulties. Zach often called after midnight because he would forget about the time zone difference. Whenever the phone rang, I literally sat straight up in bed, fully awake, as though someone had thrown a bucket of cold water in my face.

On one such morning at about 3:00 a.m., Zach called in a panic to tell me that he was standing outside the dorm because there was smoke inside of his room. When I asked whether any firetrucks were there, or could be heard in the distance, Zach replied in the negative. Nor, was anyone else from the dorm standing outside with him.

"My dear son," I told him. "There is no fire. People in the dorm are smoking weed, and the smoke has come into your room. Be assured, there is no fire. You can stay outside or go back into your room, but unless you hear the fire trucks and are told to evacuate, you should be fine."

To add to the pressures I was experiencing, Marissa was having prolonged and severe migraine headaches that incapacitated her for days at a time, and caused her incessant worry about losing her home, and flunking out of school. Maria and I were continually looking for ways to help her. We often visited the hospital emergency rooms and the school guidance counselor, while continually praying.

The Disciplines of Disciples

Yes, we were also experiencing financial pressures. Our neighborhood was loaded with foreclosure properties throughout our lovely development, while our home overlooked the sixth hole on a beautiful golf course.

On many days I didn't feel like getting out of bed, but the Holy Spirit gave me a comforting nudge that enabled me to get up, get dressed, and move forward. I learned to read the Word of God first thing in the morning before praying, and the last thing before going to sleep at night, a regimen that has remained a vital part of my spiritual practice to this day. The Holy Spirit's voice became a constant reassurance in my heart. He encouraged me to continue applying for jobs and participating in interviews. He gave me grace; I harbored no ill feelings about my job loss, and prayed daily for the woman who eliminated my job.

Years later, the legal associate and former colleague who collaborated with the SVP of HR to eliminate my job eventually lost her own position at Trinity. I was asked by a colleague if I would help her to get an interview for a legal opening at Yale New Haven Health. I gladly helped to set up the interview. I highly suspect she was shocked that I would have done that, but the Holy Spirit gave me no choice. Were it not for the presence of the Spirit, I would not have been able to help her. As it turned out, she did not make it past the first round of interviews.

I always informed my interviewers about the circumstances regarding my former position, and approached each interview with energy and enthusiasm. The peace and power of the Holy Spirit renewed me, not only during the times I applied for a position, but during the times when I received an all-too-familiar rejection letter. The Spirit always breathed life from the Word of God into my soul. I can no longer read the Word of God as a collection of stories and ancient literature; rather, I see it as an expression of God's instructions and love letters to His children and specifically to me. This understanding gave me strength to approach each interview with optimism, regardless of the constant rejections.

I now read scripture as though I am reading family history, especially about my spiritual family members who knew suffering, and how God walked with them, and inspired them. I knew that the same God who walked with them, walked with me through my trials and tribulations. During my 1 ½ years of joblessness, I was motivated to a deeper intimacy with the Spirit through the Word.

I began reading the Bible from a present-tense, here and now mindset, versus a past-tense perspective. I became intimately acquainted with biblical characters and looked at them as brothers and sisters in the Spirit, which helped me to receive comfort and learn from their encounters. Their words and experiences spoke directly to me and continue to encourage me each time I meet them in the Word. The Bible is my manual for walking in the Spirit, even while living here on earth.

Reading the Bible from cover to cover proved to be a powerful spiritual practice for me, but reading it once was not enough. When athletes prepare for competition, they spend countless, grueling hours repeating exercises, strengthening their bodies, conditioning their minds, and rehearsing for their upcoming events. Preparation is paramount. Our spirit requires similar spiritual development. A transfer of spiritual power emerges when we immerse ourselves in the Word of God with an open and seeking heart. In too many cases, we have not been taught how to properly prepare our souls to grow and mature. Nowhere in my educational, religious, or business experiences was I taught how to develop my soul.

> *"Then he added, Son of man, let all my words sink deep into your own heart first. Listen to them carefully for yourself. Then go to*

*your people in exile and say to them, 'This is what the Sovereign
LORD says!' Do this whether they listen to you or not."*

Ezekiel 3:10–11

After almost seventeen years, my family is still recovering from
that painful period of walking through the lonely, searing, hot, but
holy desert. Yet I am still sustained by the lessons I learned during
that period of solitude with God. I continue to develop and mature
as I heed the voice of the Holy Spirit. I am far from being at total
peace, but I continue to grow.

> As we move from this life to the next, our spirit is preparing for our next stage of existence and fulfillment. . . . Preparation enables those who trust in Jesus to replace any fear with expectant faith and hope for that which lies ahead.

Many of my challenges early
in life gave me strength and
confidence that the Holy Spirit
would sustain me through hard
times. My spiritual development
continued, even though at times
I was unaware that the Holy
Spirit was by my side. The next
step is for me to grow to a place
where I consciously await instruction from the Spirit, and allow Him
to use me as He desires.

I spoke with my former pastor, Pastor Fred Sindorf, from North
Shore Assembly of God in Skokie, Illinois, years ago, and he told
me about one of his deacons, Deacon Lloyd, who just before dying,
said, "I have lived my entire life for this moment." That discussion
elevated my understanding of what it means to walk with and truly
trust the Holy Spirit. This deacon had an intimacy with the Holy
Spirit, and it was the same intimacy I witnessed with Pastor Fred
when he died years later. As we move from this life to the next, our
spirit is preparing each of us for our next stage of existence and
life after death. *"For this world is not our permanent home; we are looking
forward to a home yet to come"* (Hebrews 13:14).

Peace in Relationship with the Spirit

I can't imagine knowing the peace Jesus exhibited in Matthew
26 as He faced His adversaries in the Garden of Gethsemane.
As I grow stronger in my faith, I desire more of that type of

relationship with the Holy Spirit. I embrace joyful anticipation as I look forward to going home! Preparation enables those who trust in Jesus to replace fear with expectant faith and hope for that which lies ahead. A heavenward focus is an indicator that our spirit is maturing. As we move from this life to the next, we are preparing our soul to return to its natural state and to our spiritual Father, who resides in heaven. *"Above all, you must live as citizens of heaven, conducting yourselves in a manner worthy of the Good News about Christ."* (Philippians 1:27).

As I matured, I also realized that God led me to join specific churches over the years in order to teach my spirit the lessons I needed in order to serve and edify each respective body of believers. These lessons, as we have seen, regarding spiritual maturity are taught in the parable of the seed in the workers who produced thirty, sixty, and one hundredfold returns.

During the 1 ½ years I was out of a job, I was embarrassed to tell people I was unemployed, or to answer their question yet again about finding a job. I became so connected to my role as a vice president, that I no longer felt like myself when I wasn't working. In some people's eyes, my identity and value had in fact changed, and it was a battle for me not to believe this lie.

Our heavenward focus is a sign that our spirit is maturing.

My sole support and advocate throughout this desert experience was the Holy Spirit, this is typically true when people are broken. In our brokenness, only the Holy Spirit can fill us and heal us. Christians can be prone to criticizing people "of this world," but often church members themselves are blind idolaters. Our jobs and careers can take on such priority in our minds that we sacrifice everything else to gain a position or salary we worship.

The world sees us through the lens of our work and our titles. When we first meet someone, we typically ask them, "What do you do?" Our "doing" overshadows our "being" in contemporary culture. We don't ask, "How are you?" "What do you do in your spare time?" "Who are you?" or "What do you value?" No. Our assessment of identity begins with a measurement of our tangible output, often devoid of the factor of life influence.

Letting Go to Embrace God

A purging takes place whenever we lose a job. In the past when I was job searching, I always had multiple offers to consider. I was wanted and valued. But this time there were no offers. My skills and job history seemed to have become irrelevant, and my education and credentials held no significance. These were devastating blows to my ego, not to mention examples of bias in hiring practices.

By the grace of God, I found healing from reading the Bible. Immersion in the Word transformed me and gave life to my soul. It stirred my heart to move forward and infused my soul with hope. I learned to discipline my spirit not to become bitter or angry. Focusing on the Word of God gave me patience that turned to peace.

David is the only person in scripture who is described as "a man after God's own heart." He committed his life to pursuing God. Yet when we read Psalm 69, we see David ostracized from his family. During his time tending his father's sheep in the pastures, he learned to lean on the Holy Spirit and develop intimacy with God. David learned to slay giants long before he met Goliath.

As you read the upcoming verses, pause between verses to let the words move beyond your mind, and settle into your heart. Let the stillness of the moment overtake your mind and body, and let your spirit control you. Listen in your heart and through your spirit. Recognize that the words of scripture are not mere words, they are alive, powerful, and Spirit-filled. David talked with God as a real person through the Holy Spirit, who inhabits the Word of God. It is easy to memorize scriptures; however, when we come to know the power beyond the words, the scriptures will awaken our hearts and souls like nothing else in all creation. The power of the Holy Spirit inhabits not only the Word, but also our own souls. Reflect on the following verses and allow your spirit to be still as you read the words of King David, a man after God's own heart:

"So as David stood there among his brothers, Samuel took the flask of olive oil he had brought and anointed David with the oil. And the Spirit of the LORD came powerfully upon David from that day on."

1 Samuel 16:13

"The LORD is a shelter for the oppressed, a refuge in times of trouble. Those who know your name trust in you, for you, O LORD, do not abandon those who search for you."

Psalm 9:9–10

"I will bless the LORD who guides me; even at night my heart instructs me."

Psalm 16:7

"Even when I walk through the darkest valley, I will not be afraid, for you are close beside me. Your rod and your staff protect and comfort me."

Psalm 23:4

"The LORD is a friend to those who fear him. He teaches them his covenant. My eyes are always on the LORD, for he rescues me from the traps of my enemies."

Psalm 25:14–15

"Morning, noon, and night I cry out in my distress, and the LORD hears my voice."

Psalm 55:17

"Yes, you have been with me from birth; from my mother's womb you have cared for me. No wonder I am always praising you!"

Psalm 71:6

Evil people are not only in the streets. They can also be found in media, corporations, government, academia, as well as the church.

This is another reason why we need the protection and discernment of the Holy Spirit wherever we go. We can count on Him for wisdom. The Holy Spirit's voice can be seen and heard in the stars in the heavens, the birds in the air, the flowers in the fields, the fish in the sea, the mountains and oceans, and the people around you. Everything that breathes and grows is filled with God's Spirit. Ask God to help you sense His Spirit in the depths of your soul. Don't be discouraged if this doesn't happen immediately. The "eyes" of our souls often become distracted or closed by the harried pace of modern life. Be patient and give yourself time to see through spiritual eyes.

I realized after the fact, that had I read through the Bible only once in 2006, the year I lost my job. I knew that reading the Bible cover to cover helped me overcome the spiritual battles that are a part of life on earth, and I attributed much of my success to my discipline of constant prayer and consistent reading of scripture. For some reason I did not immerse myself in the Word of God in 2006, and I realized that I was not adequately protected by the Holy Spirit as I faced powers that were filled with the spirit of this world.

During this period, I was spiritually vulnerable and under significant attack. My spirit was weak, and I was unable to protect myself and my family. However, when I remembered to reengage and read the Bible consistently, my heart was soothed and revived, and I received deep assurance that my situation would be rectified. I felt God's peace and His strength from reading.

When I was young, I believed that my prayers were sufficient to protect me, even when I was engaged in worldly and dangerous behavior. Although I was not growing spiritually during those years, prayer provided spiritual protection. However, when we find ourselves doing God's work, spiritual challenges come in many forms, and it is crucial that we have the covering of Jesus Christ through His Spirit. Our battle is not against flesh and blood, and we must always be armed and ready.

> *"For we are not fighting against flesh-and-blood enemies, but*
> *against evil rulers and authorities of the unseen world, against*

mighty powers in this dark world, and against evil spirits in the heavenly places."

Ephesians 6:12

The Protection of The Word

I realized that I was accountable not only for my well-being, but also for my family. My spiritual responsibility was greater, and I was not doing my part to keep myself and my family under the protective care of the Holy Spirit. As the head of my household, I neglected my responsibility to fully protect my family, which included the physical, mental, and spiritual aspects.

In 2007, I read the Bible cover to cover eleven times. I accomplished this by dividing the number of pages in my Bible by the number of days in the month and then disciplined myself to read the required pages each day. This isn't that difficult if you are committed to knowing the Holy Spirit. I found that it took me on average approximately seventy hours in order to read the Bible cover to cover.

I quickly discovered that reading the Bible from Genesis to Revelation required me to have conversations with the Holy Spirit because I was engaging the entire scripture. I wasn't reading the Word as separate books or chapters, but as a complete and coherent work. Reading scripture is a way to immerse ourselves in the Spirit of the Lord, as modeled by King David. Our ongoing discussions of my reading allowed me to be in constant dialogue with the Spirit. This was the way I survived 1 ½ years of unemployment and constant rejections from potential employers, friends, and even family members. I also carried the spiritual and emotional pain of my wife and children. I experienced greater appreciation of what Job must have experienced, and I now read his book with a very different perspective.

I kept a journal of the people I contacted and the interviews I completed, which yielded over 400 names of people I contacted through email, telephone, or online sites such as LinkedIn. Yes, I fought depressive thoughts and a sense of worthlessness after experiencing rejection upon rejection, but I found strength in reading the Word of God. My desire was to know the Holy Spirit. After I read and pondered Acts 1:4, "Once when Jesus was eating with His disciples, He commanded them, "Do not leave Jerusalem until the Father sends you the gift He promised, as I told you before," the Spirit gave me a revelation. It was clear to me that the gift which Jesus spoke about in this verse pertained directly to the Holy Spirit.

When God takes His children through the desert, it is with the intention of revealing Himself when they have no one else to depend on. There isn't anything in the desert except heat, sand, predators, arid conditions, and scant nourishment. Sometimes the only way for God to get our attention is to get us away by Himself, as He did when He took the Israelites into the desert.

I wish I could tell you that God purified and filled me with perfection while I searched for a job, but He didn't. I still have a lot of the same quirks and shortcomings as before. However, He made me more aware of His presence in the form of the Holy Spirit. Flying to fifteen states, for forty job interviews, and thirty-nine rejections was a learning experience I would not have wished for. This all happened in the twilight of my career, when I was fifty-three years old and had relocated my family to a job from which I was certain I would retire. However, God's plans and our plans are not always aligned and when they are not, His plans are infinitely better. Despite comfort from the Holy Spirit, something deep in my spirit kept asking the question, "Do you truly trust Him?"

Comfort and Direction

Did I truly trust God? Do you?

I knew I had to keep pushing myself to read the Word, talk to the Holy Spirit, meditate, and pray to keep moving forward. Eventually my spirit finally started to slow down and became more attentive to the things of God. I noticed details in nature and felt a deeper appreciation for the insects, birds, and animals I saw each day. I also paid more attention to my breathing, my emotions, and the thoughts beneath my thoughts. I started to notice little things, along with the startling realization that God is concerned about the smallest details of our lives. I began watching birds fly, ants crawl, or squirrels chase each other, recognizing that God is in all things, including even the inanimate, like the wind and rain.

I took a deeper interest in the characters I read about in the Bible and began to recognize them as more than just characters and stories. I saw them as real people who had gone through similar challenges in their lives, and whose examples could help me deal with my problems through my relationship with the Holy Spirit. I also took a deeper interest in the people around me. I started asking them questions about themselves and their walk with God.

I eventually recognized that the purpose behind my unemployment period was to remind me that the Spirit of God was continually with me, as He had been when I was a child, and bad things had taken place in my life. Somehow God helped me to be content with the little I had in those early years. He must have seen the need to remove certain distractions from my life in order to make me dependent on Him. This may not be true for everyone, and I am thankful He was with me the entire time.

As I mentioned previously, part of the reason I ended up working with Trinity Health was the attraction of a job with a good title, a great salary, in a faith-based organization located in the lower-cost-of-living Midwest. I had often said that I would never, ever take a job for money.

But guess what? I changed my mind because the offer looked so attractive.

God holds certain individuals to differing standards, and I now believe I made a decision that went against His will for me when I took the job at Trinity Health. One reason that I returned to the East coast was to take the job with Merck so I could be closer to my mother, who lived alone in Allentown. When I got the offer from Trinity, I figured I could fly her out to Michigan and she could stay with the family for months on end, whenever she decided. We indeed had the space, which made the move to Trinity even more attractive. I coveted the title and a chance to make more money. I went back on my promise not to accept a position for money, because I believed I could negotiate the details with God, so that

He would be pleased. Instead, I committed idolatry, something we don't talk enough about in the church.

As my plans began to unravel, I knew I needed to depend on the Holy Spirit. However, this was not the way I planned to grow close to Him. When we read the Word of God consistently, He speaks to us in a variety of ways. Sometimes He speaks through others, which did not happen for me during my job search. Sometimes He speaks directly to us in an audible voice, which He also did not do in my circumstances. Sometimes He speaks in dreams, which He did with me on occasion. Primarily, He spoke directly to my heart, because I read the Bible daily, I could hear the Spirit's voice intuitively. He also spoke to me through journaling and fasting.

I started journaling in 1986, but my writing became more intense during 2006. The written word possesses power, and by reflecting on our journey, it reminds us of the places we have been and helps us discern our growth pattern.

Fasting is another powerful tool for connecting with the Holy Spirit. I have completed liquid fasts of 3, 7, 14, 21, 30, and 40 days. I encourage you to speak with your doctor before embarking on an extended fast. Improper fasting can have harmful physical and emotional effects. Fasting done in a healthy manner and with biblical guidelines can be an effective means of communicating with God.

The Spirit taught me that impressive job titles, credentials, degrees, and wealth are fleeting goals that can vanish in an instant. God is all I need, and He is the only dependable Person and force in this world. My 1 ½ years in the desert enabled me to grow to a deeper level of spiritual maturity.

Mark 4:13–20 describes various levels of spiritual maturity. Verses 14–17 describe two levels of darkness, followed by a level of dimness in verses 18–19, and multiple levels of light in verse 20. I believe my experience allowed me to see the entry level of light, and the importance of experiencing the fullness of the Holy Spirit. Jesus explains this in Matthew 5 when He talks about those whom God blesses. He declares in verse 14, "You are the light of the world, like a city on a hilltop that cannot be hidden." In A.W. Tozer's words:

"It is in the Word you find the Holy Spirit. Don't read too many other things. Some of you will say, "Look who's talking!" We'll go ahead and say it, I don't mind; but I am reading fewer and fewer things as I get older, not because I am losing interest in this great big, old suffering world, but because I am gaining interest in that other world above. So I say, don't try to know everything. You can't. Find Him in the Word, for the Holy Ghost wrote this Book. He inspired it, and He will be revealed in its pages."[9]

When we pursue the Holy Spirit, He illuminates His presence in our hearts, and we radiate His essence. Being cast into the desert and stripped of my title and position forced me to become acquainted with the Holy Spirit. He reminded me of my purpose and who I am. The children of God should never walk in fear; this was one of the lessons the Holy Spirit taught me. Never during those 1 ½ years was I afraid. Although I was depressed, I did not fear. He told me in His Word that He would never leave nor forsake me, and I saw that promise fulfilled every day.

The reason I say I was not afraid is that I always moved forward, even when my rational mind told me to quit. Fear can stop us dead in our tracks, but faith overcomes fear through each step we take forward. I never stopped moving. One of the verses I turned to most often was 1 John 4:18: "Such love has no fear, because perfect love expels all fear. If we are afraid, it is for fear of punishment, and this shows that we have not fully experienced his perfect love." The Spirit reminded me that, if I reflected and looked back, I could see His footprints during the times He had been with me.

One key lesson when reflecting on life is to refrain from idealizing our past, which can be dangerous when we relish and yearn for the good old days. This idealization can cause confusion, bitterness, and depression. We can't change the past, or go back and relive it, but we can learn from it. Too many people forfeit joy because they can't let go of the past to see where God is taking them. I needed to pause, to reflect, and to remember from whence I had come, so I could properly focus on where I was and where I was going.

Pursuing the Holy Spirit is not a part-time job. His peace is available to each of us. It is a gift from God reassuring us that no matter what happens, we can rest in the knowledge that He has worked out all things for our good.

Consider

- ◆ What is your definition of peace?
- ◆ Do you take the time to notice the people around you? As you go through your week, focus on observing people, their facial expresions, body language, manner of speech, clothing choices, etc. What do you see that lies beneath the surface?
- ◆ Identify a time when you were most at peace. How would you describe that time?
- ◆ What role do you think the Holy Spirit played in that time of peace you described?

Chapter Eight

Pruned by the Holy Spirit

"I am the true grapevine, and my Father is the gardener. He cuts off every branch of mine that doesn't produce fruit, and he prunes the branches that do bear fruit so they will produce even more. You have already been pruned and purified by the message I have given you. Remain in me, and I will remain in you. For a branch cannot produce fruit if it is severed from the vine, and you cannot be fruitful unless you remain in me. Yes, I am the vine; you are the branches. Those who remain in me, and I in them, will produce much fruit. For apart from me you can do nothing. Anyone who does not remain in me is thrown away like a useless branch and withers. Such branches are gathered into a pile to be burned. But if you remain in me and my words remain in you, you may ask for anything you want, and it will be granted! When you produce much fruit, you are my true disciples. This brings great glory to my Father."

John 15:1–8

Pruning involves cutting off or removing dead or living parts or branches (of a plant, for example) to improve shape or encourage growth. Pruning removes or cuts out the superfluous. In my previous position as Vice President and Chief Learning Officer, I had the opportunity to meet many people from across Connecticut and throughout the nation who worked in corporations, churches, universities, hospitals, and government. Most were seeking to be the best possible leaders in their areas of expertise. One aspect of good business leadership involves pruning, removing, or cutting out the

140

superfluous. This aspect of management, while painful, is critical to organizational success.

My primary focus in my professional life has been coaching, developing, and teaching fundamental leadership principles and vital spiritual lessons that are crucial for leading organizations. I have enjoyed over 35 years working with incredible leaders from across the globe and in amazing organizations such as Allstate Insurance Company, Ernst & Young, Merck Pharmaceutical, University of Pennsylvania, Yale New Haven Health, Yale School of Management, Scholarship America, North Shore Assembly of God, Center for Creative Leadership and others. I often mentor those who come to me for help, regardless of title.

I had an amazing administrative assistant, Maritza, who always found ways to make sure no one with a need or question who came to my office door was ever turned away. I believe this to be a foundational principle of leadership. Leaders must possess a strong spiritual foundation in order to cope with the magnitude of change and stress that surrounds us today. For this reason, I focus on spiritual principles that are foundational to life.

As an example, I offer the story of a woman named Kay who came to my office to visit me five years ago. The following was written in her words:

Kay and the Power of the Word

"I walked into the office of Dr. Jay Morris, hoping to acquire a business lead. But I left without the connection, disappointed and thinking I had received nothing of value for my time, at least from a business standpoint. Honestly, I left a bit confused.

Our conversation never got to the subject of business. Instead, we discussed topics like emotions, working with people, and God.

Yes, God.

At the end of our meeting, Jay extended an invitation for another conversation, which left me befuddled. What could he want to discuss? But strangely enough, I accepted. Everything I heard about him told me he was a kind and respectful man, which alone was a novelty to me. And I was curious about whatever the conversation would be about. I was at a point in life where I was looking for something, but had no idea what it was.

My life was a hot mess. My struggling business had just started creeping toward stability, but I still felt unfulfilled. What's more, my fiscal survival rested on a single contract that would soon end.

Add to this, my son (and only child) was having issues adjusting to school. Painfully. In addition, I told a family member to vacate my house after I (regrettably) absorbed months of selfish behavior from them. And I was twenty-three years into an emotionally abusive marriage that showed no sign of hope. In fact, our relationship was spiraling downward.

I felt trapped and tormented, and I cried daily. Day and night, I grappled with unending thoughts about how to fix my collapsing world. Divorce was not an option. And although I hoped for God to miraculously restore my marriage, as in stories I heard, I didn't see signs of healing on the horizon for my husband and me.

In my second meeting with Jay, he told me a bit about his life and asked a few questions about mine. Although we focused our conversation on God, after a short time Jay switched gears and challenged me to read the Bible from cover to cover until this became a daily routine in my life.

God often uses circumstances as a pruning process to cut away superfluous or damaging elements in our lives to bring us back to health or increase our effectiveness for His kingdom.

What on earth was that request about? I asked myself as I stared at him from the far side of his desk and sipped my coffee. *Read the Bible from Genesis to Revelation? What could be more boring?*

The idea felt strange, comforting, and intimidating all at once. But suddenly I realized that Jay was asking to *mentor* me in biblical principles. In that moment, I realized that not one positive male role model existed in my life. The realization was painful, especially since I was forty-eight. And now a gentle, respected man from our business community offered to mentor me about how to know God better through the power of the Holy Spirit.

The realization brought me to tears. Although I love and respect my father and honor his role, I could not name a strong man who had positively impacted my life. All of my mentors were women. How did I manage to grow to adulthood without knowing any positive male role models? Even the older men I knew were embroiled in self-destructive behaviors or living with the consequences of bad life decisions. They had unhealthy relationships with their wives and mothers, and demonstrated zero emotional intelligence.

As I recognized this truth for the first time, I suddenly felt cheated. Yet here was a patient, godly, soft-spoken, safe man who was willing to teach me.

I accepted Jay's challenge and began reading the Bible cover to cover.

My marriage once again reached a boiling point, and I knew I had to leave. The verbal abuse and infidelity were too much. I was a frazzled wreck inside with a huge smile on the outside. My smile masked my immense emotional pain.

It wasn't uncommon for me to cry all night and then to get up the next day and do my job as though my life were perfect . . . all while I was dead inside. A piece of me was fighting to find the light, struggling to free the rest of me from the hell that became my life.

The man in the office conveyed strength and hope to me, even though I had not shared my circumstances with him. I couldn't bring myself to reveal the horrible private details about my life. I hardly knew the man in the office, and besides, ours was a professional relationship, albeit with spiritual significance. I couldn't admit to him that the Bible reading was boring. I couldn't seem to connect with it, but we kept meeting, and he encouraged me to keep reading and to be on the lookout for scripture in which the Holy Spirit spoke to me. He told me to look at the struggles of the people in the Bible and pull lessons from them for my life.

I was so consumed with my marriage that I couldn't see the great things God was doing in my business. Contracts were coming in, and I was experiencing favor with companies and associations. I assumed leadership positions in a community organization and was given advisory board appointments. But my family was still so broken that my business advancements meant nothing. I wanted my family.

I finally worked up the courage to share my troubles with this stranger, but I offered a sanitized version because I was ashamed of my situation. How could I remain in such an unhealthy environment? But his words of encouragement turned out to be balm to my soul. I looked forward to our visits, at which I could empty the pain of my soul as he listened and encouraged me. Each time we met, he asked me how my Bible reading was coming. When I didn't complete my goal, he didn't scold or shame me, but encouraged me to keep trying. And I did.

The more I read the Bible, the calmer I became. Then one day when I sat down to read, I recognized that my crying had subsided and that I was smiling. I started to entertain the thought that my marriage was over, that it was time to move on. However, I decided to wait until my son left for college two years later. To be honest, I was scared. I had spent my entire adult life with my husband, and I didn't trust God (or myself) enough to think I could make it on my own. So, I deliberately set two years to save and prepare.

It took me about nine months during this period of preparation to get through my first reading of the Bible, but I did it! I kept meeting with Jay for mentoring and to discuss what I was learning, and I shared my joy over having completed my reading of the entire Bible!

He smiled before telling me to start reading again, beginning in Genesis.

What?

I couldn't have heard him right. But we had talked so much about the importance of scripture in a believer's life that I knew Jay wasn't joking. So, I dove back into Genesis again and pretended it was a juicy novel. I was growing emotionally stronger with each chapter, but I still wasn't perceiving personal insights. For instance, I found the book of Chronicles as dry as a dusty desert; I got stuck slogging through its sands, and my reading slowed down. I missed a few days, but I kept reading. Sometimes I would crawl into bed after forgetting to read and then get back up before midnight to read at least one page. But reading the Bible had become habit.

It was now one year since I met Jay, and I was still changing. The Bible reading was making me stronger, but I still didn't see clearly. I always believed God and trusted Him, and my trust increased significantly with the reading, but I wasn't sold out. I was still angry about my marriage and my family. I trusted God for parking spaces, contracts, and healing people, but I did not trust Him to take care of every other aspect of my life. I had stuffed God into neat compartments that worked for me. But my family and marriage were components about which

> The more I read the Bible, the calmer I became. Then one day when I sat down to read, I recognized that my crying had subsided and that I was smiling.

I couldn't understand why God was silent, and they continually fueled my inability to let go and relinquish to Him my entire life. I was bitter.

Then a series of incidents occurred in my house in April of 2019 that assured me it was time to leave. Right after one such incident, I talked to God again and started my exit plan. Within thirty-six hours I secured an apartment and told my husband I would be leaving him. I left the very next day.

That was the best and worst day of my life. I was scared but knew that something had to change. No one should put up with emotional abuse and infidelity. I felt sorry for both of us. He had his issues and I had mine, and we were not equipped to make a marriage work, much less a family. We were both wasting away in a dead arrangement, and I could clearly see his pain. I still loved him but knew it was over.

Three and a half years after leaving my marriage, I was totally transformed. We filed on Christmas Eve, both agreeing to waive the waiting period, and our divorce was finalized in two weeks. Because of God's love, I learned what it feels like to be cared for, pampered, and loved and to have someone anticipate and fulfill my needs before I asked. My life became a wildly joyful adventure. Most importantly, I learned to talk to God as I would to a friend sitting in my car.

My soul is still healing, but joy now bubbles up from within. God has proven time and again that there is no substitute for trusting

Three and a half years after leaving my marriage, I was totally transformed. . . . Most importantly, I had learned to talk to God as I would a friend sitting in my car.

Him. My blessings are endless, and His favor is so heavy on me that my family members sit back and shake their heads. Since I have started reading through the Bible, the following things have occurred:

- ◆ My business has exploded and will surpass $2MM plus this year, my best year ever, compared to my former best annual income of $200K
- ◆ Business leads seem to be falling from the sky
- ◆ In the middle of the pandemic, God gave me the idea to move to Florida—a plan that came together within two weeks
- ◆ I now live close to five beaches, which is critical for me
- ◆ I mentor twenty highly professional and spiritually mature women across the country on growing closer to the Holy Spirit

I now believe I can find healthy love. I can't say I want to find love again because I'm not sure I ever experienced love in my marriage. But if it's God's will, I'm open to the possibility of experiencing a healthy love relationship in time . . . but not until I have further time to heal and God offers His approval.

I will never be able to repay Jay for caring for my bruised and battered soul with the Word of God over these last five years. He served as my Good Samaritan, mentor, friend, father-figure, confidant, and spiritual adviser. I am now on my tenth reading through the Bible cover to cover; completing the entire Bible three to four times a year is my current goal. The power of this discipline has radically changed my life.

When people come into our lives, we cannot foresee the role they will play, but God can. Had I not met my mentor, Jay, and partnered with him in reading through the Bible cover to cover, I don't believe I would be sitting now in Florida, poised for adventure and full of hope, with a clear vision for my life and peace that defies explanation. Jay became a friend who extended his time, talent, care, faith, and spiritual guidance to me *to show me that my life could be different.*

I now encourage other struggling people with the same simple assignment: read the entire Bible from cover to cover. The lessons my mentor taught me must be shared. His instructions were simple: read the Bible; get to know the Holy Spirit, and He will teach you. You have no idea where He may ask you to serve Him. I am now leading a group of twenty highly professional and spiritually mature women from across the country on Sunday evenings. One of our primary objectives is to read the Bible from cover to cover and experience the presence of the Holy Spirit. This experience has been beyond words. This is church!

Multiplication Through the Spirit

I was amazed at the transformation in Kay's life after only one year of her consistently reading scripture and praying. I also witnessed her impact on the lives of her clients and others around her.

I met a young woman in one of Kay's classes who talked about her dream job of one day becoming a doctor. As a result of sexual abuse, this young woman could not touch another person without becoming physically ill. Something as simple as shaking someone's hand at a mock interview was dreadfully difficult for her.

However, Kay was able to work with this young woman, helping her gain confidence to secure a job and provide for her two children. The power of consistently reading the Word and applying its lessons transformed Kay's life, as well as the lives of the people she touches.

I watched Kay build a personal relationship with the Holy Spirit, and she continues to do so to this day. After five years, Kay is expanding and growing her business, as well as her spiritual maturity. She sent me a recent note that read, "Jay, I just got the following from one of the students you met in my class: 'Hey Mrs. Kay, how are you? You won't believe this. I'm releasing my first book, called H.O.E., *Heaven on Earth*. I was hoping you could be one of the first to preorder yours. We're only releasing 100 copies, and I wanted you to be among the first to get one."

Kay is a leader who is now developing leaders, one of the most powerful signs of true leadership. She is currently mentoring godly, professional women from across the country to develop and mature their souls and the group is expanding internationally.

God gives each of us specific experiences to teach us the lessons we need to learn to further His work. His ways of teaching us are not like the teaching methods of the world. Like our brothers and sisters in the scriptures, many of us go through the furnace to learn God's lessons. God uses the hardships we encounter as real-life laboratories for spiritual lessons and spiritual refinement.

The Spirit in the "Detours"

When I graduated from college, I was at my wit's end because I couldn't find a job. Nick, the executive director from the Boys' Club, identified a job driving a dry cleaner's van. Although I knew he was trying to help, there was no way on God's green earth that I was going to drive a laundry truck (nothing against anyone who earns a living by doing so). It just wasn't the right job for me.

I graduated in May and applied for jobs, but received no positive responses. By June I was thinking about enlisting in the Air Force. No one seemed able to help me land a decent job. In desperation, I gave my résumé to a good friend, Bernie, whose wife knew of two job openings in social services.

Unfortunately, more than 150 people with master's degrees and years of experience applied for the jobs. The hiring manager was an African American Woman who just happened to be a graduate of North Carolina A&T an HBCU (Historically Black College or University). The chances of a person of color having a professional managerial position in Allentown, Pennsylvania, in 1975 were slim.

> God gives us specific experiences to teach us the lessons we need to learn to further His work. [He] uses the hardships we encounter as real-life laboratories for spiritual lessons.

However, the Holy Spirit made it possible for me to be hired as a geriatric case worker for the Lehigh County Agency on Aging. The hiring manager saw something in me that she felt qualified me for the job. In fact, the other open position at the time was given to another fresh-out-of-school colleague who was fluent in Spanish.

What were the odds of two new undergraduates being selected over seasoned experienced professionals?

I started the job in July and began every Monday morning by reading the Allentown Morning Call obituaries, to see who had died over the weekend, so that I could clean out my files and keep my caseload current. My client base was made up of low income men and women, sixty years of age and older who struggled financially, and in most cases, battled physical, medical, and emotional hardships. One of my first clients was a female migrant worker who was dying from syphilis. Lavinia lived in a house with other migrant workers who did their best to take care of her. Ironically for me, she lived in a house on South Sixth Street that had been previously owned by an executive who worked at Mack Trucks. His son Bobby was a classmate of mine in elementary school, and their home was palatial. I had played there on a few occasions until the family moved out of the neighborhood as demographics began changing. Of course, Bobby never came to my house.

When I walked into the house, I immediately noticed that the condition of the home was a far cry from what it was when Bobby lived there. A group of poor people had obviously taken responsibility for caring for a friend in need. Lavinia's friends did their best to take care of her and provide her with a love that is rare to see, even in the church.

My job was to find resources for senior citizens in the Lehigh Valley for people like Lavinia who needed immediate assistance with medical, physical, financial, or other life threatening problems. I was so young and inexperienced that I had to lean on the Holy Spirit to help people old enough to be my grandparents with their critical needs. By the time I was assigned to Lavinia, she was extremely weak and unable to get out of bed. She did not have health insurance, however, I was able to find a very seasoned nurse in the emergency room who recommended that her friends get her drunk, so she could be examined in the ER. Unfortunately, Lavinia died shortly after being admitted into the hospital.

The Spirit Stirs Our Empathy

I spent two years helping people like Lavinia who seemed to be hopeless, trying my very best to ease their burdens. I knew a little about pain and suffering, but seeing the elderly treated like outcasts and throwaways by society was heartbreaking. The agency was committed to helping its clients as much as it could. Our biggest need was funding. Without the proper finances, all I could do was to listen, and figure out how to ease the suffering with the sparse resources at hand.

At the time I didn't realize that the Holy Spirit was helping me discern where to go and how to help my clients. I looked at each person as though he or she were a family member, a characteristic that has always been a part of my spiritual DNA.

God uses our broken hearts to help us see, identify with, and extend His love to those who are suffering.

Another client by the name of Renaldo was being evicted by the City of Allentown as a result of multiple health-code violations. I learned that he was a very successful businessman who had a number of different ventures in the 1930s, but lost everything through an unfortunate business transaction. He had no family, so I was the only person available to help him. He would often come to my office to visit. Eventually, the city condemned his home and removed dump trucks full of garbage from his home. I was informed that many of the workers who had entered Renaldo's house were infected with lice. I transported Renaldo in my car to the Sacred Heart ER and was never infected with one louse. I was informed that the hospital had to throw away all of his clothes because of the infestation.

I cried at Renaldo's court hearing because the judge refused to let him sit in the court room and confined him to the hallway as a result of his unsanitary condition. Renaldo lost his home and was placed in a mental institution after his hearing. It hurt me to see that people could be treated this way because of their socio-economic circumstances and age. The Holy Spirit used those two years to teach me how to engage with people from the heart. This job required me to work with people whom society seemed to have tossed aside. My heart was crushed when the agency received a call about a woman with ten adult children who had dropped their mother off at the door of the ER, because none of them had the time to take care of her.

God uses our broken hearts to help us see, identify with, and extend His love to those who are suffering. Each person has a story. When we take the time to listen, we discover that all of our stories have a common theme: we all need to be loved.

The Heart of Jesus and the Reality of Trauma

Because I cared about people, I tried my best to fix their problems, but seemingly to no avail. There were just too many needs, and I was acting in the role of an extended family member. I later realized that I had been somewhat traumatized from seeing the pain inflicted on one of the most vulnerable groups in society, comprised of the old, the poor, and the forgotten. It was too much to bear, which was probably one of the reasons I started hanging out in the streets even more.

The hardships I had experienced earlier in my life enabled me to handle the conditions of my clients. However, one of the hardest things I had to do was to personally place Pop in an alcohol rehabilitation center at the age of eighty-three. Seeing my grandfather in this diminished condition was difficult for me. Dad was unable to handle this situation, so the responsibility fell to me at the age of twenty-three. Such situations often present us with experiences we cannot comprehend in the moment, but as time passes these hardships produce fruit. In the midst of these battles, we learn to rely on the power of the Holy Spirit.

I helped my step-grandmother, Ruth, take care of Pop's funeral arrangements when he died in June of 1978. As he was dying, he repeatedly cried out and asked Jesus to have mercy on his soul. I knew in my heart that he was forgiven for all the wicked things he had done in his life. I spoke at his funeral service, which was my second occasion to be in the pulpit and spoke again from 1 Corinthians 13. I am confident that Pop is in heaven and that God has forgiven him for all of the wicked things he did. I love my grandfather and felt a part of his heart that was not experienced by Dad or Nanna B.

Seeing What's in the Heart

When we walk in the Spirit, He enables us to discern the hearts of those around us. Unfortunately, many so-called Christians judge other people by what they see with their eyes, think in their minds, and not what they perceive through the Spirit's stirring in their hearts and souls. God looks on the heart, as stated in 1 Samuel 16:7, in which we are told that Samuel based his decision on the outward appearance of Jesse's oldest son, Eliab and had to be reminded that God looks on the heart. The heart that is warmed by the Spirit of Christ is able to see into the hearts of those around them, whether those hearts are cold and dead, or alive and bearing fruit.

Kay questioned why God would have allowed her to enter a marriage that would fall short of what she had envisioned. She and I discussed reasons couples should make sure they are compatible and seek spiritual counseling before marriage.

Although God did not change my friend's situation, He changed her heart. Because she wanted to obey Him, God planted thoughts about life/personal changes in her heart that helped her see that light can indeed pierce darkness. All of this changed as she started reading the Word of God on a regular basis. The pruning was painful, but it brought forth abundant fruit.

Kay sent me a note telling me that she had spoken to five hundred leaders from Europe and Africa about the challenges of living and leading through crisis. She mentioned that she felt the presence of the Holy Spirit as she spent time in scripture preparing for this international gathering. Through the power of the Spirit, Kay's story was used by the Spirit to inspire five hundred Christian leaders from around the world.

While working at the County Agency on Aging, I saw goodness in the hearts of struggling people and didn't find myself distracted by their lice, syphilis, or other illnesses. I attempted to embrace them as God saw them. This was a challenge for a kid fresh out of college who thought he knew everything. Although the problems

I encountered were overwhelming, the Holy Spirit guided me through those two years at the agency. I was able to see the hearts of the people, in conjunction with the heart of God, bringing about a solution, unaware that the Holy Spirit was teaching me about His grace and mercy. I also learned that the decisions we make without the Spirit are often the result of who we are, and the way we think, and that those unguided decisions can at times produce unfortunate outcomes.

Optimism and the Holy Spirit

During my years at the agency from 1975 to 1977, I observed that less than 10 percent of my clients demonstrated optimism in the later stages of their lives. The other 90 percent were pessimistic and had given up on life, including one man who kept his loaded shotgun on his television to remind me that I was unwelcomed to visit his mother in his home. (I guess I was too young and naive to be deterred because I kept returning.)

> The Spirit ministers to us in our suffering to teach us lessons to benefit those He entrusts to our care.

Sometimes it helps to be young and blind to danger. Looking back over my childhood and youth, I realize the ways in which death and dying were major parts of my life. After pressing forward through hardships, I look back in confidence and assert that the Holy Spirit guided me. I often struggled during the times when I wasn't praying and seeking the Lord. It was during these times when I attempted to carry my clients' burdens alone, that I struggled the most. Some of my clients relied on me to the point of finding my phone number and calling me at home.

One client, named Estella wanted to remove her son from her will and add me on as her beneficiary, which was not permissible. I started suffering from gastrointestinal bleeding and decided to move to Atlanta because my job stress had become too overwhelming. The lessons I learned were real and powerful, but more than I could bear.

My hardships propelled me into experiences that taught me spiritual competencies that prepared and enabled me to work on

global problems and engage people from all backgrounds. My challenges as a poor kid taught me tremendous life lessons that opened
doors for me to work in Fortune 100 Companies and engage with
CEOs and leaders of major institutions. I could have accomplished
none of this on my own. The Holy Spirit led me to my employers,
and the lessons I learned equipped me to walk corporate hallways
of major corporations. He was my mentor as I took on tasks I had
neither seen, nor done before.

Most people who know me will tell you that I am a quiet, behind-
the-scenes kind of guy. My goal is not to be seen but to be present
enough to make a difference.

God often uses difficult times in our lives to prepare us for the
work He has ordained for each of us. This process is the same for
all of His children. The Spirit ministers to us in our suffering to
teach us lessons to benefit those He entrusts to our care. *"I have told
you all this so that you may have peace in me. Here on earth you will have many
trials and sorrows. But take heart, because I have overcome the world "* (John
16:33).

Consider

♦   Can you identify a time when you faced a major challenge? What
    lessons did you learn?
♦   How were you able to get through your challenge?
♦   Can you see how and where the Holy Spirit may have been involved
    in this situation?
♦   What did you learn from the challenge?

Chapter Nine

Path of the Holy Spirit

"This is the route the Israelites followed as they marched out of Egypt under the leadership of Moses and Aaron. At the LORD's direction, Moses kept a written record of their progress. These are the stages of their march, identified by the different places where they stopped along the way."

Numbers 33:1-2

Remarkably, Moses and the Israelites encamped at forty-two different sites during their forty years of wandering through the desert. They depended on God to lead them, feed them, respond to their many needs, and protect them over four taxing decades. God requires total dependency on Him, the expectation He places on *all* of His children. He doesn't typically hand us roadmaps, especially when we feel we need them the most. It is interesting that the Israelites followed God and trusted His direction whenever he ordered them to move, and that Moses recorded their progress.

Perils on the Path

We often hear the Holy Spirit calling us in transitional and soul-stretching situations. God taps us on the shoulder, as He did to Moses, and opens our eyes to the plight of people He places in our path. He gives us insight to see the suffering of others, as well as the desire or motivation to respond. The Holy Spirit also uses our wanderings to stir awareness of His loving care, teach us valuable life lessons, ease the suffering of others, awaken gratitude, and deepen our empathy.

Most scared, wounded people lack the strength to tend to their weakened spiritual condition. We are too busy battling trauma, fending off crises, and erecting defenses against the world. We don't know whom to trust when we feel ourselves to be at the end of our ropes. Scared, wounded men and women are not limited to the fragile, forgotten people we see under overpasses, or clustered in homeless shelters, or living in tents.

Many of our nation's greatest personal and institutional spiritual battles are being fought in the ivory towers of renowned financial, political, and economic empires. Yes, this applies to churches as well, perhaps to an even greater extent, based on our tendency to accept blind religion in place of Spirit-driven faith.

Money and power are incapable of procuring the more elusive qualities in life, like love, joy, and peace, the things that we crave most in our inner beings, treasures the heart produces only by the fruit of the Spirit. Tragically, far too often the Spirit of God is absent in many of today's churches. Our responsibility as God's children is to ensure that the Spirit is present and active, and that His role is honored in our daily lives and in our places of worship.

> **Money and power are incapable of procuring the more elusive qualities in life like love, joy, and peace that we crave most in our inner beings; treasures the heart produces by the fruit of the Spirit.**

The Spirit is Our Roadmap

The night before I left for NCCU, I got into a fight at the Allentown fairgrounds, thanks to my good friend Pipe. I was generally a quiet, reserved person who didn't fight unless I was provoked. Somehow, Pipe got into an argument with two tobacco-chewing guys from Texas who were running a concession booth. I had been drinking Colt 45 malt liquor while hanging out with "my boys", and was feeling pretty good after a few drinks as I contemplated leaving for Durham, North Carolina, early the next morning.

The last thing I wanted was a fight. As I walked around the corner with thousands of other people strolling throughout the exhibits and concession stands, I heard Pipe shouting at the top of his voice: "Here comes Jay! Now let's see what you have to say!"

My (questionable) memory tells me that the Texan threw the first punch, and he and I definitely destroyed a couple of booths in the scuffle. When it was over, my expensive, brand new red, white, and blue shirt that I had just bought for school was stained by the blood running from his nose. I also ended up with a badly bruised eye. As soon as the fight ended, the motorcycle police arrived, and I disappeared into the crowd with an eye that was almost swollen shut, while squinting through my glasses, somewhat intoxicated. God's grace allowed me to leave without facing police intervention.

"Why didn't you just knock him out?" shouted the voice of one of the guys.

"Yeah, why did you wrestle him?" came another voice as we slipped through the crowd.

If I had used my fists, I would likely have seriously injured the Texan, been stopped before fading into the crowd, missed making it to college the next morning, and very possibly faced an arrest, especially if my opponent had required medical attention. Although I wasn't aware of it at the time, the Spirit of God prevented a course correction on my journey by subconsciously prompting me not to intentionally use my fists.

I witnessed a fight years earlier in middle school when one of the guys from the neighborhood slashed a sailor at a high school football game that was held in a stadium two blocks from the fairgrounds. The young sailor nearly died. I vividly remember seeing the glare of the streetlights reflected from the shiny blade before it cut the sailor twice and then disappeared back into the assailant's pocket. Detectives came to our locker room at Harrison Morton Junior High School early the next morning, just before our football game, and took several team members to the police station for questioning. No one saw me in the crowd that night. The young man who nearly killed the sailor spent years in a reformatory school and was incarcerated years later for having murdered a woman. I thank God my own fight was over in a matter of minutes and without serious injury that night.

The next morning Mom and Dad drove me to the bus station, and neither asked me about my swollen black eye. I had tears in my eyes when I climbed onto the bus and stared out the window as it slowly drove away. Suddenly, I felt so alone as I watched Mom and Dad waving . . . as they slowly disappeared when the bus turned the corner onto Hamilton Street. The feeling of sadness soon faded as I started to think about North Carolina and what college would bring to my life. It took almost two days to get to Durham, with overnight stops in Washington, D.C. and Richmond, Virginia.

I had never traveled that far before and was tired of sitting in the bus terminals during my stops in D.C. and Richmond. I looked for bars or clubs to hang out since I had layovers both nights and spent hours walking the empty streets unable to find anything open, not even a local bar.

Coincidence? I think not.

Limitless Grace

When I finally arrived in Durham, North Carolina almost two days later, I knew immediately that I was going to enjoy my new life. I retrieved my trunk from the bus and caught a taxi to campus. It was about 8:00 a.m., and Al Green was singing "I'm So Tired of Being Alone" over the taxi's radio as my inaugural welcome to the Bull City.

Minutes after the taxi had dropped me off at Chidley Hall I immediately met other freshmen on my floor. Otis and Dip were two of the young men who would be residing on the third floor in my dormitory and they both became a big part of my life over the next four years. I started my freshman year with a bang and a grade point average of close to 4.0. But by the time I graduated, my grades had consistently slipped every semester, finally leveling out at a 2.95. While my grades weren't stellar, they were good enough to help me achieve my goal of graduating on time. However, compared to my high school grades, I looked like a scholar.

College wasn't easy, especially as I was totally responsible for my tuition and living expenses. I bought a 1966 Pontiac Tempest the second semester of my freshman year and drove it back to

Durham. I worked every summer and sometimes held two jobs at a time. One of my first jobs was on the weekends as a housekeeper at the University of North Carolina Hospital in Chapel Hill.

The weekend job was tough because I had to report to work by 7:30 a.m. on Saturday and Sunday mornings. How in God's name I was going to keep this fast-paced schedule, only He knew. It wasn't unusual for me to party until 2:00 a.m. and make it to Chapel Hill by 7:29. I was never late for work and paid for my education by working, garnering loans, and finding scholarships. I put forth *just* enough effort to maintain that 2.95 grade point average.

I was very blessed to find a very intelligent, cute girlfriend, Rita who was a responsible student and graduated magna cum laude. Her studious nature influenced me to attend classes and complete my assignments on time. Rita kept me anchored through my sophomore, junior, and first semester senior years of college. Although I didn't attend church at that time, she kept me focused on attending classes and away from whatever craziness I would have entertained. If not for her discipline and love, I would not have made it through four years of college and graduate on time. She was a godsend. I repeated Pop's prayer every night before bed, no matter what condition I was in.

I drove to Allentown on a Thursday morning to get Mom and Dad, so they could attend the graduation ceremony at 10:00 a.m. on the upcoming Sunday. I knew they would not be able to travel on their own and get to Durham on time.

Big Neesee needed a ride to Philadelphia, so she rode with me as we headed north on I-85. We smoked weed from the time we left Durham until we reached Philadelphia. We were both high, ripped, and blind as bats, when we drove into the City of Brotherly Love. I was listening to WDAS, 105.3 on the FM channel, while driving my white, two-door 1970 Volkswagen on Broad Street. After I turned onto Market Street I quickly noticed flashing red lights in my rearview mirror. To my surprise, I was pulled over for driving on the wrong side of the street.

I was so distracted by the flashing red lights that I didn't think about rolling down the window before the officer approached the car. It was too late! When he got to the car he tapped on the window, probably because he wasn't able to see anyone inside through the thick cloud of smoke.

When I rolled the window down, a huge cloud of weed escaped out of the window to greet the officer. My braids were hanging over my shoulders and were tied down by a red bandanna. I was wearing torn jeans and a red shirt emblazoned with a big white star on my chest, while sporting three-inch black and gray platform shoes. I had not shaved in months. My backseat was obscured by my stereo system. Big Neesee sat quietly, totally unaware, on the front-seat passenger side. I was not able to comprehend the seriousness of the situation at that moment.

I just stared at him and said, "Hello." The officer informed me that I was driving on the wrong side of the street.

By this time, two other squad cars pulled up. The officer walked back to his car, and never asked to see my driver's license or registration card. I sat waiting, still not comprehending the gravity of the situation. After what seemed like a very long time, I decided to get out of the car and walk to the police car. This action clearly demonstrated that I had no control over my mind. After having been pulled over for a motor vehicle violation by a Philadelphia Police Officer, a driver (or a passenger) should *never, ever* get out of their vehicle and approach a police officer's vehicle without having been invited, especially in Philadelphia. Any sense I had ever possessed had disappeared in those billows of smoke.

The officer was looking down and writing on a pad of paper as I approached the car, and I casually asked him if he was going to give me a ticket. He never looked up, but asked me if I wanted one.

That's interesting, I thought to myself. *Was it a trick question?* I said "No" and then stood silently, trying to figure out what to do next.

The officer continued writing. I awkwardly stood looking at him for a few more seconds, then turned and hesitantly walked back to my car. I quickly got in, shut the door, and sat frozen for a few minutes, not knowing whether I should wait, or drive away. I finally started the car, pulled out, and slowly drove away, all the while gazing into my rearview mirror. I was beyond baffled. I was driving down the wrong side of the street in Philadelphia, in possession of weed, smoking weed, and was obviously in an altered state of mind. Yet the police officer let me go without so much as a warning.

Bewildered, I drove Big Neesee to the bus station at Sixteenth and Arch Streets while I pondered, what had just occurred.

"Can you believe what just happened?" I asked her.

"Believe what?" Big Neesee responded.

"The cop didn't give me a ticket."

"What cop?" she asked.

At that point I realized that it wasn't worth the time to explain to Big Neesee, since she had no clue what I was referring to. So, I dropped her off at the bus station without thinking once about how she would get home. In fact, I had no idea where Big Neesee was heading. That was the last time I ever saw her.

Looking back, I remember thanking God for so many things that night. Although I couldn't have put into words whom I was thanking or for what I was giving thanks, I now know: God's limitless grace to His children and His Spirit's protection in our foolishness.

> Although I couldn't have put into words whom I was thanking or for what I was giving thanks, I know now: God's limitless grace to His children and His Spirit's protection in our foolishness.

I was on the road Friday morning to take my parents to Durham in Dad's 1972 Grand Torino. This was the first time my parents had visited campus, and looking back, I am embarrassed to admit that I did not show them the campus, or introduce them to any of my friends. On Saturday I took them by the home of one of the older men, a coworker at one of my weekend jobs for a visit, and bought them something to eat. Then I dropped them off at my apartment and was back on the streets to indulge in the last remaining parties.

Not only that, but one of my dearest friends, Tricie, had invited her family to town for graduation, and I didn't introduce my parents to Tricie and her family. This was one of the few times in my life when I felt embarrassed about how poor I was. I was ashamed to introduce Mom and Dad because they weren't as educated and refined as her family. She and I continue to stay in touch. She is a powerful woman of God and a dearly beloved friend.

Years later, I felt extremely guilty when I contemplated my behavior on that graduation weekend. I realized that graduation was a unique event in my life that focused on success and achievement, and I suddenly became disconcertingly concerned about what others thought about my parents. After receiving my diploma on Sunday, I got back on the road with Mom and Dad, and returned to Allentown without saying goodbye to anyone, not even my closest friends, or my roommate, Otis. I was obsessing about getting home and finding a job. I was totally exhausted after driving over fourteen hundred miles in four days with very little sleep. I insisted that Dad drive the remaining one hour from Philadelphia so we could all get home alive.

Availability, Oversight, and Guidance of the Spirit

One of the most life-impacting characteristics about the Holy Spirit is His constant, unfailing availability to His children. I experienced this soon after coming home from college. I was running wild in Allentown, and Mom could see the deterioration in my lifestyle. I was committed to my job, but was hanging out on weekends in Philadelphia, New Jersey, and after-hour clubs with all types of characters.

Because of God's goodness, I was hired into a job for which I was not qualified and spent two crazy years in Allentown working at the Lehigh County Agency on Aging. In the midst of everything, I was introduced through friends to a remarkable young woman named Maria. She soon became a friend, and I took her out to dinner, movies, and concerts. She was refined, smart, and gorgeous. She was also a Christian. I told her I was planning to move to Atlanta, and she asked if she could ride with me to see what the city was like. How could I say no?

As we were driving through King of Prussia, Pennsylvania, an hour south of Allentown, in April 1977, the Spirit of God suddenly overwhelmed my spirit regarding the remarkable, gorgeous, insightful, Christian woman sitting beside me. Seconds later, I heard a voice asking her to marry me.

The Proposal

In total shock, I glanced toward the rearview mirror to see who could have proposed to the woman in the passenger seat. "Stunned!" I looked over to see Maria in the passenger seat crying. *Jesus!! What in God's name just happened?* I asked myself.

I glanced backward to see who could have proposed to Maria. In all my years I never thought about marriage, and yet it seemed as though I had just proposed to her. I was unaccountably reminded of the scene in Numbers 22:28, when the Lord allowed Balaam's donkey to rebuke him, but somehow the Spirit of God used my own mouth to speak, what I had been in no way prepared to say. I didn't say much for the rest of the drive. As crazy as this sounds, I was baffled as to how I could have proposed to Maria.

Maria flew back to Allentown, and we were married on June 12, 1977. After six years in Atlanta working for Allstate Life Insurance Company as an underwriter and supervisor, I was promoted to the position of field underwriting manager and sent to Northbrook, Illinois, for twelve years. It was during my time in Illinois where I became grounded and rooted in the Word of God. From Illinois, our family of four moved to Skillman, New Jersey, for seven years, where God enabled me to travel internationally while working with Merck as the global director of organizational development.

From New Jersey we moved to Northville, Michigan, where I lost my job at Trinity Health and encountered one of the most challenging times in my life. My next job choice was between Lagos, Nigeria, as a consultant with a former boss where I could have made a whole lot of money and traveled between Africa and the U.S.; or New Haven, Connecticut, where I ended up living for fourteen years. My initial plan in 1977 before proposing to Maria was to briefly live in Atlanta, then head to Denver, and eventually move to Los Angeles, where Fred, one of my earlier college roommates and a fraternity brother, had relocated. God, as we know, had other plans for my family and me.

I have been blessed to have worked in some of the best companies in America and given opportunities to be discipled in the things of God, while meeting giants of the faith. I attended North

Shore Assembly of God Church in Skokie, Illinois, led by Pastor Fred Sindorf, who became the senior pastor in 1986. I sat on the deacon board for ten years. While there, I learned about a missionary named Len, who lived in Kabul, Afghanistan, and heard about the unbelievable Bible meetings he held with Afghan guerrillas, who sat in his living room praying and learning about the Bible.

I learned as well from Vera A. Stephens, who became a missionary at the tender age of sixty-six and went to the mission field in Monrovia, Liberia, during a civil war. She founded the Child Evangelism Fellowship of Liberia and the Bethesda Christian Missions School, an orphanage to which children walked hundreds of miles to live. Many traveled from around the world to attend her memorial service in Chicago to honor and testify about this woman of God who left her home to share the gospel of Jesus Christ.

I was taught by Brother Doug, who lived at the Zion Faith Home Church in Zion, Illinois, a place where staff members did not receive a salary, but lived on the promises of God. When Brother Doug's daughter was diagnosed with cancer, his family lived on faith because they did not have health insurance. Yet God supplied all of their needs according to His riches in heaven. I was blessed to have been taught by people who followed the Great Commission and gave their lives to serve the Lord.

Our youth pastor, Kevin, who had been a missionary in Kenya, once spoke about a time when guerrillas threw a hand grenade into the front yard of his house where he and others were gathered, only to have it fizzle out in front of them. I saw and felt the presence of God as I listened to these missionaries' incredible stories and experienced the Holy Spirit in a brand new way.

Although I didn't realize it, God was using my time at North Shore Assembly to provide me with the greatest spiritual development I have ever received. It was during my time at North Shore when I was filled with the Holy Spirit, learned from spiritual giants about walking with the Holy Spirit, and began reading the Bible cover to cover.

On July 3, 2022, I flew to Phoenix, Arizona, to visit Pastor Fred on his deathbed. Despite receiving morphine shots every two hours, his anticipation of going home was evident, and he encouraged me as he lay dying from cancer. He died on July 7th with the same excitement that Deacon Lloyd had expressed just before his passing. I saw firsthand what it means to walk with the Holy Spirit. God's path is a glorious one, even when we are unsure of what lies ahead.

As we have seen, the young servant girl in Naaman's household, as well as Joseph, David, Peter, James, John, and a host of others, spent intimate time with the Holy Spirit. When we yield our hearts to God, He rewards us with more of His Spirit. The most precious gifts we have are not material things, but our soul and our time. God gives us time, and what we do with it dictates our life's legacy. The children of Israel all too often devoted their time to things that separated them from the Father and became lost.

As children of God, we don't always know where our path will lead, but we can confidently step out on the narrow road. As we develop our spiritual sight, we will discern the next step on the path where God is leading us. Even when we can't see far ahead, we can trust that God has both designed and designated the path we walk.

For most people, getting through a typical day involves battles, but God's children can rest in the assurance that both eternal resolution and reward lie ahead. As we mature, we learn to sit and soak in the presence of the Holy Spirit. His presence is one of the greatest joys a child of God can experience. Our souls are drawn to His essence, and when we bask in the presence of the Father, His Spirit embraces us. The world cannot understand fellowship with the Father through the ministry of the Holy Spirit, but those who hear the voice of the Holy Spirit and commune with Him know and understand the calling of the Father.

I have been blessed by God's chosen path for my life. As I prepare to walk the final stage of my journey in my post-retirement years, I am refining my focus. What is God's purpose for this part of my life? I now have the opportunity to laser-focus on my legacy and kingdom ministry. Where will this new bend in the path take me?

When I look back to see from whence I came, I recognize that, apart from the Spirit's protection and presence, I never would have accomplished all that God has done through me.

The path God's children walk is not easy. However, when I look back, I see that God's Spirit has been beside me with every step, and I stand in awe of His mercy, grace, protection, and loving discipline. May you know this same joy.

Consider

- ◆ Looking back, at what points in your life has the Holy Spirit intervened and demonstrated His mercy and protection?
- ◆ What have you noticed during these times?

Chapter Ten

Provisions of the Holy Spirit

"So you have not received a spirit that makes you fearful slaves. Instead, you received God's Spirit when he adopted you as his own children. Now we call him, 'Abba, Father.' For his Spirit joins with our spirit to affirm that we are God's children. And since we are his children, we are his heirs. In fact, together with Christ we are heirs of God's glory. But if we are to share his glory, we must also share his suffering."

Romans 8:15–17

Because we are heirs of God, the Holy Spirit interconnects with our soul and reveals our spiritual identity to us. He assures us that there is no fear in God; therefore, we His children need not be afraid. Inheritance, blessings, and abundance await us, as through Jesus, God's Son, we share the DNA of our heavenly Father. The light cast into the world by our daily behavior should manifest His attributes. Think about it.

> As God's children, our power should be drawn from the Spirit of God and should display His love, joy, and peace in everything we do. The closer our relationship with the Holy Spirit, the more we should look like Him, love like Him, think like Him, talk like Him, and act like Him.

Reflecting on Our Spiritual DNA

Does your behavior (and mine) illuminate the world with the Spirit of God? As God's children, our power should be drawn from the Spirit of God and display His love, joy, and peace in everything we do. The closer our relationship with the Holy Spirit, the more we should look like Him, love like Him, think like Him, talk like Him, and act like Him.

Paul tells us that God's children have souls that are not fearful, but are filled instead with the power of the Holy Spirit. Possessing confidence in the power of the Holy Spirit clearly demonstrates that we are children of God and possess the same attributes as our Father. The confidence that comes through the power of the Holy Spirit should enable us to press forward, even in the face of adversity. We are so intimately loved by the Father that we can call Him Daddy, "Abba, Father," an indication of our cherished standing in His eyes.

Many of us have had earthly fathers with whom we never experienced a close relationship. My father was physically present in my life, but wasn't able to express his thoughts. He was a good and kind father, who made certain that I had food to eat, clothes to wear, and a bed to sleep in. My earthly father was physically present but emotionally detached, a detachment due not to a choice, but to a limitation.

When I became a father, I suddenly realized my own shortcomings as a parent. I didn't establish the spiritual connection with my children that they needed. My children were raised in the church, but I left many of my responsibilities to spiritually nurture and teach them to the church. I should have done a better job of teaching my children the spiritual lessons I am writing about today. However, I did encourage them to continuously read the Bible cover to cover when they were both twelve years old, a practice they have maintained as young adults.

I inherited many of my earthly father's positive characteristics, including his interest in problem solving, reading, hard work, taking responsibility, courage, and humility. You will be surprised when I confess that I also inherited some of my earthly father's negative characteristics, like picking my nose. There, I actually admitted this disgusting habit in writing.

Yes, my dad had many honorable qualities, like always providing for our family's needs. He always found work, even if it was a menial job like washing dishes in a restaurant, cleaning floors, or driving trucks for the City of Allentown to ensure that our family had a safe place to live. He taught me to always work hard and bring my very best to whatever job I was given. This philosophy served me well throughout my entire career. I learned early to work as unto the Lord (Colossians 3:23).

Despite his good qualities, my dad was also unable to help me grow spiritually because he struggled to understand the fundamentals of walking with Jesus. When he was growing up, Dad didn't attend church regularly, so he didn't receive an education regarding spiritual things. He accepted Christ when I was in college, so he was new in the faith when I was hitting my early twenties. When I was growing up, he couldn't teach me about God because he never learned about these things himself; he was still a babe in Christ.

> Looking back and examining my life, I can see where and when the Holy Spirit intervened on my behalf to teach me critical lessons and offer me crucial choices.

Looking back and examining my life, I can see where and when the Holy Spirit intervened on my behalf to teach me critical lessons and offer me crucial choices. The choices we make, define the life we will live; because we must bear the consequences of our decisions for the rest of our lives here on earth. These consequences can also have eternal impact.

The Holy Spirit led me down paths on which my spirit found nurturing. I didn't have a strong background in the church, but when I did attend as a child and teen, the Word of God deeply impressed my soul. The Lord gave me a passion for His Word and for the godly people He had chosen to be a part of my life. As I spent time with Pop, I watched how he took an interest in the people around him. He always asked how they were doing, and listened intently as they shared their hearts.

I have no doubt that Pop was called to the ministry. His younger brother, Bishop Benjamin Troop Morris (Uncle Bud), had been ordained by Bishop Charles Harrison Mason, the founder of the

Church of God in Christ, the largest Pentecostal denomination in the U.S. Uncle Bud was the Bishop of the Church of God in Christ congregation for the state of New Jersey. I have his Bibles and his gold cross on my keychain. I noticed at a young age that Uncle Bud often sought the advice of Pop, his elder brother who was a brilliant and spiritual man.

However, it was Dad, who finally broke the generational curses of alcoholism and abuse. He was committed to his marriage and provided a stable home for me. He set the path for me to pick up and grow in my faith, and I know that wasn't easy after growing up in an abusive and alcoholic household, and experiencing Normandy in World War II. It was clear to me that Dad possessed Pop's spiritual DNA, absent the drinking and did his best to pass it along to me. I pray that I can pass on this spiritual heritage to my own son and daughter.

Equipping for Life

I experienced times when the Holy Spirit directed my steps, even though I had no idea what He was doing, or where He was leading. The ten years I spent at the Allentown Boys' Club were years during which God developed my leadership skills and the discipline I would need to solve business problems. I was hired in my junior and senior years of high school to manage the weight room, where I spent weeknights strengthening my body to play football and leading the younger boys. This experience also kept me off the streets and away from the temptation that lurked in my neighborhood. I worked with the younger boys and was able to interact with the men who worked at the club and learn from them. These men influenced me in ways I did not realize at the time.

> *"For I know the plans I have for you,' says the LORD. 'They are plans for good and not for disaster, to give you a future and a hope. In those days when you pray, I will listen. If you look for me wholeheartedly, you will find me."*
>
> *Jeremiah 29:11–13*

God has a plan for each of His children. However, to know that plan, our souls must remain open, and in tune with His Spirit. How could that have been possible for me when I wasn't even aware of His voice?

The answer is that my soul has always been connected to the vine. The Father is spiritually connected to His children in the same way His breath resides inside our bodies. The Spirit communicates with our spirit,

> **God's ways are higher than ours, and we couldn't begin to understand His mind. But we need only look at Jesus' death on the cross to know that we can trust His goodness and love.**

even when we are unaware of His presence. This is one reason it is important to acknowledge that each of us has a soul, which is infinitely more important than our body and mind. When our soul leaves our body, we are considered dead in this life, but our soul is crucial to our eternal existence. To ignore it is an earthly mistake that leads to eternal death, not just death in the physical realm.

> *"Teach these new disciples to obey all the commands I have given you. And be sure of this: I am with you always, even to the end of the age."*
>
> *Matthew 28:20*
>
> *"I will never fail you. I will never abandon you."*
>
> *Hebrews 13:5*

We have the promise of Jesus that He will be with us always; it comes to us from the presence and indwelling of the Holy Spirit. There are times when the Spirit of God leads us and we are not aware of it. God gives us a choice to accept or reject His promises. Even though a root may be far from the vine, as long as it is attached, it is still drawing strength from its source. The Spirit speaks to His children in different ways as He presses to keep us close to Him.

> *"The night before Peter was to be placed on trial, he was asleep, fastened with two chains between two soldiers. Others stood guard at the prison gate. Suddenly, there was a bright light in the cell, and an angel of the Lord stood before Peter. The angel struck him on the side to awaken him and said, 'Quick! Get up!' And the chains fell off his wrists. Then the angel told him,*

'Get dressed and put on your sandals.' And he did. 'Now put on your coat and follow me,' the angel ordered. So Peter left the cell, following the angel. But all the time he thought it was a vision. He didn't realize it was actually happening. They passed the first and second guard posts and came to the iron gate leading to the city, and this opened for them all by itself. So they passed through and started walking down the street, and then the angel suddenly left him."

Acts 12:6–10

Throughout each day, the Spirit acts on our behalf, but we are often unaware of His intervention. He watches over His children even more closely than He does over any other living creature. The Spirit is *always* beside and within us. When we walk through dark, dangerous valleys, the Spirit protects us, even when our emotions tell us we are alone or threatened. This confidence should empower us and enable us to always move forward.

When we believe the Holy Spirit is as near as a thought, we can live with confidence, conviction, and courage. God's children need never walk in fear because the Spirit of Almighty God Himself dwells within us, and He always responds to our cries for help. When we recognize that we possess the power to call on Him *as His children*, we can move forward in confidence, despite our circumstances. God *expects* us to trust Him. He doesn't explain His plans and justify His means to us *because He is God*. His ways are higher than our ways, and we couldn't begin to understand His mind. We need only look at Jesus' death on the cross to know that we can trust His goodness and love.

> When we believe we are never alone because the Holy Spirit is as near as a thought, we can live with confidence, conviction, and courage.

It is vital for us to learn to hear the voice of the Holy Spirit. To do this, we must train ourselves to REST by consistently:
1. **R**eading the Bible daily.
2. **E**stablishing a daily practice of being quiet.
3. **S**eeking the ability to listen for His inner promptings and still, small voice.
4. **T**ransitioning away from the company of ungodly people and distractions in our lives.

"It is God who enables us, along with you, to stand firm for Christ. He has commissioned us, and he has identified us as his own by placing the Holy Spirit in our hearts as the first install-ment that guarantees everything he has promised us."

2 Corinthians 1:21–22

"And now you Gentiles have also heard the truth, the Good News that God saves you. And when you believed in Christ, he identified you as his own by giving you the Holy Spirit, whom he promised long ago. The Spirit is God's guarantee that he will give us the inheritance he promised and that he has purchased us to be his own people. He did this so we would praise and glorify him."

Ephesians 1:13–14

"But you have received the Holy Spirit, and he lives within you, so you don't need anyone to teach you what is true. For the Spirit teaches you everything you need to know, and what he teaches is true—it is not a lie. So just as he has taught you, remain in fellowship with Christ."

1 John 2:27

"For God, who said, 'Let there be light in the darkness,' has made this light shine in our hearts so we could know the glory of God that is seen in the face of Jesus Christ."

2 Corinthians 4:6

God looks on the heart, and when we come to know Christ, the Spirit of God fills our hearts, as the Father and Son take up residence in us and teach us how to grow. As we are filled with the indwelling of Jesus through the Spirit, the Holy Spirit takes root in our souls, and we reflect His light to those we encounter. When God's children reflect God's light that resides in us, we fulfill our divine purpose and live out our intended destiny. The things of this earth fade in comparison.

Time spent with the Holy Spirit in prayer and daily scripture reading enables our souls to definitively hear and recognize His still, small voice. God's Spirit desires to know each of us on a deep and personal level, so that He can help us fulfill the purpose He has destined for each of us before we were born. The Word of God is our access to the Holy Spirit, and Jesus is that Word.

> *"Even before he made the world, God loved us and chose us in Christ to be holy and without fault in his eyes."*
>
> *Ephesians 1:4*

God designed a special role for each of us. Can you imagine His infinite creativity? You were crafted by God in His image to be used for a unique and special purpose in His creation. Only you can fulfill the role He has assigned to you; therefore, it is vital that we allow the Holy Spirit to speak directly to our hearts and not permit the babble of the world to drown out His voice. We have each been uniquely fashioned in the image of God and designed to carry out specific roles that will resonate through eternity. R. Buckmeister Fuller reminds us to:

> "Never forget that you are one of kind. Never forget that if there weren't any need for you in all of your uniqueness to be here on the earth, you wouldn't be here in the first place. And never forget, no matter how overwhelming life's challenges and problems seem to be that one person can make a difference in this world. In fact, it is always because of one person that all the changes that matter in the world come about. So be that one person."[10]

Keeping Our Eyes on the Prize by Journaling

Keeping a notebook or journal close at hand is good practice for developing the discipline of listening for, and meditating on conversations with the Spirit. Take time each day to note your experiences, both good and bad, and observe the way in which situations work themselves out. Journaling helps us remember and compile evidence of how the Holy Spirit actively works in our lives. By observing your trials and triumphs, you will begin to notice patterns in your life. The ability to recognize and value your accomplishments will strengthen your walk and trust in the Holy Spirit as a reminder of when you experienced dark and difficult days.

Too often, we become distracted by voices that tell us what we should and shouldn't do. Voices of the world influence us to act in ways that are in opposition to the things of God. As a young boy, I remember observing the older guys in the neighborhood who had money, cars, and women. A lot of us looked up to them as though they were celebrities and many of my peers emulated their lifestyle. God miraculously removed me from Allentown in order for me to experience Him in a personal way.

When I was in elementary school, I was a very good student who loved to read. I was blessed with outstanding teachers who cared about my peers and me, and pushed us to do our very best. My teachers instilled a passion for excellence at an early age. Teachers like Mrs. Nicholas, Mrs. Brett, Mrs. Hixon, Mr. Torba, Mr. Coyle, and Mr. Sam Miller, who was my middle school principal, required nothing short of excellence, and the seeds they planted in me grew.

These teachers were all Caucasians, dedicated to their profession, who saw more in us than we could see in ourselves. I honor them for who they were. I never had a teacher of color until I attended NCCU, and it was here where I first learned about my heritage as an African American.

Reading was a skill I had learned from Pop and Dad. I read a lot of comic books, which strengthened my desire to read. In fourth grade, a reading teacher challenged the entire grade to read books and write one-page book reports. I read over sixty books that year and practically lived in the library at Ninth and Hamilton Streets. Although I didn't realize it at the time, my love for reading and writing would remain with me for the rest of my life. One of my dreams was to one day write a book . . . and here it is!

Unfortunately, as you already know, I was distracted by sports and partying, and my grades consistently eroded as I slowly distanced myself from academics and the things of God. People don't often realize the power of the flesh, but it is clearly in opposition to the things of God. From the age of eight until the age of twenty-four, when I was on the road to Atlanta, sports, partying, and women dominated my vocabulary, my mind, and my environment. I loved the partying life!

Interestingly, some parents from our neighborhood didn't allow their sons to socialize with my friends and me. Two of those young men attended Ivy League Schools, and a third went to a private school. Mind you, none of these young men were smarter than me. Their parents made sure they focused on their education and prepared them for college. I, in turn, allowed the things of God to fall by the wayside and cared little about school. Fortunately, Pop planted the seed and the Holy Spirit took care of the rest.

Mrs. Rodgers, a sociology professor, once told me that I should be ashamed of myself for doing half-baked work, although her language was more stinging than that. She was right, I did just enough to get by, and that was fine by me. She could clearly see that I had the ability to do extraordinary work, but was satisfied with just getting by. Through the work of the Holy Spirit, God kept His hands on my life as I meandered through undergraduate school. It was even more astonishing that He allowed me to graduate from high school and find a college that would even accept me.

I believe the Holy Spirit has always guided my steps, even when I was outside of His will. I had to activate His power in my life by accepting Jesus Christ as my Savior. A spiritual battle wages daily in the hearts of each of us, as I often think about my friends who died young and wonder why God allowed them to perish at such early stages of their lives.

When our hearts are knit close to brothers and sisters in Christ, the bond of love cannot be truly broken. This gift lasts long after they are gone and remains as evidence of love's power.

Why was I not among their number? Only God knows and perhaps one day I will learn the answer.

The Sunday before Dennis was killed, he drove to Fountain Park and found me walking around the park. It was unusual for me to be up that early and even stranger for him to seek me out on a Sunday.

We cruised to Pottstown in "Tippin In", which was about thirty miles south of Allentown, to enjoy the drive and listen to music. I later learned that he took his fiancée, Alice a dozen yellow roses on the following day. He was killed on Tuesday and his death crushed my heart, but having him in my life strengthened my soul. His spirit loved me as only a brother in Christ could have done. Dennis was a brother to me, and I struggled when God took him from this earth. However, I have learned that when our hearts are knit close to brothers and sisters in Christ, the bond of love cannot be separated, not even by death. This gift lasts long after they are gone and remains as evidence of love's power.

Mrs. Blanks, Dennis' mother asked me to deliver a message for the youth day program at St. James on November 14, 1976. This was my first opportunity to stand in a pulpit and deliver a message in a formal church setting. My message was from 1 Corinthians 13, that beloved passage on love. I had never picked up the Bible before, other than to read a few verses here and there. As it turned out, the Holy Spirit touched the hearts of two teenagers who were in the service that morning, and they joined the church after hearing the sermon. Something changed in my spirit the moment I stepped into that pulpit. It has been one of the most profound experiences in my life, as I felt the joy and peace of the Holy Spirit.

From Death to Life

The Holy Spirit girds us and pierces our hearts to make it stronger. By giving me the opportunity to grow up surrounded by violence and exposed to aging, disease, and constant death, the Holy Spirit gently taught me that death is not to be feared, especially for those of us who have been sealed with the Holy Spirit. Although we may experience death and decay on our journey, we see that life and joy still abound when we allow Jesus to lift our earthbound veil and see sorrow, suffering, and death through His eyes.

We are responsible for nurturing our own souls to maturity, and we are also responsible for nurturing a Christ-centered response to suffering and death. Our spirit will never die because it is a gift from God as part of His grace. God's Spirit enables us to be a source of joy and peace to others in their pain and suffering. This is what it means to be light in darkness.

"Do not love this world nor the things it offers you, for when you love the world, you do not have the love of the Father in you. For the world offers only a craving for physical pleasure, a craving for

everything we see, and pride in our achievements and possessions. These are not from the Father, but are from this world. And this world is fading away, along with everything that people crave. But anyone who does what pleases God will live forever."

1 John 2:15–17

The fragrance of Christ should emanate from our speech, our being, and from the depths of our souls in order to eradicate the stench from sin that clings to this earth. The scent of the Holy Spirit should rise from within our hearts to generate an aroma that fills the places we inhabit. God has sealed our identity as His children. We are the light of the world, and we are where He has placed us, in order to reach the hearts and teach the souls of those who don't know Him. We are living water and living scriptures sent to touch the lives of the lost and hopeless.

In order for the Spirit of God to make me an effective vessel of ministry, the Word must be sown deeply in my soul and the seed nourished daily so that my spirit grows to be more Christlike. I must recognize the Holy Spirit's voice, authority, and role in my life and submit myself to His direction to fulfill my purpose.

This means seeking Him in all things, listening for His voice, obeying Him, and trusting His direction. I must allow Christ to drench me with His Holy Spirit and become saturated by His presence. This happens only when I abide in God's Word and allow it to overtake my will. This is how the Spirit works.

When we begin to comprehend the gifts we have received from the Father, our only response can be to rejoice, knowing that God has given us the most precious treasure life can offer. Not only do we possess the gift of eternal life, but we also possess the most precious treasure humans can be offered: the presence of God's Spirit dwelling within us.

We have access to God's glorious riches through the Holy Spirit, and an open door to a personal relationship with the Almighty, Omnipotent God of the universe, who loves us dearly. All we must do is believe, receive, and follow His guidance in order to fully experience His indwelling.

All God asks is that we repent of our sin-saturated addiction to doing life our way, lay down our will, and give Him full control to lead us for His purpose. In a divine exchange, God takes our sins and casts them into the outer limits of oblivion. In return, He gives us Jesus' perfection, the continual presence of the Holy Spirit, and eternal love as His child.

Unfortunately, many people die without having received this gift, spending their lives in a futile search for meaning. A story is told in Napoleon Hill's book, *Think and Grow Rich* about a young man who sold his property to search for diamonds. He died in a distant land, and the person who purchased the property the young man sold, found a huge chunk of coal on the grounds, which was later discovered to be the site of the Golconda Diamond Mines. The young man had gone in search of treasure that had already existed under his feet. He had already owned untold riches, but hadn't taken the time to explore what he already possessed. If we take the time to search our souls and connect to God's Spirit, we are certain to find treasures beyond our imaginations. Within each of us lies the breath of God, a treasure unto itself.

The Holy Spirit has been with me all of my life. Unfortunately, only a few people shined the light of Jesus into my early life and bore His heavenly scent. They have come and gone, but the fragrance of their lives remains with me. They showed me how to radiate the Holy Spirit's love in the way they lived. Some of their lives were brief, but I watched them fulfill God's purpose. Over time, I realized their love resonated with my spirit. Their souls touched my soul, and an inexplicable heart connection was made that continues to this day. My soul personally experienced God's presence through them.

These people, although physically removed from me, are still close to my heart. This is one reason I approach death as a continuation of this life. Death is not an end point, but a renewal and continuation of relationships that are anchored in our souls. Even now I feel more connected in spirit with two very dear sisters in Christ: ReeRee, Junebug's sister, and Debbie Sampson, both of whom have gone on to be with the Lord. Even now as I think about them,

I value our relationship and know they are both in the presence of the Lord. Death is not the end, but a transition in our existence to an eternal form and phase of life. This, without a doubt, is one of the reasons I look forward to reuniting with my parents, grandparents, and friends when I leave this body.

I have slowly learned that it is crucial for me to be still and listen for the voice of the Holy Spirit. As this world quickly heads toward the purpose God has prepared for it, it is critical that His emissaries, in this case His children, are prepared to carry out His bidding. We must be attentive and ready to do His work, regardless of where He places us.

The wonderful news is that the fruit of the Spirit consists of love, joy, peace, patience, kindness, goodness, faithfulness, gentleness, and self-control. The children of God have access to the things the world truly craves, while those who are of the world devote their lives to working for material things that will only decay and tarnish. The things of God grow brighter and more majestic as time moves on (1 Corinthians 7:31).

As we move closer to the time when Jesus returns, sin will become even more rampant, yes, even in the church, and the love of many, including Christians will grow cold (Matthew 24:12). The end of this present world is coming sooner than we realize. The rising level of hatred, bitterness, and hardness of heart that exists within our nation and world today warns us that we are rapidly heading toward the end times, as detailed in the Word of God. Therefore, be earnest and disciplined in your prayers. Most important of all, continue to show deep love for each other, for love covers a multitude of sins (1 Peter 4:7).

We grow more like Christ through our relationship with the Holy Spirit. Oh, what joy and gladness awaits those who have been pierced by the Holy Spirit. We are a fragrance of life to those who are eternity bound, and a stench of death, to those whose hearts are bound to this world. We live in the confidence that there is no fear in love, for perfect love drives out fear. The children of God are joyous people of hope!

Consider

♦ What are you most passionate about?

♦ Are you developing your passion? If yes, how are you doing so? If no, why not? What do you need to do to develop it?

♦ Have you taken this to the Holy Spirit?

Chapter Eleven

—————————————

Fruit of the Holy Spirit

Knowing Yourself–Cluster One

"The Holy Spirit produces this kind of fruit in our lives: love, joy, peace, patience, kindness, goodness, faithfulness, gentleness, and self-control. There is no law against these things!"

Galatians 5:22–23

In Matthew 7:20 Jesus teaches us that we can learn a lot about a person by observing their actions and behaviors. This principle also applies to trees.

"Yes, just as you can identify a tree by its fruit, so you can identify people by their actions."

Matthew 7:20

We identify trees by their fruit and this can also be applied to identifying people by their attitudes, speech, and behavior. The marvelous news is that the work of the Holy Spirit in us empowers us to bear *unlimited* fruit for God's kingdom; however, a believer's fruit-bearing capacity is always tied to their degree of spiritual maturity. Interestingly, the fruit of the Spirit operates somewhat like a spiritual gauge that measures our level of spiritual maturity. Our fruit is observed in the choices we make (or don't make), the things we say, and the way we walk through everyday life.

Don't forget the way we respond to aggressive drivers or comport ourselves when our favorite sports team loses. Or the times when we don't get what we think we deserve and are entitled to receive. And what about your reactions to the obnoxious and belligerent person who cares only about their concerns and belittles you for being ignorant? Our actions often display our spirit and can be used to help us to identify and understand our level of spiritual maturity.

Fruit of the Spirit at Work—Maturity

The fruit of the Holy Spirit's work in our lives is visible to the world in several ways. The Holy Spirit draws people to Christ through us because God's love shines through us, and He enables us to enjoy life as God designed. To help us better understand this fruit, or character qualities, I have grouped the fruit of the Spirit, as listed in Galatians 5:22, into three categories:

> **Cluster 1: *Knowing* Yourself Through** *Self-Control, Gentleness, and Faithfulness*
> **Cluster 2: *Sowing* by Serving Others with** *Goodness, Kindness, and Patience*
> **Cluster 3: *Glowing* from Your Soul with** *Peace, Joy, and Love*

The fruit is presented in ascending order, with qualities of love stated as the most powerful and clearest demonstration of God's power. It is important for us to assess our effectiveness in demonstrating each fruit, and to ask the Holy Spirit to help us grow more effective in reflecting Jesus and serving those around us in a spirit of loving compassion.

> *"Oh, the joys of those who do not follow the advice of the wicked, or stand around with sinners, or join in with mockers. But they delight in the law of the LORD, meditating on it day and night. They are like trees planted along the riverbank, bearing fruit each season. Their leaves never wither, and they prosper in all they do."*
>
> *Psalm 1:1–3*

> *"The godly will flourish like palm trees and grow strong like the cedars of Lebanon. For they are transplanted to the LORD's own house. They flourish in the courts of our God.*

Even in old age they will still produce fruit; they will remain vital and green."

Psalm 92:12–14

In the discussion to follow, I have reversed the order of Paul's presentation of the fruit in Galatians 5:22 in ascending order where the tree begins to take root. Putting down new roots is often the hardest part of our growth process. I also reversed the order so you can immediately start planning how to demonstrate the fruit of the Spirit in your life. One of the most effective ways to begin seeing growth is to apply and practice the principles for using the fruit every day, beginning now.

The fruit of the Spirit operates much like a spiritual barometer that demonstrates our level of maturity as God's children.

Paul lists the fruit beginning with love, our ultimate goal, however, before we can love, we must have the fruit of self-control in our lives. We must learn to crawl before we walk and eventually run. We will start with the first cluster.

Cluster One: Knowing Yourself—Self-control, Gentleness, and Faithfulness

This first cluster focuses on our inner life and examines the way we manage our personal lives and behaviors. We must discipline ourselves to make deliberate, godly choices about our attitudes, decisions, values, morals, character, and responses to life. It is shocking to see how many Christians float through life with only the most basic biblical knowledge (not the same as wisdom) and interact with the world without knowing how to think and act according to a biblical worldview. Self-control, gentleness, and faithfulness are developed in us through the trials and tests that require self-sacrificing choices. This is the path to growth. Our spirit works in partnership with the Holy Spirit in our growth, and in strengthening our love for God. We see this process in the lives of Joseph, David, and Moses. I have also seen it evolve in my executive coaching with leaders like Kay.

However, many of us do not take the time to enlist the power of the Holy Spirit to guide us along the way. When we decide to follow Jesus, we need the Holy Spirit more than ever, one moment, and one day at a time, but it all begins with you. Change must be internally focused, and learning to change is often the most ignored aspect of our lives. Learning to die to self is the central element of change for a child of God. Learning discipline in order to follow Jesus is not easy, but all things are possible with God.

Internally Focused Fruit—Being Our Best Selves

Self-control

Self-control is the ability to control one's behavior or emotions. It is the ability to manage and control our impulses, feelings, and behaviors so we can reach our desired outcomes in life. Our level of self-control is demonstrated in willpower, which enables us to prioritize our attention and efforts in order to achieve specific outcomes.

We all demonstrate characteristic behaviors in our lives from the time we are born until the time we die. The question is: What *motivates* our behaviors and emotions? As children, we are taught to manage our reactions to certain stimuli. We are told early on that we cannot have everything we want, and that some things are not good for us. Without the self-control we gain from childhood guidance, and loving discipline, we can lack the inner compass that steers us away from situations and decisions that can be detrimental and unsafe.

Without the self-control we gain from childhood guidance and loving discipline, we can lack the inner compass that steers us away from situations and decisions that can be detrimental and unsafe.

In Galatians 5:18, Paul talks about the flesh, and the things against which children of God must fight. Disciplining ourselves to master basic fundamentals is not easy. Kay, who started reading the Bible from beginning to end, had to prioritize her Bible reading on a daily basis. Developing spiritual discipline is no different from attempting to get our bodies in shape and working out. It requires that we establish a routine, follow it, and enlist others to help us if necessary.

Engaging in the Battle

Engaging requires us to identify habits, rituals, behaviors, and thought patterns that subvert our attempts to create new, disciplined routines, and habits. It is important to identify deceptive thinking patterns, and behaviors as we focus on our spiritual development. We must take inventory of everything that stands in the way of changing bad habits. This requires quiet, reflective time, so we can explore the layers of our motives and discover the places where our thinking and actions don't align with living a godly life.

If possible, find a compassionate, trustworthy accountability partner who can encourage you, keep you on track, and loves God. Don't overwhelm yourself unless you need to make urgent lifestyle changes that may prevent danger to yourself or others. Start with small things, like following through on commitments, practicing gentleness, or expressing gratitude, which is an aspect of joy. Developing self-control is crucial because it affects almost all areas of life.

Surrounding yourself with positive influences is crucial. You might need to make hard decisions about the people, places, and activities you choose. Self-control may sound easy, but it is usually one of the hardest fruit to produce, and requires sincere, diligent commitment. Monitor your practices and keep your goals at the forefront of your mind.

I learned long ago to journal. This practice has helped me monitor progress toward my goals, stimulated creativity, and provided examples and reminders of God's goodness. I also use a journal to celebrate accomplishments as a reminder that I am moving forward.

Letting go of bad habits and influences is key to growing fruit. Seeds need water, light, soil, attention, and pruning in order for them to sprout and grow. Some of the toughest decisions you will have to make will be about pruning the negative company you keep. The attitudes of family, friends, and other people heavily influence your decisions and focus. Listen to the Spirit as you read the following passages regarding pruning, self-control, and other deceptive thinking patterns:

"To acquire wisdom is to love yourself; people who cherish under-standing will prosper."

Proverbs 19:8

"Those who control their tongue will have a long life; opening your mouth can ruin everything."

Proverbs 13:3

"Don't befriend angry people or associate with hot-tempered people, or you will learn to be like them and endanger your soul."

Proverbs 22:24–25

"Don't copy the behavior and customs of this world, but let God transform you into a new person by changing the way you think. Then you will learn to know God's will for you, which is good and pleasing and perfect."

Romans 12:2

"For God has not given us a spirit of fear and timidity, but of power, love, and self-discipline."

2 Timothy 1:7

"Understand this, my dear brothers and sisters: You must all be quick to listen, slow to speak, and slow to get angry. Human anger does not produce the righteousness God desires. So get rid of all the filth and evil in your lives, and humbly accept the word God has planted in your hearts, for it has the power to save your souls."

James 1:19–21

Knowing Yourself. My recommendation for building self-control is to learn how to read the Bible cover to cover on a regular basis. Without discipline and self-control, it is nearly impossible to move to the next level of fruit bearing, which is gentleness. It is crucial for us to discipline ourselves to read God's Word daily, whether for five minutes or an hour or more. Planting the Word helps us grow in knowledge and teaches us to discern the voice of the Holy Spirit, who leads us. Grounding ourselves in the Word is one of the most important things we can do as we strive to walk more closely with God. As Eugene Petersen reminds us:

> "The Christian Scriptures are the primary text for Christian spirituality. Christian spirituality is, in its entirety, rooted in and shaped by the scriptural text. We don't form our personal spiritual lives out of a random assemblage of favorite texts in combination with individual circumstances; we are formed by the Holy Spirit in accordance with the text of Holy Scripture. God does not put us in charge of forming our personal spiritualities. We grow in accordance with the revealed Word implanted in us by the Spirit."[11]

Start by reading the Psalms. I would recommend starting with Psalm 27, Psalm 37, Psalm 91, or Psalm 139. I also recommend reading John's Gospel, or identify the scriptures that resonate and encourage you. Read and meditate on them. They will help discipline you to walk more closely with God. As you sustain this practice with the help of the Holy Spirit, you will see spiritual growth in your life.

When we discipline ourselves to read the Bible from cover to cover, we grow in knowledge of the Word. Every Christian should institute this practice because the Word of God is like manna, food directly from our Father, communicated to us by the Holy Spirit.

Reading the Bible from cover to cover connects our souls directly with the Holy Spirit, the inspired author of the Bible. When we read the Bible on a consistent basis, we begin to notice changes in our soul, especially when we read it at least three times consecutively cover to cover on a regular basis. It is our manual for learning how to function as a child of God. It is God's instruction book, teaching us how to be more like Him. We must also read the Bible with total reverence and not read it like we read the Wall Street Journal or Google News. We must recognize the holiness of the Word of God; words that have come directly from the mouth of the Father. When this happens, our spirit rises to its appointed level of maturity.

What could be more exciting than having face time with the One who breathed out God's love letter to us? Kay noticed a change in her soul after having read the entire Bible four consecutive times. The experience of when and how the reading affects our soul is different for each person. It took me more than ten times to begin to recognize the power of this practice, and yes, it makes a huge difference in my life.

Consider

♦ What thoughts, attitudes, and actions keep you from demonstrating self-control?
♦ What do you need to do to ensure that you remain consistent in your Bible reading?
♦ What might be a potential result if you don't remain steadfast?

Get into the habit of reading the Bible every day. If it seems too difficult, start with the Psalms and read through them before embarking on a cover-to-cover challenge. Start by reading five minutes a day and slowly increase your time. Notice what happens when you start reading consistently. The goal is to read the Bible annually from Genesis to Revelation and develop intimacy with the Holy Spirit.

Gentleness

Gentleness is the quality of being kind, careful, and even-tempered. Gentleness may also be translated as *meekness*, but note that this is not synonymous with weakness. Gentleness involves humility and thankfulness toward God and a polite, restrained, servant mindset toward others. The opposite of gentleness is anger and a desire for revenge and self-aggrandizement. Gentleness requires the self-control to not, become angry when people do things that cause us to become upset and lose our ability to remain rational and objective. It is restraining our anger without seeking revenge. It is the ability to stay in control of our emotions, especially as tempers rise. Billy Graham reminds us that:

"Gentleness may be the most tangible sign of greatness displayed in us. You and I may never be respected as voices of authority; we may never gain the plaudits of the world; we may never rule or swing the baton of power. But one day the meek will inherit the earth (Matthew 5:5), for no one can take away our rightful share of God's divine and delightful bequest to us."[12]

When we look at the state of our nation and the world at large, we observe that gentleness is often regarded as a weakness or a character flaw. From childhood, we are taught to be aggressive and forceful and not to let anyone take advantage of us. We are taught to be protesters, not to take "it" lying down, and to fight for our rights. We were not instructed on how to develop a spirit of gentleness.

Gentleness is a key attribute in becoming more like Jesus. He tells us in Matthew 11:29 that He is *gentle and humble* and we should learn from Him.

If we step back and respond gently when we are arguing or fighting, we reflect Jesus, who often responded to His false accusers with silence. It requires a discerning heart not to be intimidated and pulled into the arena of anger. Jesus was always in control and exerted spiritual power in the midst of animosity and hatred. Gentleness is an indicator of self-control demonstrated even within the context of bitter entanglement. It is a sign of true strength, discernment, self-control, and Holy Spirit power. It allows you to keep a clear mind and not be drawn into angry discourse.

Gentleness corrects in love and not in anger. It refuses to argue a divisive point of view, but instead, relinquishes power to the Spirit. Gentleness is a path to forgiveness that focuses on the heart of the other person and the power of our God. Forgiveness sets aside personal needs and desires in order to listen intently to the emotions and pain that pour from someone else's heart. Gentleness equips us to be like Jesus and to love another person even when they are not loveable.

Listen to the Spirit as you read the following passages and stop to reflect on what the Spirit is saying:

"Take my yoke upon you. Let me teach you, because I am humble and gentle at heart, and you will find rest for your souls."

Matthew 11:29

"A gentle answer deflects anger, but harsh words make tempers flare."

Proverbs 15:1

"Now I, Paul, appeal to you with the gentleness and kindness of Christ though I realize you think I am timid in person and bold only when I write from far away."

2 Corinthians 10:1

"Always be humble and gentle. Be patient with each other, making allowance for each other's faults because of your love."

Ephesians 4:2

"Since God chose you to be the holy people he loves, you must clothe yourselves with tenderhearted mercy, kindness, humility, gentleness, and patience. Make allowance for each other's faults, and forgive anyone who offends you. Remember, the Lord forgave you, so you must forgive others."

Colossians 3:12–13

"You, Timothy, are a man of God; so run from all these evil things. Pursue righteousness and a godly life, along with faith, love, perseverance, and gentleness."

1 Timothy 6:11

As you proceed through this reflective process, take breaks if you feel overwhelmed. Read your Bible daily, even if it is only five minutes a day. Pray, and let the Holy Spirit prompt you. Practice being gentle with yourself. Identify people who provoke angst in your soul, and pray for wisdom. Then listen quietly for the Spirit to speak to you through the Word, an inner prompting or voice, dreams, a sermon, or a conversation with a friend. Recognize that, as with any other learning process, developing the fruit of the Spirit takes time.

If you know people who demonstrate gentleness, spend time with them to learn how they have mastered this behavior. Also identify the people who provoke the greatest challenges to your ability to demonstrate gentleness. What is there about a particular individual that makes it hard for you to be gentle with them? Practice not needing to have the last word. Identify circumstances in which you will yield to the Spirit and step back from anger. Remember to call upon the Holy Spirit and remind yourself that He is with you even in the midst of conversations with this person.

Knowing Yourself. Pay attention when you notice that you are in the process of getting angry. Stop and invite the Holy Spirit to help you. Reflect on your thoughts and emotions when you are speaking with others. Are you less patient with some people more so, than with others? Take the time to notice the modulation in your voice and mood when speaking to those with whom you don't feel aligned. Listen to the emotion in your voice when you get upset. Learn to listen to the sound of your voice when you might be out of sync with the Holy Spirit. Slow your breathing down and try to determine the cause of your internal conflict, and how it may be creating a reaction in the listener. Remember that the Holy Spirit is present and ready to assist you. Practice asking Him to help you in real time.

When you are in a heated discussion, call on the name of Jesus and ask the Holy Spirit to calm your thoughts, quiet your spirit, and stop your tongue. If appropriate to the situation, apologize to the person with whom you were speaking and tell them you need to be still for a few seconds to pray. Recall one of the verses you have read and slow your breathing. Think about the results you hope to take from the discussion. Practice and learn.

Consider

- Identify the people who anger you the most.
- Why do you become angry in their presence?
- Slowly cultivate gentleness by making conscious efforts to better understand the person or persons who trigger your anger. Is it some thing about you that angers them? Note your progress in interacting

with them and review it from time to time. Remember, the Holy Spirit is as close as the air you breathe.

Faithfulness

Faithfulness is the quality of being faithful or remaining loyal to someone or something, being constant, staunch, steadfast, and resolute. Faithfulness requires firm adherence to whomever or whatever an individual owes allegiance. Faithfulness implies unswerving loyalty to a person, or thing, or to the oath or promise by which a tie has been contracted.

The word *fidelity* is also used to define faithfulness; it means strict devotion to getting something done. Faithfulness means making a commitment that will remain intact until either a goal has been reached, or a task completed. When you think about self-control and how to become successful, note that both desires necessitate committing to, and controlling your behavior, while expressing gentleness. Listen to the Spirit as you read the following scriptures:

"The eyes of the LORD search the whole earth in order to strengthen those whose hearts are fully committed to him."

2 Chronicles 16:9

"The faithful love of the LORD never ends! His mercies never cease. Great is his faithfulness; his mercies begin afresh each morning."

Lamentations 3:22–23

"The master said, 'Well done, my good and faithful servant. You have been faithful in handling this small amount, so now I will give you many more responsibilities. Let's celebrate together!"

Matthew 25:23

"If you are faithful in little things, you will be faithful in large ones. But if you are dishonest in little things, you won't be honest with greater responsibilities. And if you are untrustworthy about worldly wealth, who will trust you with the true riches of heaven?"

Luke 16:10–11

"God will do this, for he is faithful to do what he says, and he has invited you into partnership with his Son, Jesus Christ our Lord."

1 Corinthians 1:9

"If we are unfaithful, he remains faithful, for he cannot deny who he is."

2 Timothy 2:13

"So God has given both his promise and his oath. These two things are unchangeable because it is impossible for God to lie. Therefore, we who have fled to him for refuge can have great confidence as we hold to the hope that lies before us."

Hebrews 6:18

God has endowed each of us with gifts and talents to serve and bless those around us. When we don't invest these gifts and talents wisely, they do not bear fruit and bless others. This grieves the Holy Spirit. Wasting God's gifts is unfaithfulness. If you think back to the parable of the seeds and the sower, the individuals who were mature produced thirty, sixty, and one hundredfold investment fruit.

God gives each of us a purpose. Are you prepared to walk into your destiny, or will you continue to tread water and do things that won't bring you peace and joy? Do you desire to get to the place at which you engage in the things the Holy Spirit places in your heart, and effectively invest the gifts and talents you have been given? God *wants* us to live the satisfying life He has designed for us.

To what are you most committed? Do you participate in activities without having to work up the motivation because you enjoy them? Why is your commitment so strong to a certain person or activity? What does it require for you to maintain your highest level of commitment to this person, activity, or thing? How committed are you to your faith? Your church? How much time do you devote to reading the Word and praying? How much time do you spend alone with God? These questions are not about legalistic activities or meant to condemn you. It is my hope they will help you assess your commitment to God's Word as you move toward cultivating the fruit of the Spirit.

Sometimes we are not able to be faithful to our purpose because *"A person without self-control is like a city with broken down walls"* (Proverbs 25:28). Too often we do not take the time to prioritize the most important things in life (faith, family, people, activities, time, values, legacy, etc.).

Knowing Yourself.

♦ What are your top three values?
♦ Are you able to clearly articulate your top three values?
♦ What values drive your life and the way you want to live?
♦ Are your actions aligned with your values?

If family members closest to you were asked to identify your top three values, would the values they identify match yours? I have included a lot of questions because questions are powerful and get us to stop and reflect. Commit to reviewing your values and beliefs on a regular basis. This simple discipline will teach you much about yourself and the things that are most important to you.

Consider

♦ Are your values consistent with the way you live day-to-day? How easily could an observant person identify them?
♦ Is God one of your top three values? If yes, why? If no, why not?

Cluster One

♦ As you reflect on Cluster One, what have your learned about your walk with the Holy Spirit? In what ways are you more aware of His presence now than you previously were? What can you do to grow more into becoming your best self?
♦ Have you started to practice any of the spiritual disciplines you have read about? If your answer is yes, what are they, and what results have you observed?
♦ See Appendix A and complete the Fruit of the Spirit Survey questions 1–3.

Chapter Twelve

Fruit of the Holy Spirit

Sowing by Serving—Cluster Two

"When the ten other disciples heard what James and John had asked, they were indignant. But Jesus called them together and said, You know that the rulers in this world lord it over their people, and officials flaunt their authority over those under them. But among you it will be different. Whoever wants to be a leader among you must be your servant, and whoever wants to be first among you must become your slave. For even the Son of Man came not to be served but to serve others and to give his life as a ransom for many."

Matthew 20:24–28

Cluster Two: Sowing by Serving—Goodness, Kindness, and Patience

The first cluster focused on self, and building strong roots that produce spiritual fruit and growth on our spiritual journey. Our maturity equips us to follow the person of the Holy Spirit so we can confidently obey God's Word and His leading. With this confidence, we can better serve the needs of the lost souls we meet. Faith in God also prepares us to work on Cluster Two: goodness, kindness, and patience. Our goal is to serve as Jesus served when we help those around us.

Goodness combines virtue and holiness in action. It results in a life characterized by deeds motivated by righteousness and a desire to be a blessing in the name of God.

This cluster transitions us from an internal focus to an external focus on the lives and souls of the people near us. Jesus not only focused on the spiritual health of people, He was attentive to their emotional and physical condition. His purpose was to love people and set the captives free from the sin that enslaves humanity.

Goodness

Goodness is simply defined as virtue, or the quality of being morally good or acting out of an upright heart. Goodness is about being morally excellent and obedient to God's commands. It is also a form of kindness that involves doing what is right and sometimes turning attention from ourselves to others.

Goodness combines virtue and holiness in action. It results in a life characterized by deeds motivated by righteousness and a desire to be a blessing to others. Someone demonstrating goodness desires to serve others. Showing goodness enables others to see that we are different from the people of this world. When we demonstrate goodness, we reflect God by doing what pleases Him without expecting anything in return. We manifest the Holy Spirit when we seek to do good to others, regardless of how they treat us. Through our acts of goodness Jesus becomes real to the world. Jesus came to serve and not to be served, Matthew 20:28.

Blessing others and doing little things for them without expectation is an example of goodness. Holding the door for someone or helping someone clean up a mess is a simple act of goodness. Smiling and asking someone how they are doing, and taking the time to listen to their response is another demonstration of goodness. We become the hands and feet of God through both random, and planned acts of goodness. Focus intently on the things you can do to make the lives of those around you a little better without looking for anything in return. It is putting others before yourself, and trying to understand things from their perspective. Notice what this practice does in terms of your soul.

Read the following scripture verses and write down whatever speaks to your soul regarding goodness:

> *"Love your enemies! Do good to them. Lend to them without expecting to be repaid. Then your reward from heaven will be*

very great, and you will truly be acting as children of the Most High, for he is kind to those who are unthankful and wicked."

Luke 6:35

"We know that God causes everything to work together for the good of those who love God and are called according to his purpose for them."

Romans 8:28

"Don't copy the behavior and customs of this world, but let God transform you into a new person by changing the way you think. Then you will learn to know God's will for you, which is good and pleasing and perfect."

Romans 12:2

"Don't just pretend to love others. Really love them. Hate what is wrong. Hold tightly to what is good."

Romans 12:9

"Therefore, whenever we have the opportunity, we should do good to everyone—especially to those in the family of faith."

Galatians 6:10

"For we are God's masterpiece. He has created us anew in Christ Jesus, so we can do the good things he planned for us long ago."

Ephesians 2:10

This is how goodness shows up as we notice, interact with, and learn about the people God places in our path.

What motivates you to do good? Does goodness come naturally for you, or is it something you have to work on? Do you take time to notice the needs of those around you? Do you spend more time focusing primarily on yourself, or noticing the needs of others? Are you able to see the individual qualities that make people unique? Are you attentive in terms of noticing the problems and burdens they carry?

I coached an emergency room director at Yale New Haven Health who told me about a time when he arrived at the hospital at around 6:30 a.m. A security guard noticed Dr. C's sagging shoulders, slow gait, and lack of a smile.

"Hey, doc," the guard called out. "Are you okay? You don't look your usual self."

Some hospital personnel might have thought the question a bit odd. It isn't typical for security guards to have casual relationships with physicians. Dr. C wasn't a typical doctor, he was special. Dr. C always created a welcoming presence because he exuded goodness and openness, he cared deeply about others.

He quickly realized that his shoulders were sagging, and that he was in a surly mood because he was thinking about the many problems awaiting him that day. He quickly shifted his mood and prepared to rise above the challenges of the day, dealing with each situation as it occurred. The doctor made it his goal to get to know the people in his environment, so that he could help meet their needs. He often took the time to ask others how they were doing and showed genuine concern for both his patients and his colleagues, regardless of their position within the hospital. It wasn't unusual for employees in housekeeping, or food and nutrition to seek professional or personal advice from Dr. C.

This is how goodness shows up, as we notice, interact with, and learn about the people God places in our path. The simple interaction between two men noticing and getting to know each other made such a strong impact on him, that Dr. C took the time to share this story with me.

I had the privilege of attending the 105th birthday of Frances Hesselbein via zoom on a Sunday in November 2020. Frances died on December 11, 2022, at the age of 107. Her motto was "I live to serve." Frances was the Executive Director of the Hesselbein Institute, formerly the Peter Drucker Institute, and was a prominent global expert on leadership. She received the Presidential Medal of Freedom for her work as the CEO of Girl Scouts of America, and was recommended for a Cabinet position in the White House under the Ronald Reagan administration. In three simple words, Frances embodied goodness.

Sowing by Serving. Blessing others with anonymous efforts of being kind without expectation of return. It is also a way to show God's love to people and demonstrate that others care about them. Both random and planned acts of goodness seed kindness into a world greatly in need of the Spirit of God.

The Spirit convicted me one day after I had gotten off a zoom call with a friend I had been helping for a few years, who was doing quite well. My friend offered to help me, but time passed, and he didn't make any significant steps to follow through on his offer. I became irritated, since I had gone out of my way on numerous occasions to help him, but he did not return the favor when he had opportunities.

The Holy Spirit nudged me, saying, "Your blessings come from Me, not him. Serve without expecting anything in return."

Dying to self is difficult without the help of the Holy Spirit. Putting others first is a contradiction in today's world. Putting God first enables us to get strength through the Holy Spirit and to serve as Christ served.

Consider

♦ Do you take the time to notice when people are discouraged and feeling down? How do you respond?
♦ How easy is it for you to serve those who ridicule you?
♦ Do you go out of your way to help others? If yes, why? If no, why not? Is self-denial something that comes easily to you?

Kindness

Kindness is the quality of being friendly, generous, and considerate. Kindness also includes benevolence, affection, gentleness (which we have already discussed), warmth, concern, and care. A kind person is loving and giving. Kind people typically have a high level of optimism and genuine regard for others.

Those who are kind often demonstrate a great deal of patience with those who are unlikeable and sometimes even cruel. They have learned how to look past a person's behavior to glimpse into their heart. Yet we often see people in authority disdain those who may not appear to be as intelligent or well-off as the majority. At times we may secretly look down on certain classes of people and hold them in low regard. Jesus had a strong affinity for the poor, widows, orphans, foreigners, and people who were considered different or cast off from society. These people needed Him, and He would not turn them away. His love for them was palpable.

Like Jesus, we should seek out the poor and the outcast. The life and legacy of Mother Teresa provide evidence of the power of the Spirit's love and the fruit of kindness. She stated:

> "Be kind and merciful. Let no one ever come to you without coming away better and happier. Spread the love through your life, but only use words when necessary."[13]

Through the power of the Word and the Holy Spirit, we have been bestowed with compassion and kindness to equip us to care for the poor, lost, and hurting souls. Being kind to untrusting, self-protective people can be challenging. We are equipped with the power of the Holy Spirit and Jesus' love to serve all. Still your mind and meditate as you read the following verses:

> *"But the LORD was with Joseph in the prison and showed him his faithful love. And the LORD made Joseph a favorite with the prison warden."*
>
> *Genesis 39:21*

> *"You gave me life and showed me your unfailing love. My life was preserved by your care."*
>
> *Job 10:12*

> *"Love is patient and kind. Love is not jealous or boastful or proud or rude."*
>
> *1 Corinthians 13:4–5*

> *"In a burst of anger I turned my face away for a little while. But with everlasting love I will have compassion on you, says the LORD, your Redeemer."*
>
> *Isaiah 54:8*

"Don't you see how wonderfully kind, tolerant, and patient God is with you? Does this mean nothing to you? Can't you see that his kindness is intended to turn you from your sin?"

Romans 2:4

"So God can point to us in all future ages as examples of the incredible wealth of his grace and kindness toward us, as shown in all he has done for us who are united with Christ Jesus."

Ephesians 2:7

"Be kind to each other, tenderhearted, forgiving one another, just as God through Christ has forgiven you."

Ephesians 4:32

"Since God chose you to be the holy people he loves, you must clothe yourselves with tenderhearted mercy, kindness, humility, gentleness, and patience."

Colossians 3:12

Do you find yourself able to display kindness toward people who are mean and rude? People who disagree with you and see things from a radically different perspective? Unfortunately, this is difficult for most of us. When we regard other people as children of God, despite their behavior, we acknowledge them as our brothers and our sisters, who God dearly loves. Kindness means giving our resources, including our time, gifts, and finances, *without hesitation* whenever prompted by the Holy Spirit. This level of investment is godly goodness. It is serving at the highest level.

Sowing by Serving. Pray for those who have hurt you. One of the hardest things I had to do was to pray for the HR SVP who eliminated my job. Just praying for this person and asking God to bless her was a challenge, but doing so kept me from harboring bitterness in my soul. Pray specifically for those who have hurt you. Notice how difficult this is to do in the beginning. Kindness takes strength and intentionality. It requires work and the help of the Holy Spirit, but it builds spiritual character and spiritual maturity.

Consider

- ♦ What was the most recent act of kindness you displayed? What prompted you to demonstrate this act, and how did it turn out?
- ♦ Why is it hard for you to display kindness to people who are mean and rude? Are you able see them as individuals who are often miserable and in deep pain, or do you tend to see them as people who need to be put in their place?
- ♦ Identify a person who you do not like. Begin praying for them.

Patience

Patience is the capacity to tolerate delay, trouble, or suffering without getting angry or upset. Having patience means that we can remain calm, even when we have done everything we can do to make sure we have responsibly handled our end of a situation. Patience is often referred to as longsuffering, forbearance,

> **Patience is developed as we go through hardships and trials because we are forced to draw on power and resources beyond ourselves.**

or endurance. It is not giving up in the face of anger. Patience, far from being passivity or resignation, is power.

Patience, as well as the other fruit, are in direct conflict with our worldly nature. When we become selfish, we put our needs ahead of others. It is during these times that we need to ask the Holy Spirit to intercede on our behalf and strengthen us to endure. Having the Word of God in our hearts is critical for practicing patience. We must also draw from the other fruit, especially self-control. Patience requires that we increase our ability to demonstrate goodness and kindness. Without these previous steps, and fruit, it is near impossible to be patient with people you do not like.

Patience is developed as we go through hardships and trials because we are forced to draw on power and resources beyond ourselves. It is in the furnace that iron is purified, and this process is the same with our souls. Prayer, scripture reading, and solitude are tools that help us learn patience. Learning from our experiences is also necessary for breaking old and unproductive habits.

It is never easy to learn to endure when those around us are ridiculing and accusing us unfairly. Please note that I have experienced these things firsthand and can attest that they are not easy to accept. However, I am still learning to be patient, especially with those who deliberately set out to discourage or harm me. I can assure you that ongoing practice and reflection will enable you to develop patience, with the help of the Holy Spirit. Allow the Holy Spirit to speak to your heart as you reflect on the following verses:

> *"Wait patiently for the LORD. Be brave and courageous. Yes, wait patiently for the LORD."*
>
> *Psalm 27:14*

> *"Be still in the presence of the LORD, and wait patiently for him to act. Don't worry about evil people who prosper or fret about their wicked schemes."*
>
> *Psalm 37:7*

> *"Be still, and know that I am God! I will be honored by every nation. I will be honored throughout the world."*
>
> *Psalm 46:10*

> *"But those who trust in the LORD will find new strength. They will soar high on wings like eagles. They will run and not grow weary. They will walk and not faint."*
>
> *Isaiah 40:31*

> *"Rejoice in our confident hope. Be patient in trouble and keep on praying."*
>
> *Romans 12:12*

> *"Love is patient and kind. Love is not jealous or boastful or proud or rude. It does not demand its own way. It is not irritable, and it keeps no record of being wronged."*
>
> *1 Corinthians 13:4–5*

> *"Always be humble and gentle. Be patient with each other, making allowance for each other's faults because of your love."*
>
> *Ephesians 4:2*

Sowing by Serving. Waiting upon God is a privilege, but it is never easy. If you are careful and observant, you will see God's responsiveness, even when circumstances don't turn out the way you envisioned them. It is vitally important for you to be gentle, kind, and good to yourself as you practice the fruit of the Spirit, remembering your spiritual DNA. Do not become discouraged when you feel impatient. Identify previous situations in which you didn't get the results you had expected, but things eventually worked out. What behaviors did you demonstrate during those situations? Pray and ask the Holy Spirit to support you as you develop stronger patience.

Consider

♦ Are there certain individuals who test your patience more than others? Why is that?

♦ What, specifically, have you done to improve your patience?

Cluster Two

♦ As you reflect on Cluster Two, what have you learned about your spiritual fruit? What progress, if any, have you seen in yourself?

♦ Operating at the highest levels of Cluster Two will produce evidence of fruit, perhaps it is only 5 percent, 15 percent, or 25 percent, but bear in mind that fruit is fruit. People will respond to goodness, kindness, and patience in a world that is far too often bitter, cold, and angry. You will bear fruit when you serve and trust the Holy Spirit.

♦ See Appendix A and complete the Fruit of the Spirit Survey quetions 4–6.

Chapter Thirteen

———————————

Fruit of the Holy Spirit

Glowing in the Spirit–Cluster Three

*"When Moses came down Mount Sinai carrying the two stone
tablets inscribed with the terms of the covenant, he wasn't aware
that his face had become radiant because he had spoken to the
Lord. So when Aaron and the people of Israel saw the radiance
of Moses' face, they were afraid to come near him."*

Exodus 34:29–30

Cluster Three: Glowing in the Spirit–Peace, Joy, and Love

The third cluster of fruit encompasses peace, joy, and love and reflects
the very character of God. When we reach this level of fruit bearing,
we are fully aligned with the Holy Spirit. These virtues are examples
of the way Jesus walked the earth. He was filled with the Holy Spirit's
power and used these qualities to attract people to Himself.

Developing these virtues is a building process that requires spiritual discipline, and maturity, beginning with self-control. When
God called Moses to lead the children of Israel out of Egypt, as
we read in the book of Exodus, Moses did not yet have the level of
maturity he showed in the book of Deuteronomy, where he pleaded
with God to let him enter the promised land. God had initiated
Moses' spiritual development when He exiled him from Egypt for
forty years after he killed an Egyptian. After that interlude, God
brought him back to Egypt, fully equipped to lead the children of
Israel to the promised land.

Producing abundant spiritual fruit happens in only one way:
when we grow close to God through His Word, Jesus, and the

Holy Spirit. Growing into a deep, personal relationship with the Holy Spirit requires a high degree of spiritual discipline. When we look at the life of Moses, we see a man who underwent many challenges in his forty years in the wilderness with the children of God (his second forty-year interlude), challenges that forced him to rely on the Spirit of God for every step and every need. Moses, we could say, *glowed* the Holy Spirit. When we receive God's peace, it will overflow with a joy, that radiates love. This cluster allows God's Spirit to fill and overflow us and release *the rivers of living waters* described in John 4:14.

By the time you reach this cluster, you should have identified some of your gifts and talents, and have begun to apply these gifts and talents in your efforts to serve others. In this cluster we are producing much fruit for the kingdom, whether 30 percent, 60 percent, or even 100 percent of what God has invested in us. Even if the numbers are 5 percent, 10 percent, or 20 percent, we are still producing fruit and serving. We will one day personally hear God say to us, *"Well done, my good and faithful servant. You have been faithful in handling this small amount,*

Producing abundant spiritual fruit happens in only one way: when we grow close to God through His Word, Jesus, and the Holy Spirit.

so now I will give you many more responsibilities" (Matthew 25:23).

Peace

Peace may be defined as quietness, tranquility, mental calmness, serenity, or freedom from disturbing thoughts or emotions. Peace is also a state of security or order within a community that is provided by law or customs. Being at peace can also mean being strong and grounded in the face of discord. We spent time in chapter seven talking about the peace of God.

Find a quiet, peaceful place to be still. As you read the scripture verses for this cluster, note in your spirit what it is you experience. Do you feel peace in the depths of your soul as you read each verse slowly and deliberately? Allow time between verses for each verse to rest in your spirit.

"In peace I will lie down and sleep, for you alone, O Lord, will keep me safe."

Psalm 4:8

"Those who love your instructions have great peace and do not stumble."

Psalm 119:165

"You will keep in perfect peace all who trust in you, all whose thoughts are fixed on you!"

Isaiah 26:3

"I am leaving you with a gift—peace of mind and heart. And the peace I give is a gift the world cannot give. So don't be troubled or afraid."

John 14:27

"Since we have been made right in God's sight by faith, we have peace with God because of what Jesus Christ our Lord has done for us."

Romans 5:1

"So letting your sinful nature control your mind leads to death. But letting the Spirit control your mind leads to life and peace."

Romans 8:6

"Let the peace that comes from Christ rule in your hearts. For as members of one body you are called to live in peace. And always be thankful."

Colossians 3:15

"Now may the Lord of peace himself give you his peace at all times and in every situation. The Lord be with you all."

2 Thessalonians 3:16

As you slowly read the scriptures and allowed it to sink into your heart, did you notice any effect in terms of the quietness of your soul? If not, that is okay. Start spending more time noticing your spirit and practicing stillness. Begin noticing how the Word of God refreshes your soul. I vividly remember as a five-year-old boy sitting all alone by the Little Lehigh River and listening to the water running over the falls and down the river. The sound of the water instilled a sense of peace that settled deep in my little soul. For some reason it produced in me an assurance of love and comfort beyond words and a reassurance that, no matter what happened, God would be with me. The Word of God brings us that same guarantee, but we must spend time with Him to experience His peace and His presence.

Peace is the ability to sit in the midst of chaos and experience the calm of the Holy Spirt in our hearts. It is the ability to rest in the flow of the Spirit and not let go of His presence. Peace is steadfastness that anchors our souls. We learn to experience peace as we go through the heat of the furnace in which we experience God's presence. This is where we learn to recognize the still, small voice of the Father, 1 Kings 19:12. This won't necessarily happen at the outset, but eventually, if you remain faithful, the Word of God through the power of the Holy Spirit will soothe your soul and speak directly to your heart. The Holy Spirit's voice will become clearer because He speaks directly from His Word which is now beginning to saturate your spirit.

> We learn to experience peace as we go through the heat of the furnace where we experience God's presence. This is where we learn to recognize the still, small voice of the Father (1 Kings 19:12).

This effusion of peace can be seen and deeply felt by others. It also demonstrates the foundation of our faith and can manifest itself in a physical presence. It can be seen and felt when chaos abounds and a person of peace steps in and brings a calm. People notice and can feel the effect of this person's presence. That sense of calm is noticed. This peace rests in the certainty that *Jesus is our peace*. It is the ability to remain still and yielded, and to possess overwhelming tranquility, just as a nursing baby does when resting contentedly in their mother's bosom.

It is a tranquility that knows no fear when the enemy surrounds us and it looks as though the end is near. We will find ourselves able to remain confident in the Holy Spirit's protection. His peace surpasses all understanding, and we know without a doubt that He protects us every minute.

"Jesus often withdrew to the wilderness for prayer" (Luke 5:16). Jesus often went to quiet places to be close to God. Learning to get away from the noise and distractions of the world is important for our relationship with the Holy Spirit. It is in the quiet moments that God's Spirit speaks to us.

Glowing in the Spirit. As you reflect on the past, can you identify situations when you felt overwhelmed, yet things worked out well? What can you learn from such a situation? The Spirit of God has been hovering over your life since birth, and will continue to do so for as long as you have breath, even if you decide you don't want anything to do with Him.

He has never forsaken you and never will; even if you have walked away from Him, He will never turn away from you.

Consider

♦ What does it mean to have peace? Describe peace in your own words?
♦ When was the last time you experienced true peace?
♦ Do you have a secret place where you go to find peace?

Have you ever felt a peace so pleasant and captivating that it seemed as though you were dreaming and never wanted to wake up? Immerse yourself in the Word of God and begin to notice how this affects your peace. Find a quiet place to meditate on God's Word. Spend the initial minutes noticing your breathing. Slow it down. Clear your mind and allow the Holy Spirit to speak to your heart through the Word of God and prayer every day.

Joy

Synonyms for *joy* include *jubilation, triumph, exultation, exhilaration, rejoicing, ecstasy, euphoria, bliss, radiance,* and *ebullience.* Joy in its fuller spiritual meaning of expressing God's goodness involves more. It is deep-rooted, inspired exuberance that flows from gratitude. Joy is not based on things or people or circumstances. It is rooted in the depths of our souls and flows directly from the Holy Spirit. We all may know someone who makes us smile whenever we see or speak to them. These joy-givers leave us with a warm glow. They overflow with the joy of gladness.

Such people draw their joy from the ever-flowing fountain of the Spirit; recall Jesus sharing that "living water" with our sister at the well in Samaria. James 1:2 directs us, *"Dear brothers and sisters, when troubles of any kind come your way, consider it an opportunity for great joy."* The only way we can have joy in the midst of our trials is to lean on the Holy Spirit and draw that overarching, undergirding joy directly from Him. This requires total dependence on Him. It also requires that we have an ongoing relationship with Him as our teacher, counselor, and advocate.

The fruit of the Spirit begins to glow after we relinquish to Jesus' authority over our lives and begin working on self-control. If we diligently nourish our relationship with God, the Holy Spirit begins to work within us as soon as we become a new creation in Christ. This requires commitment and hard work. The seed of faith is planted when we accept Jesus. As with any other seed, it needs fertile soil, sunlight, and water in order to sprout and grow. Our souls need the Son's light, the Word of God, the indwelling of the Holy Spirit, and constant prayer in order to develop and flourish. Without these ingredients, the seed will stagnate, or worse, it will die. We have an older brother, Jesus, to whom we can take all of our troubles. He will show up for us in the form of the Holy Spirit. Whether or not we are aware of and attuned to Him, He is always with us.

When we are ready, the Spirit directs us to our purpose in life. We begin to see the benefits and results of walking in God's purpose, which gives us great satisfaction when we see progress in our growth as the fruit of the Spirit expands in our life. The blessings of the fruit of the Spirit resonate in our souls. Joy is now both a choice and a reality. While joy and happiness are wonderful feelings, they are different. Joy is consistent because it is driven internally by the Holy Spirit and independent of our circumstances. Happiness is short-lived. Joy is eternal.

Joy is present when we experience peace, patience, kindness, gentleness, faithfulness, and self-control. Joy manifests when we begin to produce fruit because we are aligned with who we are and our purpose for being. This speaks to our identity as a *Masterpiece*.

Happiness tends to be driven by externals like people, money, power, titles, and circumstances. Happiness is situational and targets the passing pleasures and distractions the world pursues. Joy is not based on circumstances, but is instead based on exuberance that flows from the depths of our soul, regardless of our circumstances. Our joy is contagious and can also be felt by those around us.

I developed a habit of giving cash to homeless and needy people on the streets. Of course, there are those who take advantage of people like me, but there are also many disadvantaged people who truly appreciate being acknowledged. I have on occasion given people fifty, seventy-five, or one hundred dollars. Seeing their reactions has tremendously blessed my soul, but the greatest blessing is when they sincerely respond with "God bless you." Their eyes, hearts, and bodies communicate genuine joy.

The opportunity to give has been a precious gift to me and somehow has always brought joy to my heart. When I pray for the homeless, I often remember Tiffany from Ohio, a young Caucasian woman who told me that she was the older of two girls and ran away from home. She had cancer and was being treated in Smilow Cancer Center at Yale New Haven Hospital. I haven't seen her in eight years and want to believe she returned home to her mother and sister in Ohio. She was a precious soul, and I could tell in her voice that she was special. Her smile brought me joy.

I started gifting people when I was eight and able to make money by shoveling snow. I would go shopping alone on Hamilton Street at Christmas to buy and wrap gifts for my parents and my grandparents. I felt joy watching others receive my small tokens.

Ponder the level of joy in your heart as you read the upcoming scriptures. Also think about how to incorporate joy into your daily life. Read these verses and allow the Holy Spirit to guide your spirit regarding ways to develop a strategy to increase His joy in your heart.

"I pray that God, the source of hope, will fill you completely with joy and peace because you trust in him. Then you will overflow with confident hope through the power of the Holy Spirit."

Romans 15:13

"Nehemiah continued, ""Go and celebrate with a feast of rich foods and sweet drinks, and share gifts of food with people who have nothing prepared. This is a sacred day before our Lord. Don't be dejected and sad, for the joy of the LORD is your strength!"

Nehemiah 8:10

"Take delight in the LORD, and he will give you your heart's desires."

Psalm 37:4

"Satisfy us each morning with your unfailing love, so we may sing for joy to the end of our lives."

Psalm 90:14

"I pray that God, the source of hope, will fill you completely with joy and peace because you trust in him. Then you will overflow with confident hope through the power of the Holy Spirit."

Romans 15:13

"Always be full of joy in the Lord. I say it again—rejoice! Let everyone see that you are considerate in all you do. Remember, the Lord is coming soon."

Philippians 4:4–5

"We do this by keeping our eyes on Jesus, the champion who initiates and perfects our faith. Because of the joy awaiting him, he endured the cross, disregarding its shame. Now he is seated in the place of honor beside God's throne."

Hebrews 12:2–3

"Dear brothers and sisters, when troubles of any kind come your way, consider it an opportunity for great joy. For you know that

when your faith is tested, your endurance has a chance to grow.
So let it grow, for when your endurance is fully developed, you
will be perfect and complete, needing nothing."

James 1:2–4

Glowing in the Spirit. Unspeakable joy awaits those who walk in the Spirit. It is beyond our mental comprehension, but is present and evident in those who walk in the fullness of the Spirit. It takes us into spiritual depths far beyond words. Joy is faith-based and operative even in the face of fear because it has glimpsed into the realm of holiness. One of the ways to invite joy is to recognize and acknowledge your blessings. Praising God in worship is a way to develop joy.

Consider

- ♦ How do you define joy?
- ♦ Are others able to experience your joy? In what ways?
- ♦ Are you able to make a distinction between joy and happiness? What is the difference?
- ♦ When was the last time you were truly joyful? What contributed to your joy?

Take time throughout the day to praise and worship God. Develop a heart of thankfulness. Notice what happens after you spend time worshipping God. Thankfulness is another way of identifying your blessings and realizing how present the Holy Spirit is in your life. How often during the course of a day do you practice being thankful?

Love

"The greatest of these is love" (1 Corinthians 13:13). Our culture casually throws around the word *love*. We treat it as an object, something that can be turned on with a switch or purchased at random. Do you and I truly understand the power of love? Can we visualize loving something or someone so much that we would be willing to die for? Even when the person hated us with all of their strength?

Agape is love that is felt deeply in our soul and is the ultimate expression of God's love. It is beyond our comprehension, while expressed by Jesus dying for someone like you and me on a cross. It is the kind of love that accepts, forgives, and believes for our, and their greater good. Agape is unconditional, spiritual love; the purest form of love that is devoid of personal desires or expectations, regardless of the flaws and shortcomings of others.

Following are seven levels or categories of love (with brief descriptions) that human beings can express. As you read each level, think about your level of engagement at each of the following levels:

Level One

♦ **Ludus or Playful**—This form of love is depicted in playful forms, such as flirting and teasing.
♦ **Eros or Erotic**—This love is usually represented through sexual passion or desire and is manifested in physical acts.
♦ **Philautia or Self**—This form is seen in self-care and embracing all of one's gifts and flaws.

Level Two

♦ **Philia or Affectionate**—This love is represented through friendship and loyalty, as that shown within teams.
♦ **Storge' or Familiar**—This love is seen with parents, children, and family members.
♦ **Pragma or Enduring**—This love is seen with couples who have been together for long periods of time and have matured together.

Level Three

♦ **Agape or Selfless**—This is the purest form of love that is given directly from God through the Holy Spirit. The living water that Jesus shared with our Samaritan sister at the well in John 4 demostrate agape love. This love flows from the Holy Spirit through us to others.

Reflecting on Love

Agape love represents a love that ultimately embraces others as they are, and requires selfless sacrifice for others. This is the love Jesus Christ demonstrated when He died to bring us salvation and save our souls.

As you read the following scriptures, reflect on your definition of love. Think about the level of love that dominates your life and determine what will be required of you to move to agape or selfless love:

"Be very careful to obey all the commands and the instructions that Moses gave to you. Love the LORD your God, walk in all his ways, obey his commands, hold firmly to him, and serve him with all your heart and all your soul."

Joshua 22:5

"Love your enemies! Do good to them. Lend to them without expecting to be repaid. Then your reward from heaven will be very great, and you will truly be acting as children of the Most High, for he is kind to those who are unthankful and wicked. You must be compassionate, just as your Father is compassionate."

Luke 6:35–36

"So now I am giving you a new commandment: Love each other. Just as I have loved you, you should love each other. Your love for one another will prove to the world that you are my disciples."

John 13:34–35

"Owe nothing to anyone—except for your obligation to love one another. If you love your neighbor, you will fulfill the requirements of God's law."

Romans 13:8

"Always be humble and gentle. Be patient with each other, making allowance for each other's faults because of your love."

Ephesians 4:2

"Most important of all, continue to show deep love for each other, for love covers a multitude of sins."

1 Peter 4:8

"If someone has enough money to live well and sees a brother or sister in need but shows no compassion, how can God's love be in that person?"

1 John 3:17

"If someone says, 'I love God,' but hates a fellow believer, that person is a liar; for if we don't love people we can see, how can we love God, whom we cannot see?"

1 John 4:20

As you read through the different verses of love, did you notice anything in your spirit? Perhaps you thought about the relationships you have experienced over the years and how you conveyed love, or bitterness, or disdain, or indifference toward certain individuals.

In the midst of love, hatred often rises in its ugliest form. This can be seen when we look at the Civil Rights Movement of the early sixties. I attended the 35th anniversary of the bombing of the Sixteenth Street Baptist Church in Birmingham, Alabama where four little Black girls were killed in a bombing in 1963. I met Reverend Fred Shuttlesworth who was very active in the Civil Rights Movement during the 1960s. This man and his wife had been beaten multiple times, and his home had been bombed, yet he continued to love those who hated him. To love in the face of hatred is not an easy thing. This love can only come from the Holy Spirit. Reverend Shuttlesworth loved God.

Agape love is from God. Can you recall a time when you truly felt loved? A time when nothing else mattered except being in the presence of the one who loved you, and you them? This is what draws me to the Word of God and the presence of the Holy Spirit. This is what it will be like when we get to heaven, true bliss, beyond our imagination. However, we can still experience overflowing agape love through the Holy Spirit, just like Jesus when He talked with our Samaritan sister at the well.

Glowing in the Spirit. " **1)** *Love is patient and kind.* **2)** *It is not jealous or boastful or proud or rude.* **3)** *It does not demand its own way.* **4)** *It is not irritable, and it keeps no record of having been wronged.* **5)** *It does not rejoice about injustice but rejoices whenever the truth wins out.* **6)** *Love never gives up,* **7)** *never loses faith,* **8)** *is always hopeful, and* **9)** *endures through every circumstance,"* 1 Corinthians 13:4–7.

Have you taken the time to assess yourself against each of these attributes? This was my first sermon. I preached this message in 1976 and am amazed today that God is allowing me to begin to understand, after forty-seven years, the true meaning of this scripture. To love is to serve as Frances Hesselbein did throughout her life.

Consider
- What do you sense in your soul as you think about love?
- Which level of maturity have you achieved?
- What do you need to consider as you reflect upon this kind of love?

Cluster Three
- As you reflect on Cluster Three, what have you learned about your spiritual fruit? What is one thing you will do to improve your maturity in this cluster?
- Who can you identify to help you mature in this cluster?
- See Appendix A and complete the Fruit of the Spirit Survey, questions 7–10.

Review of the Fruit of the Spirit
- Cluster One—Knowing Yourself: Self-Control, Gentleness, and Faithfulness are demonstrated in the way we manage our behavior.
- Cluster Two—Sowing to Serve Others: Goodness, Kindness, and Patience are indicated in the way we serve others.
- Cluster Three—Glowing in the Spirit: Peace, Joy, and Love reflect God's essence and power and are displayed in our hearts.

If we carefully meditate on the fruit, we will see that each one produces characteristics that encourage and lead to the growth of the next fruit; it is like watching branches growing on a tree. Growth begins with a seed that sprouts and matures into different stages. The seed of self-control, for example, steadily grows until it matures into gentleness, which grows into faithfulness, etc. The world will know we are Jesus' disciples by the way we live and love. Accepting Christ is the means by which the seed is planted. The sanctifying Holy Spirit enables the growth through each fruit, one at a time.

Consider

- Which cluster are you most concentrated on right now? Why is this cluster showing up?
- What do you need from the Holy Spirit in order for you to develop and mature?

Chapter Fourteen

Promises of the Holy Spirit

"Teach these new disciples to obey all the commands I have given you. And be sure of this: I am with you always, even to the end of the age."

Matthew 28:20

The Word of God promises that the Holy Spirit's presence will dwell with His children, no matter where we may be. To effectively conduct ourselves as God's *Masterpiece* requires our wholehearted participation.

You and I must have faith that His Spirit dwells within us twenty-four hours a day, seven days a week. Producing fruit requires us to remain connected to the vine, our source of life.

Producing fruit also means disciplining our souls to obey and follow the Spirit of God, and not the spirit of this world. Jesus tells his disciples to obey all of the commands He gave them. This requires us to keep God in the forefront of our minds and hearts wherever we go. This was demonstrated when God required the children of Israel to gather manna *each* day, except for the Sabbath day of rest. It is important that we read the Word and pray *daily,* so that we don't drift away from Him.

Serving is a key manifestation of love. As a result, we are given His protection and resources, no matter our situation. We have access to all we could ever need, whenever we need it, and however we need it, through the omnipresent Holy Spirit. We are to die to self, in order to produce fruit for the kingdom.

So, why is it that God's children have so many challenges in this life? One of the primary reasons is that this world is not our home.

"This world is not our permanent home; we are looking forward to a home yet to come."

Hebrews 13:14

"I am only a foreigner in the land. Don't hide your commands from me!"

Psalm 119:19

"We are here for only a moment, visitors and strangers in the land as our ancestors were before us. Our days on earth are like a passing shadow, gone so soon without a trace."

1 Chronicles 29:15

"Dear friends, I warn you as 'temporary residents and foreigners' to keep away from worldly desires that wage war against your very souls."

1 Peter 2:11

A major conflict is taking place in the world, good versus evil, and darkness versus light, and you and I live in the middle of this conflict. The spiritual realm is beyond our limited comprehension, but we must spend time with God learning about the most crucial aspects of our being. Those who worship God must learn to worship Him in spirit and in truth because His Word is truth. We as His children must learn to look at the world through our spiritual lens and walk in the light. This means learning to shut our physical eyes, and our logical minds, in order to see God in the Spirit.

"All who are led by the Spirit of God are children of God."

Romans 8:14

The other challenge for the children of God is that we often walk in fear and worry, not by faith and conviction. If the Spirit of God is within us, we should never fear. The more fruit we produce, the closer we move to faith, and further away from fear.

"God has not given us a spirit of fear and timidity, but of power, love, and self-discipline."

2 Timothy 1:7

"Such love has no fear, because perfect love expels all fear. If we are afraid, it is for fear of punishment, and this shows that we have not fully experienced his perfect love."

1 John 4:18

"This is my command—be strong and courageous! Do not be afraid or discouraged. For the LORD your God is with you wherever you go."

Joshua 1:9

We have the promise that God is with us and that we should demonstrate the power of faith, believing that we have the victory, no matter what problems we might face. Children of God must learn to use the gifts of God and manifest the fruit of the Spirit.

"I pray that from his glorious, unlimited resources he will empower you with inner strength through his Spirit. Then Christ will make his home in your hearts as you trust in him. Your roots will grow down into God's love and keep you strong."

Ephesians 3:16–17

When we, the children of God, grow closer to our Father, we begin to resemble the Son, but this can only happen through the power of the Holy Spirit. The Spirit of God teaches us the very things of God, and we display His glory. The question to ask is: "Why do so few of God's children represent the Father in the fullness of His glory?" Especially after Jesus confirmed this reality when He said:

"I tell you the truth, anyone who believes in me will do the same works I have done, and even greater works, because I am going to be with the Father. You can ask for anything in my name, and I will do it, so that the Son can bring glory to the Father. Yes, ask me for anything in my name, and I will do it!"

John 14:12–14

When we realize who we are, and whose we are, we are on the path to doing great things for God. This also means that we as children of God must set ourselves apart from the world in our thinking, behaviors, and choices. We cannot serve both God and the world. In the Old Testament, God wanted the children of Israel to separate from the people around them so they would not become godless, as their worldly neighbors. However, in the very last verse in Judges, we read to our dismay, *"In those days Israel had no king; all the people did whatever seemed right in their own eyes."* This is the very situation we are witnessing today. Without the presence of the Holy Spirit, we cannot live according to God's standards. The attraction of sin in this world is more powerful than any of us.

We are called to shine like stars in the sky and lights on a mountainside in order to display the pure love of Jesus. When we are disciplined in the Word and ways of God, we will be given the power of the Holy Spirit. When Jesus Himself says we will do greater things than He, He means just that. However, these words also require that we display humility and love in order to access the power required for these behaviors. We must die unto ourselves, relinquish our selfish ambitions, and desire the things of God alone. The world tells us to behave differently, so that we may prosper according to its standards. But our sights should be set on things higher than anything this world can offer. We must set our sights on the things of God.

> *"My thoughts are nothing like your thoughts, says the LORD. And my ways are far beyond anything you could imagine. For just as the heavens are higher than the earth, so my ways are higher than your ways and my thoughts higher than your thoughts."*

> *Isaiah 55:8–9*

God will not give His power to just anyone. A worthy vessel must be filled with the Spirit, as Jesus was, and be obedient to the will of the Father. Servants of God are held to a higher standard, just as God held Moses to a higher standard and, as a result of Moses' failure to adhere to it, God did not allow him to cross the Jordan River even though he pleaded with God to go over, (Deuteronomy

3:26–27). God was angry because Moses did not honor Him at Meribah, (Numbers 20:12) where he and Aaron had brought forth water from the rock. God will not allow anyone, or anything to usurp His glory.

When we walk in the Spirit, God speaks to us heart to heart, directly to our souls. This is where spiritual maturity is developed and the place where the Holy Spirit reveals His wisdom. When God's children walk in the Spirit, we display the power of God through the Holy Spirit and bring God's beauty to a lost and dying world. As we learn to walk in the Spirit, we cultivate the fruit of the Spirit, as delineated in Galatians 5:22: love, joy, peace, patience, kindness, goodness, faithfulness, gentleness, and self-control.

These gifts are lacking in our world. To stand in the face of bitterness, hatred, racism, sexism, and darkness and display the fruit of the Spirit requires that we be empowered through the Holy Spirit. The world seeks the fruit of the Spirit through alternative pursuits, but the children of God have direct access to the true beauty of life, available only through the Spirit. As our fruit ripens and matures, it provides protective power for us as fruit bearers. The more strength we draw from the vine, the more we become integrated into the vine, and the more we resemble Jesus.

As I thought about the individuals in my life who have demonstrated the fruit of the Spirit, I found my list to be very short. Is the list short because so few people in my personal life have fully surrendered to the Holy Spirit? Is it because we have so few role models to follow? Committed believers are all around us, but they must be awakened to their identity, their calling, and the promises God has made to us. Is it because very few people recognize the presence and purpose of the Holy Spirit, and understand His position in the Trinity? I believe this to be the case.

On Sunday, December 5, 2010, while visiting Fred, my college roommate, I attended a morning church service at Faithful Central Bible Church in the Los Angeles Forum and listened to Bishop Kenneth Ulmer deliver a message from Romans 8 in the 7:00 a.m. service. The congregation of approximately three thousand listened in rapt silence as he spoke. At a pivotal moment, Bishop Ulmer read:

> *"God knew his people in advance, and he chose them to become like his Son, so that his Son would be the firstborn among many brothers and sisters. And having chosen them, he called them to come to him. And having called them, he gave them right standing with himself. And having given them right standing, he gave them his glory."*

> *Romans 8:29–30*

My heart leaped in response to the words, and I jumped to my feet in amazement and worshiped the Lord, while the rest of the congregation remained silent (and very likely puzzled).

What happened to me as I heard the words of Romans 8:29? My spirit suddenly grasped the mind-bending truth that *I was a brother of Christ*, who had been created to follow the footsteps of the Father's only Son. I read this scripture many times before, but never grasped the full meaning, nor the true power of these verses.

This revelation shook my thinking. The closer I grew to the Holy Spirit, the more power I would have to do eternal, immeasurable, redemptive work in the world.

> *"May you have the power to understand, as all God's people should, how wide, how long, how high, and how deep his love is. May you experience the love of Christ, though it is too great to understand fully. Then you will be made complete with all the fullness of life and power that comes from God."*

> *Ephesians 3:18–19*

Our demonstration of the fruit is the evidence of God's Spirit working within us. Jesus is the farmer, and we are the seeds of His fruit and the evidence by which we build the kingdom. Time is growing short, and Jesus' return is closer than we realize. When we step into the promises of God, we step into unspeakable joy, similar to that which Paul experienced.

"I was caught up to the third heaven fourteen years ago. Whether I was in my body or out of my body, I don't know—only God knows. Yes, only God knows whether I was in my body or outside my body. But I do know that I was caught up to paradise and heard things so astounding that they cannot be expressed in words, things no human is allowed to tell."

2 Corinthians 12:2–4

Consider

♦ How do you view the promises of God? Do you believe them to be general statements, or do you see them as guaranteed commitments that will happen?

Chapter Fifteen

Presence of the Holy Spirit

"The Jewish leaders were infuriated by Stephen's accusation, and they shook their fists at him in rage. But Stephen, full of the Holy Spirit, gazed steadily into heaven and saw the glory of God, and he saw Jesus standing in the place of honor at God's right hand. And he told them, 'Look, I see the heavens opened and the Son of Man standing in the place of honor at God's right hand!' Then they put their hands over their ears and began shouting. They rushed at him and dragged him out of the city and began to stone him. His accusers took off their coats and laid them at the feet of a young man named Saul. As they stoned him, Stephen prayed, 'Lord Jesus, receive my spirit.' He fell to his knees, shouting, 'Lord don't charge them with this sin!' And with that, he died."

Acts 7:54–59

We open this final chapter with the scene from Acts seven in which Stephen is staring intently into heaven watching Jesus standing at the right hand of God. The Pharisees and the Sadducees are hysterical because Stephen claims to see God, who manifests His presence to Stephen in a personal way. In a spirit of self-righteousness, the Pharisees and Sadducees condemn Stephen and kill him, believing that they are acting on God's behalf. The word *presence* is defined in the dictionary as the state or act of existing, occurring, or being present in a place or thing. It describes a person or thing that exists or is present in a place, but is not necessarily seen.

227

God was *present, with and in* Stephen even as the religious leaders were stoning him. His Spirit is *with us, and in* us in the same intimate way.

God's Love in Everything

In Acts seven we also see one of the rare occurrences in which the Father, Son, and Holy Spirit appear at the same time and place. Stephen is filled with the Holy Spirit and speaks with such great power that the Jewish leaders are convicted by his words to the point that they attack and murder him in the very presence of God.

This is an amazing story because we see Stephen demonstrating God-given power while gazing directly into heaven and facing imminent death. There are few instances in the Bible in which people are privileged to look directly into heaven. An even more amazing part of this story is that, like Jesus, Stephen prays before he dies and asks God to forgive his murderers. God's love is present in his prayer for his murderers, and clearly indicates that the Holy Spirit filled Stephen with His power and love. We recognize the powerful presence of the Holy Spirit when we stop, look closely, and bask in the peace He brings.

My son, Zach, desperately wanted a dog when he was a child. Maria and I were able to delay getting a dog when he was very young. However, after Marissa arrived, the two of them managed to persuade Maria to get a Bichon Frise named Garth, who came from a family of show dogs. We didn't like the name and changed it to Shiloh when he came to us as a feisty six-month-old puppy.

Shiloh was a cute puppy, and when he walked, he strutted like a show dog because that was in his DNA. It was almost as though he walked with confident arrogance. On two occasions, he defecated in his crate in an almost defiant manner, both times just before I left for work. On the second occasion, I spanked him with a rolled-up piece of newspaper and then hosed him down in the backyard. I promised to take him back to the breeder the next day, but Marissa cried the entire night, and I changed my mind. After the spanking, Shiloh's demeanor changed, and he would eventually sit with me for hours on end as I quietly read scripture.

Shiloh came to us in the summer of 2006, the same year my job was eliminated. He became an endeared member of our family and a prominent figure in my life during my year and a half of unemployment. Shiloh knew when we were down and in need of his presence. Eventually, he had a bad reaction to a medication that compromised his immune system. In addition to the reaction, he had to have emergency gall bladder surgery and suffered from two bouts of basal cell carcinoma that required chemotherapy. He lived for thirteen years and was the most engaging animal I have ever seen, even when he was extremely ill.

The veterinary staff gathered in one of the rooms, and were all in tears as they watched him die. I held him in my arm and rubbed his stomach as life was slowly withdrawing from his little body. How could the Holy Spirit fill such a small vessel with so much love? I still can see our beloved pup as he drew his final breath.

Upon Shiloh's death, we received ten plants and over thirty sympathy cards from people who knew him. Although this might sound controversial, I believe the little guy was filled with God's pure love. The vet told us that whenever Shiloh visited the office, in spite of the pain that racked his little body, he had a calming effect on the entire staff. This animal was endowed with a love that was so infectious with the people he met. I am confident that the presence of God resided in the heart of Shiloh, the same presence that lives in every creature on this earth.

When we become sensitive to the presence of God, He begins to show up everywhere. This sensitivity becomes even more obvious in Cluster Three when we glow in the Spirit. The presence of the Holy Spirit is love.

> *"But the time is coming, indeed it's here now, when true worshipers will worship the Father in spirit and in truth. The Father is looking for those who will worship him that way. For God is Spirit, so those who worship him must worship in spirit and in truth."*
>
> *John 4:23–24*

"Make them holy by your truth; teach them your word, which is truth."

John 17:17

Learning from Our Past

I asked several colleagues and friends to read the first draft of this book, and one asked me, "Where are you spiritually, now that you have experienced all of these things?"

I thought about this question and came to a realization. I look in eager anticipation toward my physical death, as I realize my remaining years on this earth are fewer in number than those I have already lived. My desire is to live those remaining years in total service to God. In pursuing this goal, I continue to be a work in progress, though obedient to His calling.

When Maria and I got married in 1977, God literally yanked me out of Allentown, Pennsylvania, and sent me down the highway to Atlanta. I was as wild as wild could be, getting high and running the streets with reckless abandonment. So God sent Maria, who helped me discipline myself and find purpose for my life. In the past I did things that hurt others, and I did not recognize at that time the depth of pain I had inflicted. I didn't understand the scripture that says, *"Above all else, the heart is deceitful"* (Jeremiah 17:9).

While attending a conference in Alexandria, Virginia, almost ten years ago, I contacted Rita to ask her to forgive me for the way I had treated her my senior year in college. We were together for two and a half years when I decided it was time for me to part company, and make the most of my remaining senior semester without her.

Rita was the oldest child of three girls. After we had broken up in our senior year, her mother died in January. I attended the funeral, but I didn't see her again during our final semester. I tried to call her the following summer to make amends, but she told me over the phone that she despised me. The thing that haunted me most was remembering her very words, and the look on her face my junior year with tears streaming down her face, when she told me she loved me. Rita had shown me her heart and offered to give it to me, but I had decided to move on, to what at that time, I don't know. Hey, but college break-ups are supposed to be no big deal.

It wasn't until years later that the Holy Spirit illuminated her face in my memory, reminding me that she had truly loved me, but that I treated her love like an object for sexual gratification. I was so obsessed with my needs that I took hers for granted. I did love Rita at that time, but it was with an eros love. When I called her on the phone after all of those years, she thought it was a hoax. I had not spoken to her in almost forty years. We talked for a while, and she told me she was married and was a trustee handling her church's finances, administration, and business transactions. My heart leaped for joy when she forgave me. She reviewed this manuscript and provided her feedback.

I realized that in college my heart was cold, self-serving, and self-focused, which is what happened to Adam and Eve's hearts when they became separated from God. They were well intentioned, but when they took their eyes off God and focused on themselves, they ended up hiding from God in shame, after realizing they were naked. Their eyes had been opened to know the difference between good and evil. I also realized that emotional trauma can sometimes be more impactful than physical violence, often leaving the victim with lifelong spiritual scars.

When we have the mind of Christ, we learn that life's greatest joy comes from loving those around us, regardless of their demeanor. Loving people unconditionally is the greatest service we can provide them. Loving people helps them find their way to God because He is the source of the greatest love the world has ever known. Reflecting on my selfishness helped me to realize that I had taken someone's love for granted, which was a painful realization. This process also helped me to recognize that, despite my weakness, God still loved me. My spirit rejoiced to know that God's love for me was unconditional.

As we grow deeper in our spiritual walk, we see how profoundly connected we are to those around us through love, both in the flesh, and in the Spirit. We are ourselves enriched, and enrich the lives of others when we reflect on the pain we knowingly, or unknowingly inflict on others along our journey. We must learn to listen intently to the voice of our souls. God's love permeates every living thing, and He speaks to us in a thousand ways when we learn how to listen.

Maria and I sold our home in April of 2021 and moved into a two-bedroom apartment in New Haven, Connecticut, where we lived for fourteen months. We moved back to Georgia after that and lived in a hotel for four months, and eventually moved into our new home. We returned to Georgia forty years after leaving Atlanta in 1983, and we are still in transition. After seventy years, God is still working on me as I learn more and more to submit to His will.

When I started writing this manuscript, I was not thinking we would sell our home and wait on God to show us what to do next. As I reflect on where God has faithfully brought us, I am confident that He will lead us to the place He has prepared for us. Although I have acted haphazardly in the past, I have learned to trust the Holy Spirit in vibrant new ways. I now have more confidence that, when I listen to the Spirit, I will always land where God wants me to be. God's *Masterpiece* (those of us who are children of God), must pray for the scales of spiritual blindness to fall from our eyes so that we may see the Father's glory in ourselves, in every child of God, and in His creation. We must rediscover our birthright in the Lord!

When we meditate on God the Father, the Holy Spirit, and Jesus, the primary characteristic we observe and absorb is love.

I pray that you are sensing my excitement as I envision all that God has in store for each of us. *You* were created with a purpose: to partner with God in His master plan for the world. *You* can speak into the lives of people no one else can reach. Your Christlike influence will ripple into eternity . . . but only if you lay down your life and pick up your cross to follow Jesus, the Christ.

The older I get and the closer I grow to the Holy Spirit, the deeper my faith grows. As I watched intermittent coverage of the George Floyd murder, I came to the realization that *I have a responsibility to pray for those responsible for his death.* The realization didn't strike me until I mentioned it to my pastor, Alfred Watts, the senior pastor at the Cornerstone Christian Center, that I have a responsibility to pray for lost souls in this world.

We are not destined to spend eternity on earth. We will spend eternity in heaven, and our time on earth prepares us for that. The more we grow in the Spirit, the more we grow into the *Masterpiece* God designed us to be. Ultimately, I must pray for those who hate me, as Stephen did, but that is a lesson for another time. I wish I could tell you that I have matured to the point at which I abide at Cluster Three, *glowing in the Spirit*. Although this level is where the Holy Spirit is patiently leading me, I have yet to achieve that place in my maturity. I continue to press on!

Pure Love, Perfect Peace

I am growing in patience and still learning how to live my faith day-by-day. I have had glimpses of peace and moments of joy, but these have not been sustained to the level the Holy Spirit desires. Like you, I am a work in progress. I had the privilege to be in the presence of Pastor Fred Sindorf who faithfully resided deep in Cluster Three. He was a vital mentor who demonstrated the love of Christ in my life and helped me to build my spiritual foundation.

I flew to the Sherman Home in Phoenix, Arizona, on July 3, 2022, to see Pastor Fred, my former senior pastor from North Shore Assembly of God in Skokie, Illinois, after receiving a message that his health was failing; he was in stage four cancer. His wife, Wanda, and their three daughters, Rebecca, Rachel, and Christina were sitting around his bed. Despite receiving morphine shots every two hours, Pastor Fred was alert and smiling.

When I first entered the room, I immediately noticed that an almost palpable peace had suffused it. Although I could see that Pastor Fred was in unbearable pain, his sense of humor and joy radiated from his face. As I sat and read scripture aloud, he lay calmly in his bed, his eyes closed as he smiled, assenting to the voice of the Spirit in the verses.

People who traveled to see him brought an abundance of love that overflowed in embraces, shared memories, soft laughter, bittersweet tears, words of thanks, and tender prayers. Pastor Fred was visiting his oldest daughter, Rebecca, in Arizona when his health took a turn for the worse. Although Pastor Fred lived in Wisconsin, friends like me had flown or driven across the country to see him before he died. The only words adequate to describe my final moments with Pastor Fred are *pure love*. The room was filled with an indescribable sense of peace, the essence of God's own presence. There was no time. There was no thought. It was simply peace.

I could only imagine what my friend, Dennis must have seen before he was killed, or what Stephen saw as he gazed into heaven before he was stoned. I do know that, when the Holy Spirit is present, nothing else matters. I know that Pastor Fred is home and is rejoicing in the love of His Father. The Holy Spirit inhabited his body, and my dear friend glowed with love. The place was filled with the Holy Spirit. Recalling that, I can't begin to imagine what heaven must be like.

When we meditate on God the Father, Jesus the Son, and the Holy Spirit, the primary characteristic we observe about them and absorb from them is love. As we allow ourselves to be filled with the Spirit of God, we bring His essence of love into the world through our bodies used as temples of the Holy Spirit. *When we serve as God's temple, we truly live out our reality as His Masterpiece!*

Under Pastor Fred's leadership I developed a love for the Word and for worship in 1986. He was a saint who lived close to God and is now enjoying his heavenly home. Pastor Fred's life was a reminder that the indwelling Holy Spirit becomes powerful when we die unto self. I pray that I will continue to pursue the Holy Spirit as my highest priority as long as God supplies breath to my body.

I pray that you, too, will gain a stronger appreciation of the Holy Spirit's love for your soul, and that you will invest the time to know Him, and show Him to a lost and broken world.

I once heard someone say that, if God were to allow us to peek into heaven, we would commit suicide for the opportunity to get there sooner. Paul talks about heaven in 2 Corinthians 12:2–4:

"I was caught up to the third heaven fourteen years ago. Whether I was in my body or out of my body, I don't know—only God knows. Yes, only God knows whether I was in my body or outside my body. But I do know that I was caught up to paradise and heard things so astounding that they cannot be expressed in words, things no human is allowed to tell."

Paul's declaration is powerful, and when we spend time with the Holy Spirit we experience this indescribable joy.

You and I, my brothers and sisters, have the ability to live on earth in a heavenly, spiritual manner. As we display the fruit of the Spirit in the flesh, we enjoy the blessings of heaven and inspire others to do likewise here on earth. We can bring heaven to earth. When we live in the Spirit, you and I can experience unimaginable joy as we free our minds from fear, envy, lust, hatred, depression, addictions, and all of the other negative influences of sin we experience in this world. We can access the power of the Holy Spirit to live exceptional lives here on earth. This opportunity is available to anyone who believes in Jesus as their Savior and is willing to produce fruit.

We can know overflowing joy and a peace that surpasses all understanding. We can shine like the Son every day of our lives on earth. These things require faith, hope, and love that emanate from God the Father. They require that you step out and surrender all.

Poor Eve was duped into believing that she could be as wise as God, but she learned that her disobedience separated her from the One who loved her most. Jesus bridged that separation and brought us back to the Father through His gift of salvation and the presence of the Holy Spirit. You have the opportunity to experience life as it was designed by God, and you can shout that Good News to the world.

Get to know the Holy Spirit by reading the Word of God, reflecting on His message, and listening to the voice of the Holy Spirit as He speaks to you through the Word and prayer. In time, your soul will crave the Word as you begin to walk in step with the Holy Spirit. As you surrender your life to His glorious plan, you become the fragrance of Jesus in a lost and dying world.

How can we tell when we are in the presence of the Holy Spirit? When we are producing the fruit of the Spirit and know His love, joy, peace, and radiate a glow that flows from the inside out. God has a marvelous plan for your life, no matter who or where you are. He wants nothing but the best for you, sons and daughters of the Most High God. You and I are made in God's image, and each one of us is *a Masterpiece!*

Acknowledgments

I want to thank Gail Adams, Dr. Leon Bailey, Thereda J. Cobb-Newsome, Donna Patrice Covington-Green, Dr. Marcia Alesan Dawkins, Verona "Vee" Earl, Reverend Todd Foster, Karen Hinds, Nick Hines, Richard Louis, Steve Martin, Anthony Nicoletti, Jennifer Olson, Dr. Jerry Rabalais, Wanda Sindorf, Scotty Smith, Katie Stallard, and Mike Stallard for laboring with me through this manuscript.

Thank you Shelly Beach for helping me through the initial stages of editing the manuscript and offering resources.

I want to acknowledge my *Sisters in Soul* spiritual maturity group including Lisa Banks, Leida Centeno, Dr. Dawkins, Abigail Dunne-Moses, Holly Hughson, Dr. Maria Keckler, Jennifer Olson, and Toshia Safford for furthering the spiritual maturity group and growing their walk with the Holy Spirit. To Karen Hinds for leading my *Sisters in Soul* and for being a spiritual coach and mentor.

I thank the Lord and honor those who have encouraged me along this journey: Reverend Daniel "Pipe" Blount, Reverend James Britt, Lawrence "Cal" Callaway, Wesley Farmer Jr., Kevin Myatt, Joseph "Butch" Ransom, James Sibley, and Susan Williams.

Scotty Smith and Francine Beasley, you have been the siblings I never had.

I want to extend my heartfelt thanks to all of those who have gone on before me: Dennis Blanks, John "Junebug" Battle, LaRace Battle, Dora Smith-Brickhouse, Pastor Fred Sindorf, all of whom were a comfort on this side of the journey. This applies as well to Pop, Nanna, and Nanna B for the foundational lessons they taught me.

Mom and Dad, I am so proud to be your son, James Baker Morris, Jr., III.

Zach and Marissa, I pray you will remember what I tried to teach you and thank you for loving me in spite of my flaws. My love and thanks pour out to Maria for walking with me through all of these years, trusting that somehow all of life's circumstances would truly work out to God's glory.

To God the Father, God the Son, and God the Holy Spirit, my undying gratitude goes out for your love and mercy.

Appendix A

FRUIT OF THE SPIRIT SURVEY

Circle the answer that best describes your behavior for each of the fruit.

SELF-CONTROL

1. I read my Bible every day with the goal of reading it cover to cover.

1	2	3	4	5
Never	Rarely	Often	Very Often	Always

GENTLENESS

2. I can control my anger in every situation.

1	2	3	4	5
Never	Rarely	Often	Very Often	Always

FAITHFULNESS

3. I live from my core values each and every day.

1	2	3	4	5
Never	Rarely	Often	Very Often	Always

CLUSTER ONE TOTAL SCORE_____

GOODNESS

4. I find it easy to serve those who ridicule me.

1	2	3	4	5
Never	Rarely	Often	Very Often	Always

KINDNESS

5. I pray for those who have hurt me.

1	2	3	4	5
Never	Rarely	Often	Very Often	Always

PATIENCE

6. I am patient in every situation.

1	2	3	4	5
Never	Rarely	Often	Very Often	Always

CLUSTER TWO TOTAL SCORE_____

PEACE

7. I am able to find peace in the midst of utter chaos.

1	2	3	4	5
Never	Rarely	Often	Very Often	Always

JOY

8. I experience a heart of thankfulness each and every day.

1	2	3	4	5
Never	Rarely	Often	Very Often	Always

LOVE

9. I have a steady flow of agape love pouring forth from my soul each and every day.

1	2	3	4	5
Never	Rarely	Often	Very Often	Always

CLUSTER THREE TOTAL SCORE _____

HOLY SPIRIT

10. I am led each and every day by the Holy Spirit.

1	2	3	4	5
Never	Rarely	Often	Very Often	Always

TOTAL SURVEY SCORE FOR ALL 10 QUESTIONS_____

Total your scores by cluster to view your individual cluster results. Combine all of the scores including question 10 which will give you a maximum of 50 points. Read the following guides.

Scores between 36-50 are a strong indication you are bearing fruit for the kingdom and should mentor others.

Scores between 20-35 are a strong indication you are serving others and ready to strengthen your walk with the Holy Spirit. Consider identifying a leader who could serve as your mentor. Identify someone you could mentor.

Scores below 20 indicate you are ready to identify your gifts and find ways to grow closer to God. Identify a leader who you trust, and talk to them about their faith. Pray and seek out a mentor. Grow your fruit. Read your Bible daily and get to know the Holy Spirit.

Appendix B

Lessons from our Peaks and Valleys

Take the time to look back on your life and identify experiences and events in which the Holy Spirit has hovered over your life to protect you. Break your life into five-year increments, starting with the year you were born. For each of the time periods, identify one peak experience and one valley experience. Identify patterns and themes and note common occurrences. Write a one-to-two sentence summary for each increment. You may need to use a separate notebook or a computer to give yourself the space you need, as well as to record your answers to some or all of the questions throughout the book. Once this is completed you should create a development plan that will enable you to build spiritual strength.

If you look closely, you will begin to see themes and patterns in terms of your high and low points. Our greatest spiritual lessons often take place during the low points of life. What sometimes looks like failure can bring about some of the greatest lessons you will ever learn. The key is how you and I learn to frame life's circumstances to identify God's presence.

SPIRITUAL LESSONS

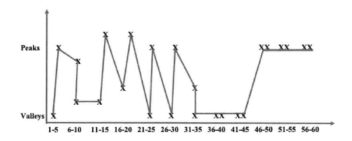

Five Year Age Increments

243

Notes

Introduction
[1] Pastor Deron Spoo.

Chapter One
[2] Kirk Byron Jones. Addicted to Hurry: Spiritual Strategies for Slowing Down (King of Prussia, PA: Judson Press, 2003), 77.
[3] Billy Graham. The Holy Spirit: Activating God's Power in Your Life (Nashville, TN: Thomas Nelson, 1978), 69.

Chapter Two
[4] Jones. Addicted to Hurry: Spiritual Strategies for Slowing Down, 55.

Chapter Four
[5] Andrew Murray. Experiencing the Holy Spirit (Hunts Valley, PA: Whitaker House, 1985), 25.

Chapter Five
[6] Andrew Murray. Experiencing the Holy Spirit (Hunts Valley, PA: Whitaker House, 1985), 25.

Chapter Six
[7] A.W. Tozer. Life In the Spirit (Peabody, MA: Hendrickson Publishers, 2009), 125.

Chapter Seven
[8] Tozer. Life In the Spirit, 101–102.
[9] Tozer. Life In the Spirit, 35.

Chapter Ten
[10] R. Buckmeister Fuller.

Chapter Eleven
[11] Eugene H. Peterson. Eat this Book. A Conversation in the Art of Spiritual Reading (William B. Eerdmans Publishing Company, Grand Rapids, MI/Cambridge, UK, 2006), 25.
[12] Graham. The Holy Spirit: Activating God's Power in Your Life, 308.

Chapter Twelve
[13] Mother Teresa.